Whi ACCESS

How to Hunt
Top Whitetail States
Cheaply & Effectively

Chris Eberhart

Published by

kp krause publications

An Imprint of F+W Media, Inc.

700 East State Street • Iola, WI 54990-0001
715-445-2214 • 888-457-2873
www.krausebooks.com

Our toll-free number to place an order or obtain
a free catalog is (800) 258-0929.

Library of Congress Control Number: 2008937708

ISBN-13: 978-089689-834-9
ISBN-10: 0-89689-834-2

Designed by Jamie Griffin and Donna Mummery

Printed in United States of America

Table of Contents

Acknowledgments   4

Introduction: By Tom Nelson   5

Chapter 1: The Dream Becomes Real   6

Chapter 2: Wisconsin: Setting out and Scouting   10

Chapter 3: North Dakota: Early Season Magic   34

Chapter 4: Wisconsin: The October Lull   69

Chapter 5: Missouri: Hunting a Heatwave and a Buck in the Rain   90

Chapter 6: Wisconsin: The Rut Is On   141

Chapter 7: Michigan: An Interlude and a Doe   155

Chapter 8: Ohio: The Late Rut in a National Forest   170

Chapter 9: Michigan: Suburbs and a Refuge in December Snow   192

Appendix: Hunting Statistics, Hunting Expenditures   206

Chapter 10 Epilogue: North Dakota Revisited: A Nomad Rolls On   208

For Linnea Montaine, who only allowed me to write while she was napping.

Acknowledgements

Every book has its beginnings somewhere. The first thoughts of writing this one came about back in November of 2004. After hunting out of my van in Wisconsin, Missouri, Michigan, and Ohio, I drove up to Massachusetts to bowhunt for a week with my good friend Ben Bailey. Over a dinner of grilled venison with some friends, we were talking of the season, about where and how I hunted, and of books. Ben said, "Why don't you write a book about your low-budget hunting road trips". And so the idea was born. Thank you, Ben, for helping me in so many ways.

Along the way, through both the adventure of the actual trip and the writing, I had a lot of help, for which I am very grateful. First, I would like to thank Susanne for her love, and tolerance of my own special sort of madness. Also I thank my brother, Jon Eberhart, for helping me take care of business. Both Dan Maurer and John Gibbons were generous enough to proof rough manuscripts. Their suggestions helped shape these pages. Tom Nelson took the time out of his busy schedule to work through my sometimes choppy writing, provide some insight and to craft a fitting introduction. Special thanks to Derrek Sigler for sticking with my book and pushing it through the system. Dan Schmidt was very helpful in this process as well.

I would also like to thank John Eberhart, Hubert Wursthorn, Bob Browne, Kim and Chad Ruby, and so many others, who, in various ways, generously contribute to my hunting, writing, and life in general. This book would have never taken shape without your help.

Chris Eberhart
2008

Introduction

What is it about large whitetail bucks that consumes bowhunters? What compels us, as practitioners of the bow and arrow, to be so obsessed with big-racked whitetail deer? Hunters will miss birthdays, anniversaries, and holidays just to get one more chance at that mystical buck.

I personally know bowhunters who have lost their jobs, wives, and almost their lives, in pursuit of this antlered adversary. Why do we hold these polished sets of headgear in such high esteem? In the majority of cases it surely is not for financial gain. On the contrary, many bowhunters spend thousands of dollars on guided hunts at premier whitetail venues across North America just hoping for a chance at a bragging-size whitetail. Some are willing to spend even more money and hunt inside an enclosure just to obtain a trophy-caliber buck to adorn their wall. Then by the roaring fire the hunter can recount his hunt to his friends, exclaiming his prowess as a hunter.

Placing a Pope and Young-qualifying buck on the wall does not benefit your health and well being. Actually, pursuing wide-racked bucks has most likely shortened my own life span. Sleepless nights, frozen toes and shattered nerves are just a few of the symptoms I have incurred while bowhunting the elusive whitetail buck. But in my perhaps infatuated mind, the price has been worth it.

There is no question that if you have the finances, you will sooner or later obtain your goal of tagging a trophy whitetail. Book a hunt with a whitetail outfitter in a big buck hot spot such as Iowa, Kansas, Illinois and your opportunity will sooner or later come about. But few of us have the financial means to year after year dole out the greenbacks necessary to enhance our chances of bagging a trophy-size buck. Factor in the time commitment needed and to most of us it is an impossible dream.

Or is it? Within the pages of this book, author, friend, and whitetail authority Chris Eberhart guides you along the trail to whitetail success that is within the resources of the average bow bender. When it comes to bowhunting trophy bucks on a budget, and in hard hunted areas, Chris has proven to be gifted. He truly has lived the life of a whitetail nomad. Sleeping in the back of his mini van even as the mercury drops well below freezing. Surviving on cookies and cans of cold soup for days on end. His only companion, a bowhunting magazine. Give Chris your pocket change and he can bowhunt for a month and, in the end, travel back home with a monster buck. He has and knows what it takes to bow kill a big buck on a small budget. He is also willing to make the sacrifices needed to fulfill his quest. This makes Chris the consummate whitetail fanatic.

While you peruse the pages of this book, keep in mind that you, too, could and can do anything Chris has done. Many of the bowhunts Chris makes are conducted on public lands open to all bowhunters. Chris does not have thousands of acres of private land at his disposal. On the contrary, he bowhunts small tracts of land and is often sharing his access with dozens of other archers and even gun hunters in some cases. He successfully fills his tags on bragging-size whitetails in hard-hunted areas in central Michigan where ninety percent of all antlered bucks are harvested every gun season. To fill your tag in this setting, you had better be willing to take the extra steps to success. Throughout this book Chris will share his proven techniques and insights for consistently taking big bucks in hard-hunted areas. As entertaining as it is educational, when finished, this book will have you packing your vehicle, donning your camo clothes, and heading towards the nearest patch of whitetail country.

By Tom Nelson (January 20, 2008)
Host of "American Archer" Television Show

Chapter 1

The Dream Becomes Real

Every bowhunter has goals and dreams. It might be a Pope and Young buck for your wall, a trip to Alaska for Sitka blacktails, or to Iowa for a corn-fed bruiser. Perhaps you want just one more trip with an old friend before the sun sets. You and I both have yearnings unsatisfied by our local haunts. Have you ever dreamed about spending one entire fall as a Whitetail Hunter, doing nothing but traveling the United States, chasing the hunting seasons across this great land while chasing large, whitetail bucks in unfamiliar forests? That was my great dream. If you share that dream, you are probably waiting for a winning ticket, or perhaps retirement before taking the opportunity to devote an entire fall to the pursuit you love most.

As a father with a young family, struggling to make ends meet as an outdoor writer and struggling small business owner, I put off the dream, always imagining another time when it would be easier to accomplish. Eventually however, as the years rolled by, I realized that the "right" time might never arrive. To reach an extraordinary goal we have to take risks, take chances, and find ways to overcome obstacles. We have to be more creative and work with the scarce resources we have. This is the story of my season-long quest for big bucks. It is the story of my experiences and includes all the details and facts a bowhunter might need to become a whitetail traveler. It is a recipe for you to follow, adding or subtracting ingredients as you cook up your own hunting adventure.

This is a wonderful time to be a bowhunter in pursuit of big bucks in the USA. Never before have there been so many hunting opportunities. Whitetails are more abundant now than they have ever been in history. There are huntible populations in just about every state and province in North America. In fact, in many areas whitetails are even overpopulated. Compared to other recreational expenses, hunting licenses, both for residents and non-residents, are in most cases reasonable, and sometimes downright cheap. Coinciding with the high deer numbers is the availability and quality of today's hunting equipment. There are several competing chains of hunting superstores that provide everything a hunter could possibly need or want. Things we take for granted, like treesteps, treestands, camouflage for every situation, and scent eliminating products are fairly recent developments.

Another aspect of modern bowhunting that makes this a great time to be a bowhunter is the availability of information. There is a complete media pallet that centers on hunting in general, and bowhunting in particular. There are books, magazines, videos, and television shows that equip today's bowhunter with more information than ever before, not to mention what is available on the Internet at the click of a button. Bowhunting information covers everything from techniques to deer biology to deer management. The bottom line is that there are more deer, more hunting opportunities, better equipment, and more hunting information available than ever before. Things couldn't be better!

There are also challenges to face. As with everything else in life, goals worth reaching never come without obstacles to be overcome. The obstacles you and I might have in common are time, money, and access. Whenever I'd start exploring the means to live my dream one or the other of these barriers would cloud my skies. For most of us, finding the time may be the most challenging obstacle to overcome. My situation may be unique, but perhaps you can find parallels that will open the door for you. As a recent father, I have a small child to parent and a wife who prefers my presence at home. She and I share a business, and like most small businesses, we struggle and don't have much money for extras. On the other hand, I am a writer who specializes in writing about hunting whitetail deer. Writing does not exactly line my pockets with extra money, but at least I could undertake the adventure with the hope that you would want to read about it. Now there is some added pressure!

This buck was the result of my very first do-it-yourself cross-country bowhunt.

Although you may not be an outdoor writer, perhaps you are single. Perhaps you are in transition, just out of college or the military, or maybe between careers. It might take a few years of saving and living meagerly, but as you will see, you don't have to save much to gain whitetail access. So by the grace of my wife's forbearance, and our frugality, the barriers of time and money were surmounted.

The Access Issue

Access to great hunting appears to be a problem for everyone except the rich and the industry insiders. Expanding whitetail populations have led to intense interest in hunting and the resultant increase in bowhunter numbers has led to more competition for those few trophy deer. This competition has caused privatization and a lot of hunters have been pushed off land that was previously available to them. The leasing rates in some of the best areas in Michigan are now going for thirty-five dollars an acre, and I have heard of property being leased for up to seventy-five dollars an acre in prime areas in Ohio, Illinois, and Wisconsin. In Michigan, where leasing was almost unheard of fifteen years ago, it is getting to the point that if you don't own or lease land, then you will not be hunting private property. This trend is pricing a lot of guys right out of hunting! With ever-increasing sprawl, hunting land is simply disappearing, in some places at an alarming rate, for instance around Chicago, Detroit, or Columbus. With ever increasing urbanization, more and more people have little or no contact with hunting. This lowers the general acceptance of hunting in society. Anti-hunting groups are attacking hunting at every turn, and their clearly stated intention is to make all hunting illegal.

One answer to the access problem is public land. There are vast expanses of public land and there are hidden gems, tucked into suburbs and among the vast tracks of great farms. Together, as I make my way from state to state, we'll explore the information you need to locate these hunting locals and the reality found on the ground when you get there. Although my preference is for hunting private land, a large portion of my hunting currently takes place on public ground. While private land often holds undisturbed deer, it is time consuming to gain access. It is also uncertain. Kill a great deer on private land, and pretty soon others may come to bid out your access. The landowner himself might close off the land to the public and open it only to family. Both have happened to me, even on this very adventure. On the other hand, it never hurts to stop and ask, make some friendly conversation, and learn more about other rural Americans.

The reality of hunting is not something you can find on a TV screen. Many hunting shows and videos create false expectations, especially for beginning hunters. The kind of hunting shown is simply unavailable to the vast majority of bowhunters. Most television hunting is done in very exclusive areas in a handful of states, either the area is hyper-managed for trophy animals, or hunting pressure is so tightly controlled that only a few fortunate hunters ever set foot there. Don't you wonder about bowhunters who have every shed antler of a trophy buck for the last three years, several hundred-trail camera photos and have named him? Sure, I know a bunch of those fellows and they are decent folks; however, they are running a business engaged in selling entertainment, they are not depicting the kind of hunting you and I can ever experience.

Public land and heavy hunting pressure on private property impose some special challenges on the bowhunter in pursuit of big bucks. That those challenges can be overcome is demonstrated in my other books. Those books are filled with detailed explanations of hunting strategies, equipment and true hunting stories of the big bucks killed. The detailed information will show you how to succeed in the midst of other hunters. If you decide to undertake a cross-country hunting odyssey or face regular hunter pressure on public land, you will enjoy learning from the experiences of my hunting family in just those situations.

So, is it possible to live the dream and hunt big bucks from one end of the United States to the other throughout an entire season? The answer is simple; yes. Hunting opportunities abound, but they do not always come easy, nor always free of charge. Equipment is great, but it does not replace skill. There is a wealth of useful hunting information out there, but it has to be filtered from thick layers of unrealistic entertainment. Private deer management practices can both help and hurt hunting. Hunting is under attack, but it isn't totally endangered. Hunting faces countless challenges; however, there are reasonable solutions to most of those challenges. Reality almost always lies somewhere between the extremes.

Navigating through the hunting world and finding a situation that is comfortable is something every bowhunter has to do. It is a simple fact that my bowhunting is constrained by a small budget. Like just about everyone else, I have commitments, and don't quite earn as much as I would like. In order to reach my bowhunting goals, I have had to be creative and compensate for my chronic lack of greenbacks. The good news is that it is still possible to hunt, fish, or simply adventure all across America on a small budget, and have good success on big bucks, heavy fish, or just good times. This is the story of the challenge and rewards of hunting three months straight on a very limited budget. Something you, too, can achieve with a little ingenuity and hard work.

What To Do
- Set a goal. Knowing what you want to do and where you want to do it is the first step.
- Set a budget that you and your family can live with. I'm not rolling in money, but knew that if I stuck to my budget plan, I could pull this adventure off.
- Do it. If you want to hunt the top states that are always featured on the TV shows, you can do it and for much less than you think. Trophy deer are available to the average hunter.

Chapter 2

Wisconsin:
Setting Out and Scouting

The drive is horrible, maddening, and burning hot down around the south end of Lake Michigan spinning around that monster known as Chicago, eight lanes of concrete filled to the brim with racing automobiles, semi-trucks, and toll booths: move with the current or die. The temperature is somewhere in the mid 90's and a bell of brown and yellow hazy smog hangs over the city. The radio drones its never ending, made-for-the-masses drabble over the invisible waves. With a broken air conditioner, I have my window rolled down in hope that moving air will be cooler air, but am soaked with sweat just the same. Like Dante's Inferno, I feel like I have dropped into the depths of hell, hoping to make the absolution that is somehow promised by the Wisconsin line, and the hunting ahead.

The journey begins…

From the state line, the drive is lighter and I drop my guard a bit. Four hours later I reach my happy hunting grounds. Long hours of concrete at furious speeds leave me drained, and with a pounding headache, as I pull off the highway well after dark. The farm is divided into three parts, the first only five miles from the highway. I arrive in a matter of minutes. As I turn onto the tractor path, my van headlights cut into the dark between walls of corn, then into alfalfa and soybeans. The glowing tapetum deer eyes reflect the intense candlepower of my headlights. A doe and two fawns stare for a split second before slipping away into the inky black, to which my own eyes have not yet adjusted. At least there are a couple deer here this year. I park my van at a corner between fields, and step outside to shake off the stiffness of ten hours on the road. Slowly my pupils enlarge, adjusting to the dark, and the stars that I had just moments ago been unable to see, slowly become visible. Sitting for a few minutes on my back bumper I enjoy the now cool comfortable September air before sliding into my van. As fatigued as I am, the business of the evening is short: a quick brushing of my teeth, a few words scribbled in my journal, and lights out. In mere minutes sleep is upon me and the day's arduous journey is being processed in uncomfortable dreams.

The morning greets me with a cloudless sky and a brilliant red sun creeping up from the southeast. A quick glance out the windows reveals fields empty of deer. Slipping out of my blankets, I slide the side door open and sit with my legs crossed, enjoying the moist morning air. It is going to be hot today; this is obvious, although it's still early. Allowing the dew to burn off some, I eat breakfast slowly: some cold bagels, and a multi-vitamin chased down with a cup of water. While brushing my teeth I mosey to the other corner of the cornfield, curious whether any deer are feeding in the adjacent beans. Nothing.

My Wisconsin camping spot between cornfields.

Back at my van I relax with the sliding door open for a few minutes just listening and watching, taking deep breaths — nothing much in mind. It is the second week of September and this is the beginning of what could be three solid months of roaming and bowhunting. As I sit, I notice that time is already changing. There is no place I have to be, and nothing I have to do for the next three months. Let the hunting begin.

Stepping to the back of my van, I open the double doors and prepare for a day of scouting. When most people think of hunting, they think of being in the woods with a weapon chasing animals. Hunting, though, goes far beyond that. Scouting is for me just another facet of hunting. It may sound strange, but I crave and enjoy scouting nearly as much as I do actual hunting. Scouting is part of the process, and the preparation is what makes a hunter the best he can be. Making the effort to learn the woods and figure out what the deer are doing, and why they are doing it, is a challenge and something that I do instinctively, almost compulsively, every chance I get. Scouting is hunting and learning. It is a sorry "hunter" who doesn't attempt to learn something every time he steps in the woods. The actual hunting season (when it is legal to kill an animal) isn't open yet anyway.

I retrieve the plastic tub labeled scouting gear. From inside the tub I pull my scouting uniform, a pair of old German army pants and an earth-colored, lightweight button down shirt with long sleeves. After dressing quickly, I turn my attention to my scouting pack. Satisfying my mildly compulsive disposition when it comes to hunting, I double-check its contents. It contains a fanny pack with a complete set of steps, a tree saddle, a safety belt for climbing, a forty-foot length of quarter inch rope, a brush saw, a compass, some reflective tacks, a pair of leather gloves, some toilet paper, and two water bottles. And, pulling them from my hunting notebook, I add a couple of Internet topo-photos of the area to the top pocket of the pack. Satisfied with its contents, I set the pack on the ground and return the plastic tub to its place

The tub labeled Scent Lok is the next. Sorting through a couple of activated carbon sacks, I eventually find a Scent Lok suit that I hunted with a few years ago, and pull it on over my scouting garb. Right now this is comfortable, but judging from the sun I will be dripping with sweat in just a few hours. The finishing touch to my clothing for this scouting foray is my lightweight scent-reduced, rubber scouting boots. My mere presence in the forest is enough disturbance, and the last thing I want to do is leave an obvious scent trail all over the place, alerting every deer within miles to my intentions. My high tech scent control armor won't eliminate all the signs that I was around, but it will perhaps leave the deer guessing. The van is quickly locked and I set out following the tractor lane between the fields.

My first destination is an area I call the back field. Last fall I breezed through the far corner of the farm and found the terrain interesting from a hunting perspective, but never had an opportunity to clear out a tree there. Booting down the tractor path, I pass through the corner of the front woods into the fields again. The path shoots straight out of the woods about a hundred yards before curving sharply left, just off the front of a grassy overgrown draw that juts about two hundred yards into the agriculture. The path ends with a turn-around at the outside corner of a wooded fencerow that separates this farm from the neighbor's place. The property lines around here are mostly irregular, with points and squares cut out of solid pieces of land. (At one time the fertile tops must have been far more valuable than the wooded slopes.) I continue straight down the edge of the fencerow. The corn is deep green and tall; several feet over my head. That there is corn here isn't unusual, but the fact the entire back field is planted in it is. I've hunted this farm three previous seasons and there has always been strip planting of crops back here. I wonder at the change, and slow step forward, keeping an eye on the ground for tracks and along the fencerow for fresh rubs. Across the fence line the neighbors have half of their field planted in corn as well. This is far more maize than I've ever seen here.

Read the Signs

Easing up to the corner of the field, I arrive at an interesting area (from a hunting perspective). Along the woods, the farmer has left an overgrown grass and brush strip that is about twenty yards wide separating the trees from the crops. A couple of draws end in this strip, so I guess it is left untilled to limit erosion. Like all three portions of the farm, these fields sit on the top of bluffs, surrounded by steep wooded hills that drop down to more crops in the wide flat bottoms below. I have never hunted here before, but it is clear that the deer use this grassy interface heavily. A well-worn runway curves around the tip of the first draw and runs parallel to the bordering woods. At the tip of the first point, under some overhanging branches, there are three scrapes with numerous licking branches above them. One branch in particular grabs my attention. It is about the diameter of my thumb; has been broken in two places; and, is hanging only by a thin strip of bark. A buck has to have some long tines in order to have enough leverage to break a branch like that. Scrapes this size in early September almost certainly mean they were initiated by a mature buck. I feel myself grinning at the sight of them. This is a good sign the bucks are here. Moving on, I traverse the length of the grassy strip following a runway cut through tall brome.

A couple more scrapes line the woods and a few minor runways shoot directly out of the forest into the corn. My goal is the far back corner of the field. Studying topo-photos in the off-season revealed that the corner should be an excellent spot. Several terrain features come together there. The fields extend to the lip of a very steep bluff, with a county road almost directly below it. Between the edge of the fields and the steep hill is less than forty yards. There are large blocks of woods to the north and east. In order for a deer to cross from one woods to the other without exposing himself in the fields, or having to cross the face of what is, for all practical purposes, a cliff, it has to pass through this point. It is a natural pinch point; at least that is what it looks like on my topo-photos.

Arriving at the corner, I look for signs to back my suspicions, and confirmation comes quickly. Several runways cross the corner; nothing spectacular from sheer use, but there are numerous good rubs along them, indicating use by a mature buck. This quick inspection is all it takes to decide that it is necessary to prepare a tree to hunt from here. As far as trees go

Comparing a computer aerial photo to real terrain.

the pickings are slim — either too small, completely in the wrong spot, or simply too large to hunt out of. After about a half-hour of inspecting trees for angle and position, I make my selection. An ash tree right along the old fence line is the unsuspecting winner. It is located slightly north of the corner. From this tree I can shoot to three runways out to thirty yards into the woods, and to the corner where the corn, the grass strip, and the woods intersect. There is scrape right at that intersection which is also about thirty yards away. Yet another runway traces the edge of the corn, ten yards from the base of the ash, crossing a very slight runway out of the corn about twenty yards away. Basically, it is the only tree where I have a chance to connect with the majority of deer movement across the pinch point, even though it is on a field edge. I almost never hunt field edges, but the presence of corn, and the shots into the woods at this inside corner, proves this spot to be an exception.

There is only one problem. This spot is going to require a great deal of work to get just right. The ash is hidden amongst a fencerow of thick growth, and is surrounded by larger maples and other trees with wide swinging branches. The branches provide great cover, but to open up shots where I need them, I will have to do some serious pruning. The tree itself is straight with a split trunk at around twenty-five feet. Five feet above the split, the left trunk has a perfect location for a tree saddle; the angle appears to be just right. The amount of work ahead of me is formidable, so I do not procrastinate.

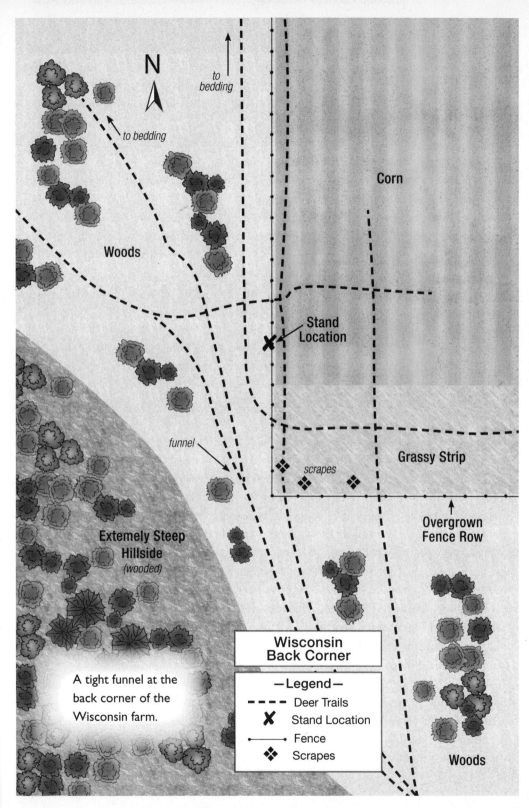

N

to bedding

to bedding

Woods

Corn

Stand Location

funnel

Extemely Steep Hillside
(wooded)

scrapes

Grassy Strip

Overgrown Fence Row

A tight funnel at the back corner of the Wisconsin farm.

Wisconsin Back Corner

—Legend—
- - - - Deer Trails
- ✖ Stand Location
- •—•—• Fence
- ❖ Scrapes

Woods

I set my pack down at the base of the tree, and pull on a last year's pair of Scent Lok gloves, my tree prep fanny pack, and my tree saddle. Now rigged for climbing, I begin setting tree steps, careful to select the side of the trunk that leans slightly away from me. For getting up the tree, I use double fold steps with quick start screws. The procedure for placing steps is for me a steady routine that I vary only under unusual circumstances. I always begin on the right side of the trunk at knee level. Here I screw in the first step. Resting my right foot on the step, I use my right knee to measure the height for the next step, on the left side. This sequence is repeated on both sides until I reach the height I intend to hunt from. I almost always use twelve steps to reach my comfortable hunting height, usually somewhere between twenty-five and thirty-five feet. Above the twelfth step, I screw in steps to stand on. My choice for this is solid, non-folding steps, or steps with a single fold at the screw. It is usually necessary to use four or five of these placed opposite one another on the trunk in order to be able to maneuver around the tree to shoot in all directions. With these last tree-steps in place, I climb up on them and attach my tree saddle. It takes me around ten minutes to complete this entire procedure.

Now, hanging safely in my saddle, I can inspect the shooting lane situation. This tree has great cover from the top. With its split trunk, I can sit comfortably attached to one trunk and rest my back against the other, sort of like resting in a lounge chair. The extra comfort of having a backrest is a bonus in this type of split-trunk set-up. The next task is to remove any branches in arms length that may interfere with a potential shot. With this accomplished, I mentally note the branches and trees that have to be trimmed in order to sufficiently open up shooting lanes on the ground. Leaving my tree saddle in the tree for reference, I scoot down and begin removing branches and saplings. This is the real physical labor of bowhunting.

Shooting lanes are a curious point of difference among bowhunters. Some hunters cut conspicuous wide-open lanes, akin to a fairway in golf, while others attempt to pick small holes to shoot through. Personally I think balance is necessary. The size of shooting lanes and the amount of cover needed to hunt a tree are situation based, and should reflect the frequency of your intended hunting. For instance, I know I will only be hunting this tree a couple of times, and it provides excellent cover with its double-trunk and background limbs from other trees, so as a consequence I open my lanes a little wider than usual to insure that if a buck passes, I will be able to get a shot. If this were a tree that I was going to hunt regularly, I would leave the lanes slightly narrower as a precaution to remain undetected. Also, in trees where one hunts lower to the ground, more cover is required.

As I clear my shooting lanes I attempt to make them as inconspicuous as possible by cutting off all saplings flat to the ground, and then covering up the "stumps" with leaves and dirt. I also drag every branch and tree away from my stand locations, and hide them where they either look natural, or integrate them into briar thickets or under wild grape vines. In doing this, I'm not so much worried about concealing my actions from the deer, as I am worried about concealing my hunting locations from other hunters. People generally don't miss, or

Preparing a tree to hunt.

notice, things that simply aren't there. There are probably ten other bowhunters on this farm, and I don't want them to know where I'm hunting, not to mention the numerous gun hunters. Whenever I discover cut saplings while scouting I immediately begin looking around for a nearby treestand. Certainly, most other bowhunters do the same thing. The cutting, carrying and dragging, climbing up and down, and cutting some more takes me a little over three hours to complete. The last things I do are remove all my steps and inspect the area one last time. All my shooting lanes are open, and, apart from some unsettled leaves, the area around the ash looks as though I was never here at all. Perfect. Time to move on.

Three hours of hard physical labor made my boots a little heavier which cause me to negotiate the walk a little slower, and now I carry my remaining water bottle in my hand. The temperature has risen, and I'm already parched. Trudging now not so stealthily down the edge of the cornfield I make for my second destination of the morning, the tip of that huge draw that juts about two hundred yards into the crops. This is a special place for me, and a center of buck activity in the area. More exactly, I want to inspect a tree dubbed the twelve-point tree.

This series of photos is meant to show how I hunt from a saddle.

1=sitting comfortably in my Saddle; 2= shooting to the right; 3=shooting to the left; 4=shooting behind; 5=when deer come you can use the trunk to hide behind; 6=when using a Tree Saddle your Treesteps as foot rests should be placed around the tree like this.

Two years ago, while on a week-long hunt on this farm, I discovered this draw. That year there were several scrapes along a well-worn runway, leading straight up the center of the draw towards the crops. I prepped a tree to intercept that runway, and to be able to shoot to the scrapes. The tree was a dying ash also towards the center of the draw. The first morning I hunted there a deer suddenly tiptoed into view about thirty yards away just after daybreak. With its head down feeding, I initially thought the deer was a doe. To my surprise, when the deer raised its head, it was crowned with a white antlered ten-point rack, with three very tall matching tines on each side, and main beams that nearly touched at the tips. He would probably have scored somewhere in the 135 range, if measured with Pope and Young style points, despite an inside spread of clearly less than twelve inches.

Judging his casual demeanor and course, I guessed the buck would follow the main runway and pass at less than fifteen yards, so I slowly swung around the tree into position for that shot. Waiting, watching. But, to my astonishment, the buck had other plans, and suddenly turned crossing the side of the ridge. He picked up the tempo so I had to act fast. I spun around the tree, found a hole that the buck would pass through, drew, estimated the distance at thirty yards, blatted, stopping the buck, and shot. The arrow was right on line, and flew right under his barrel chest. All this happened in about the same amount of time it takes to read these two sentences. Minus a tuft of brown hollow hair shaven by a razor sharp broadhead, the buck spun, took two bounds up the ridge, halted for a split second to glance back, and in a slow trot vanished into the draw, never to be seen again. At least I never set eyes on him again. It's rare to get a second chance at a pressured mature whitetail.

A couple of hours later, my mistakes became as clear as day to me. Crossing the ridge was a tiny runway that I had failed to notice while clearing out my tree. All along the runway were miniature rubbed saplings, none much larger than my little finger in diameter. With main beams that nearly touched at the tips, the buck could probably only rub small diameter trees. That row of tiny rubs was likely an indicator of this buck's regular travel route. Because I had failed to notice this runway, I hadn't checked the distance, nor cleared a shooting lane. When I shot, the buck was standing at almost forty yards, instead of the thirty I estimated. The shot was actually up hill, causing more arrow drop than usual. In judging distance from a tree I had always used the ground as a reference, but in this case of shooting up the draw, the ground wasn't flat from the tree, and the buck, with his deep chest, simply appeared closer to me than he actually was. It was a mistake that I will never forget. Sometimes learning is painful. I hunted that spot a couple more times that season and saw a couple of nice yearlings, but neither that ten-pointer nor any other mature buck revealed himself.

Pay Off

The following year, the first area I scouted on the farm was this draw. Missing that ten-point haunted me still. The situation was much the same as the year before. The well-worn runway up the center of the draw, and the small inconspicuous runway, complete with

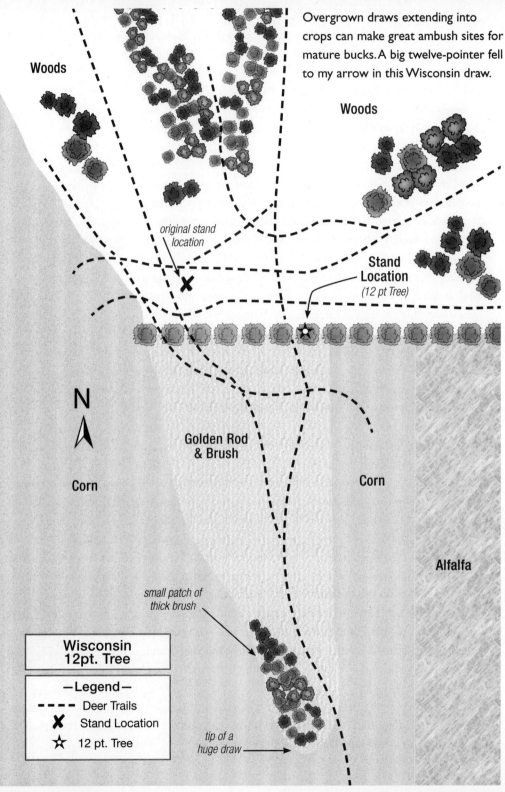

Overgrown draws extending into crops can make great ambush sites for mature bucks. A big twelve-pointer fell to my arrow in this Wisconsin draw.

Woods

Woods

original stand location

Stand Location
(12 pt Tree)

N

Golden Rod & Brush

Corn

Corn

Alfalfa

small patch of thick brush

Wisconsin 12pt. Tree

—Legend—

- - - Deer Trails
X   Stand Location
☆   12 pt. Tree

tip of a huge draw

numerous fresh rubs on tiny saplings, were both still there. Immediately, I selected and prepped a tree on the top edge of the draw that gave me a fifteen-yard shot to the smaller runway. Two days later I was perched in my new tree at about 4:30 a.m. It was a cold clear late September morning, with frost on the ground. The sun rose in a perfectly clear sky, and with it so did the temperature. By 9:00 a.m. the mercury already scratched the sixty-degree mark, and was rising. I hadn't seen a deer all morning. A bit too warm in the heat, I decided to remove my outer jacket and stowed it in my pack. While doing this I noticed my *doe in estrous* can that I had purchased just a couple days prior. On a whim, with my concentration waning from lack of action, I decided to test the call. Not expecting a response. I merely wanted to hear what it sounded like out in the great outdoors.

After tipping the can over three times I returned it to my pack and settled in, intent on sitting for a couple more hours and content to enjoy the pleasant sunny morning. Not ten minutes later a flicker of movement down the draw grabbed my attention. A deer's leg crossed between shadows, then a flash of an ear, and a second later an antler, big antler. The buck strolled up that tiny runway, stepped into my shooting lane, stopped and looked in the other direction. The arrow was on its way before I could even think about what was happening. In a burst the buck bolted straight ahead into the still brilliant golden rod that covers the tip of the draw. A half-hour later an ample, easy to follow, seventy yard blood trail led me to the buck. It definitely wasn't the buck from the year before, but instead a heavy-antlered, perfectly typical twelve pointer. It turned out to be the biggest deer killed on the farm in about a dozen years.

Arriving at the next point, I steal down to the center of the draw and back up the other side, heading straight for the twelve-point tree. I size up the situation quickly, attempting to keep my disturbance to a minimum. The deer sign is virtually the same as the previous two years, though there are fewer rubs this year, and only one half-hearted scrape. My tree is still in good shape, and the shooting lanes are all open. Though there is new growth, it hasn't filled them in yet. My main concern is that someone else will discover this spot and set up a stand here. This is probably the best hunting location on this entire portion of the farm. There isn't any sign of other hunters, so I move on.

Small sign, like this broken off rub turned licking stick can be easy to miss.

This big twelve pointer was a welcome surpise on a sunny, early season morning.

My third destination of the day, now afternoon, is at the tip of yet another draw, that drops into the same deep ravine as the point I just inspected. The ravine is absolutely huge, covering a solid mile of woods that adjoin these fields. The tip of this draw is about a half-mile walk from the first. Last fall I cleared out a tree here but never hunted from it, having filled my tag on the third day of my hunt. Arriving at the tree I notice immediately that things have changed. During the winter the farmer did some selective timber harvesting and this has effected the runway situation dramatically. The best runway from last year is blocked by the leftover tops, and the deer are now primarily using another runway that passes close to the tree, but is impossible to shoot to. There are still five runways that come together here, but they are not as tight to my stand as last year. I weigh my options. Either I have to find a new tree, or I have to subtly alter the landscape so the deer move where I want them. The search for a new tree proves fruitless. This is still the best tree in the point of this draw. Decision made, it's time to bring things a little closer together. (If you can't go to the deer, bring the deer to you.)

Bring Them to You

Deer, if they are relatively undisturbed, tend to take the path of least resistance. If faced with the choice, they will almost always select the easy route over the more difficult one. For instance, deer will travel several hundred yards out of their way to cross through a hole in a fence rather than jump over it. They also do not like walking through piled up brush. So my first action is to find dead branches to block off the main runway that I can't shoot to. There is a lot of dead stuff around, so this only takes me a few minutes. Busy dragging and stacking brush, I fail to notice the fast-approaching, ominous black clouds until the grumbling growl of thunder in the distance catches my ear. Despite the still bright sunshine above me, a mountain of thunderheads looms to the west. It looks like rain will soon arrive.

My second step is to open up the runways that have been blocked. This means cutting a path through some saplings and piling more dead branches to pinch the deer a little closer. The percussionist sky beats it's warning of an imminent summer downpour, so I hurry. It takes me about an hour to get everything just right, including opening up a new shooting lane. With just a few cuts remaining, the sky opens and lets loose it's heavy burden. Within seconds I'm drenched, but not miserable. The rain is warm, and it actually feels refreshing after roasting all morning under my Scent Lok. The water is perhaps a blessing. In such a downpour, any scent that I inadvertently left behind will hopefully be washed away. Tossing the last sapling on a pile, I start towards my van.

Upon arrival it is still pouring. Already soaked, I decide to take advantage of the suddenly plentiful water. Quickly stripped of all of my clothes, I shower in the rain. With my scent eliminating shampoo and soap I lather up right here between two cornfields. It has been two days since my last shower and this feels great. I only hope that nobody happens along to see me standing naked in the fields, so I make it quick. (You never know what other people's sensibilities may be.) My final rinse is from a plastic gallon jug of water. Feeling squeaky clean, I change into some normal street clothes, and place my soaked scouting attire in a black plastic bag. Within minutes I'm on my way to the local laundromat.

The rain has already stopped, and if it weren't for the glistening iridescent green hue of light reflecting through beaded water and the wet pavement, you would never think it had just poured buckets. Sitting in the back of my van with the sliding door open, I eat lunch. Some bread with a can of tuna fish followed by a can of fruit cocktail all washed down by the cola I just bought. Not exactly the lunch of champions, but protein, calories, a little caffeine and perhaps a couple vitamins — all for less than two dollars. When the money is gone the hunting is over, and the money is pretty thin to begin with. After eating, I dispose of my trash in the laundromat garbage can. The dryers spin their last few turns and come to an abrupt halt. Snatching my clothes from the heat, I hurriedly fold and return them to their plastic tubs.

It's early afternoon and there is still a lot of land to scout. I take the road out of the village that cuts up the side of the first steep bluff, under which the small town is nestled. Right on the top of this first bluff is the central and largest portion of the farm. I hope to catch the farmer, Greg, around somewhere. My intentions are to let him know I'm here. Approaching the main barn, I notice his old rusty red and white Ford parked in front of it. The barn is a former milking barn that has been re-styled into a calf-raising operation. After parking next to the truck, I step out. An auger is running out of one of the doors dropping silage onto the bed of a truck. At the bottom end of the auger I find Greg shoveling chopped green corn. He doesn't seem surprised to see me, and in fact he knew I was coming, just not exactly when. We shake hands and he makes me feel welcome. We talk a bit as he continues working. Perhaps not all the local farmers are like this, but Greg is one of the hardest working human beings I've ever met. In the three years I have hunted this farm, I've never seen this guy not working. He starts every morning well before daylight and stops well after dark. His farm is one of the cleanest and most orderly I've ever seen. We talk about the ride out, and the deer he has seen this summer. It's obvious after a few minutes that I am slowing his work down, so I get on my way. If there is anything that I don't want to do, it is to be any kind of nuisance to anyone who gives me permission to hunt. And besides, I have my own work to do.

From the end of the driveway I pull back onto the road that crosses the top of this bluff. Three ninety-degree curves and about two and a half miles down the road lies another parcel of Greg's land. This is the smallest of the three tracts he owns. It is a corner rectangle that measures exactly one hundred acres. Approximately eighty of the hundred acres is covered in crops, and about twenty in woods. Twenty acres isn't many treed acres, and pieces of woods this small can be hit or miss as far as deer activity goes, but this twenty has some outstanding features. Each of the last two years I've very briefly investigated this spot. My scouting and hunting, however, was very superficial.

My goal for this afternoon is to finally figure out the best options for hunting here. I have a couple destinations already in mind as I park my van and don my scouting attire. Despite the

This small Wisconsin town is home base for a couple days.

fact that my hunts here have been short, this corner has developed its own personal hunting history for me over the last two years. A couple of past encounters with mature bucks in these woods are welded in my hunting memory. Visions of these bucks scroll through my mind as I get under way.

The twenty acres of trees is roughly shaped like a right triangle, but the edge along the angled side has a couple ninety-degree turns added to it, instead of being a straight line. If viewed from the air, the edge looks like it has two irregular stair steps. A draw ends at each point of each step. The two draws merge at the outer northeast corner of the property. They are actually fingers of a deep valley that separates two very steep bluffs on the neighboring property, and extends almost a mile straight east. An apple tree punctuates each of the inside corners. The cornfield borders the woods all the way to the last point. From the last point, extending to the far corner and down the edge of the neighboring woods is a long narrow L-shaped overgrown cow pasture about forty yards wide. A lone ancient apple tree marks the corner of the cow pasture, situated twenty yards from the corn and twenty yards from the woods.

Two years ago, the first season I stepped foot in these woods, that apple tree in the pasture was drooping under the weight of its apples. There were also several scrapes under it. That year I quickly set up in the corner of the woods in a birch tree. My plan was to intercept the deer as they were leaving the woods heading for the apples, and I was certain the main runways were covered. A little too sure of myself, and convinced the deer had to get by me first, I failed to open up a good shooting lane to the apple tree itself. There was a shot to the tree, but not a really open one. I was so convinced of my plan that I didn't even walk off the distance to the apple tree.

You can probably imagine the rest of the story without me even telling it. Hubris always comes back to get you, especially if you disrespect the animal you are hunting. The first time I sat in that corner birch, a very large, heavy, wide, and dark antlered eight-pointer swaggered out of the corn, strutted straight across the fallow cow pasture, and fed under that apple tree. Try as I might, leaning, turning, stretching in my sling I couldn't get a shot. After he was gone I paced off the distance to the closest spot the buck stood, thirty-five yards, and borderline for what I consider really comfortable shooting distance. I knew right then that I had made a serious mistake, and I needed to find another tree. You have to be able to shoot to destination points. Big bucks will usually only present one opportunity and you have to be in a position to take advantage of it. This was one more lesson taught to me by a mature buck. Almost every encounter is a learning, and humbling experience. To add insult to injury, that buck left a huge rub about five yards under my tree a couple days later. I never saw him again from that spot.

Treading lightly, I trace the edge of the woods searching for deer sign. Although the field is in corn (the best possible situation), there aren't many tracks. The first of the three apple trees carries just a few apples. The second is drooping under the weight of its apples, and surprisingly the ground is littered with rotting fruit. The deer haven't touched them. There is simply too much food for deer in this area in September. With strips of corn, soybeans, and alfalfa in nearly

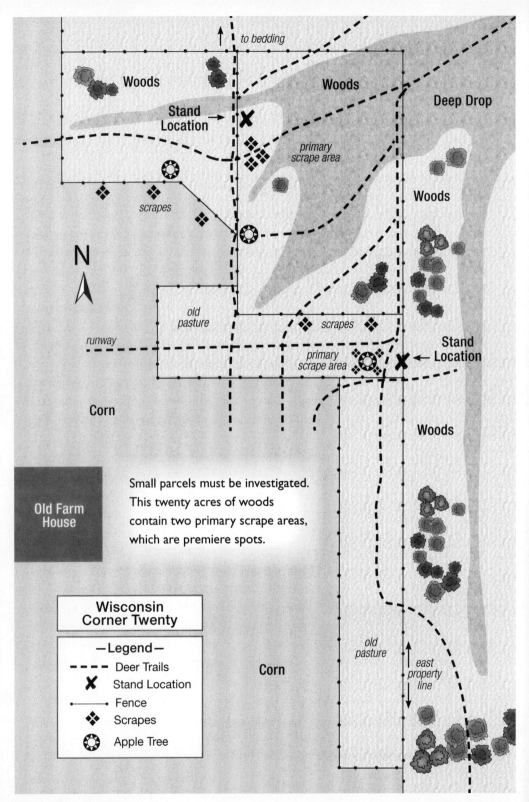

to bedding

Woods

Woods

Deep Drop

Stand
Location

*primary
scrape area*

Woods

scrapes

N

scrapes

Stand
Location

*old
pasture*

runway

*primary
scrape area*

Corn

Woods

Old Farm
House

Small parcels must be investigated.
This twenty acres of woods
contain two primary scrape areas,
which are premiere spots.

*old
pasture*

*east
property
line*

Corn

Wisconsin
Corner Twenty

—Legend—

- - - Deer Trails
✕ Stand Location
•—•—• Fence
❖ Scrapes
✺ Apple Tree

every field, combined with loaded apples trees, abundant oaks, and thick natural browse along the wooded hillsides, deer don't have to go far to fill their bellies. My first planned stop is that cow pasture apple tree. The burning question is whether, or not, it has apples this year. Absent the fruit, the hunting isn't nearly as good in that corner. Out in the pasture I stroll past the tip of the last point and anxiously peek down into the corner. Luck is with me; even from a distance it's easy to distinguish an abundance of baseball sized green apples. Following a hoof-honed runway through the mix of brome and Canadian thistle, I cut straight to the corner.

There are only two trees to choose from on the side of the fence I am allowed to hunt. The first is the larger of the two, and branches into three trunks. It would be possible to set up a sling from the middle trunk. The second is a single bowled tree within arms reach of the first. I inspect them carefully, mostly concerned about trunk lean and shot possibilities. Neither one is what I would call perfect; both of them lean slightly in the wrong direction. They both would be impossible to hunt out of with a conventional treestand. The lean of the trunks would make it impossible to hang a treestand on the side necessary to get a shot to the apple tree. After much consideration, I select the smaller tree and get to work. Following the same routine as always, while clearing out trees, I begin with setting treesteps.

Arriving at the top, I hook up my saddle and look around. Why didn't I pick this spot two years ago? From my current perspective, my original tree appears to have been a bone-headed aberration. The shot to the apple tree is now about fifteen yards, instead of the previous thirty-five. The background cover provided by the trunks of the other tree is great, and there are far more shot options than from the other spot. The only minor problem is a young maple, slightly left of center, between this tree and the apple tree. In order to get a shot on that side of the apple tree I will have to prune a couple of wide out-swept branches. From my perch, I mentally note the branches that need to go, and scurry back down to remove my steps. Clearing those

This is one of the corner apple trees.

branches proves to be far more work than I anticipated, and the cutting, dragging, and hiding consumes about two hours. In total the walk, tree selection, and setup takes me more than three hours. As I tuck the last branch in a thicket, the sun is dropping low on the horizon. It's too late to complete another location before dark, so I call it a day and hoof back to my van. Along the way a doe and her fawn are surprised to see me at the edge of the woods. One step around a corner of the cornfield, a stern stare from the doe twenty yards ahead hits me flat footed. A split-second verification glance, then white bouncing tails, and a few insulting snorts is the reaction to my rude gangly intrusion.

Changing out of my scouting clothes, I notice how sore my hands and shoulders are. Getting trees ready for hunting is real physical labor that requires muscles specific to climbing. It usually takes me a few days to grow accustomed to the work. In a day or two I won't even notice the climbing, but for now the steady burn of lactic acid in my muscles reminds me of my work. To finish out the evening I drive around the two long bluffs that contain the land I will be hunting on. Driving country roads looking for deer is a late summer ritual that I've enjoyed my whole life, starting as a small child in the backseat of my father's car. Tonight the drive is more than twenty miles without a glimpse of a single deer. There is simply too much corn hereabouts.

My last stop for the day is my sleeping spot that is tucked between cornfields. Dinner is a cold can of chunky style soup and some bread, chased down with cold water. As the sun sets I sneak along a cornfield to again check the hidden row of soybeans for deer. Peering around the stalks I spy a fawn about a hundred yards away. She is up to her shoulders in beans. With the help of my high powered binoculars I magically draw her to within an arms length, close enough to see individual hairs. I kneel down for the show. The fawn contently plucks bean pod after bean pod off the plants, chewing briefly before swallowing. The setting sun behind her creates the illusion of a golden aura around the little deer. Minutes later a mature doe emerges out of the cornfield. At perfect ease in the summer abundance, together they meander across the beans and disappear into more corn.

Mere seconds pass before a buck haunts out of the shadows of the adjoining woods. He is a young buck with about an eighty inch eight-point rack. In this area a rack of that size usually indicates a good yearling. Though there aren't terribly many deer here, this part of Wisconsin has the biggest deer, both body and antler wise that I have ever seen. Through my light gathering optics I survey the buck's every move and gesture until it is too dark to see him anymore. He is still munching on the protein rich beans as I pussyfoot my retreat. Closing off my evening, I scrawl a few words in my hunting journal; listen to some public radio; and drift off into a deep sleep.

Keep Looking

The following two days are dedicated purely to scouting from sunrise to sunset. I prepare a total of eight new hunting locations, and re-check three others. Two of the new spots are really good, among the best I've ever found. The first is a tree I immediately christen the *dump tree*. This spot is a classic funnel. It is located only a couple hundred yards behind the old farmhouse and the calve barns. At the back of Greg's property is a hidden alfalfa field that cannot be seen from any road, in fact, if I didn't actually walk back there I would never even know it exists. Right off the edge of this field the bluff drops off sharply. An old fencerow divides this field from the others. If you were to look at the bluff from the air, this particular field would look somewhat similar to a peninsula in a lake. It juts south from the longer east-west bluff line. The old fencerow runs across the top of the bluff line and extends across field. At the other end of the fencerow straight west is the biggest stand of timber on the entire farm; it contains several dense bedding areas. The hidden field and the timber are only about two hundred yards apart. Between the two is a narrow strip of woods that is bordered on the south side by very steep bluff, and on the north by more fields. At its narrowest point the strip is only about twenty yards wide. Strewn amongst the trees and brush in the strip is a variety of old discarded farm equipment and waste. There is an old metal wagon, and a pile of tires, some

I spend the last hour of light cruising around bluffs like these looking for deer, unsuccessfully! There is simply too much food and cover at this time of year.

shingles, and a several pieces of bent tin roofing. I step on an old license plate and pick it up — Wisconsin 1964. Everything back here in this dump seems to be from around then.

The tree I select is only about ten yards from the head-high pile of tires, and about thirty yards from that old metal wagon. There is also a dilapidated wooden pen about fifteen yards from my tree. From the looks of it, I imagine the pen was used to hold hogs. The main runway weaves between all of the artifacts. The tree has three trunks; the middle one being the best suited for my saddle. I run my steps up and get situated. As always while setting up a tree I try to answer the questions of why a deer would use this spot, and when is the most likely time a buck would pass through? In this instance the answers are simple. Any buck heading to or from that hidden field, which is brimming with buck sign, will have to cross this point in order to remain in cover.

The "when" portion of the question is a little more open ended. *Anytime* is the real answer, but my assumption is that mornings will be the best time to hunt this spot. Bucks probably visit that field at night and can be intercepted as they return to the big woods to bed down in the morning. Mature bucks are simply more likely to be on their feet in the daytime in the mornings on their way back to the security of their bedding areas, rather than on their way to a potentially dangerous feeding area in the evening. As I work, I imagine a big buck casually cruising down the main runway into my shooting lane presenting a perfect twenty-three yard shot. This is definitely one of the better trees on this farm.

The second truly notable tree on the farm I discover on the apple tree twenty. Two years ago I had a second encounter with that very large, heavy, wide, and dark antlered eight-pointer mentioned a while back. I was set up at the second corner near one of the apple trees. Right at the break of daylight I attempted a light rattling sequence. Just a few minutes later, that big boy was crossing the draw seeming to move in my direction. About seventy yards away, he hung up and let out a long loud wheeze. He just stood there for a long time as if to say, "I'm the boss here, and if you want a piece of me, you're going to have to come down and get it." He wouldn't come any closer despite my calling efforts. Though I tried puffing into my grunt call a couple of times, I might as well have been playing a tuba considering the buck's reaction.

Seeming agitated, he worked over a licking branch with his antlers and pawed at a scrape in rut-frenzied fashion, finishing off by pissing down his legs. Calling my bluff, he paced back and forth like a nervous prizefighter for a few minutes, and even wheezed one last challenge to his yet invisible adversary before vanishing forever. Following that morning's hunt, I crept down to where that buck stood and found six scrapes and several runways littered with rubs. A primary scrape area is one of those ephemeral spots that should cause a bowhunter's heart to drum a little faster, especially if he knows what he is looking for. Unfortunately I was unable to hunt there that year, or even prep a tree, because it was my last hunt on the farm that season

The image of that buck standing there wheezing is clearly etched in my mind as I investigate that draw. Though it is my fourth time hunting this farm, this is my first opportunity to really scour every inch of the place. My hunts the previous years have all been short, week-long excursions during season. Scouting and hunting on limited time during the season is a precarious balance act. You have to scout enough to set up in good spots, but still leave the area as undisturbed as possible so as not to disrupt daily movement patterns of the mature bucks. The consequence is that some areas may not be scouted quite as thoroughly as they should be, and some stands end up being just a little off. So far, however, my success rate here has been good: two mature bucks killed in three seasons, and three close encounters with mature bucks during that one off-year. Despite being lucky those other years, I don't want to press my luck if I don't have to. Thorough scouting leads to good hunting. I'm happy to finally have the time to seriously attempt to unravel the deer movement mystery on this farm.

Though there is only slight buck sign evident right now, in the form of a couple half-hearted rubs, the primary scrape area is, generally, as it was two years ago. A couple of the licking branches, over where the scrapes should be, have been chewed on and marked. Licking branches are the key to scrapes; the more of them there are, the more the scrape is being used. Five runways cross right here. The best tree for this spot is a century old maple. This is a centenarian that requires a lot of work, as I suppose most hundred-year-olds do. Maples tend to have many branches and this one is no exception. The first difficulty is getting up to where I want to hunt. There are numerous arm-thick branches that have to be pruned in order to be able to climb a straight shot up the trunk. This is important later for easing my bow up on its rope.

The second order of business is setting my saddle in the right position. This maple has a split trunk, and I set up on the outside trunk at a little over thirty-five feet in the air. This may seem a little high up, but the tree is on a slope and the shots to the deer trails and to the scrapes are all across the slope. Actually, my height above where the deer should be is only about twenty feet. This actually places me a little lower and closer to the deer. Fortunately, with the split trunk, there is an abundance of cover for my soon to be lurking self. Unfortunately, there are many branches that have to be removed in order to have clear shots. I get to cutting. Starting at the top and working down, it takes me an hour just to saw through all the iron-like maple branches in my way.

Satisfied with my pruning job and with my feet planted on the ground, I continue with clearing shooting lanes. I expect this to go a little faster, but am quickly disheartened. There are many more saplings and branches to remove than assumed, and as I trace all the runways I discover one well used trail is a little too far away to shoot to. This out-of-range deer trail must be blocked off in order to push the deer closer. I steadily cut, look, cut, look. The clearing takes me some time, but eventually all the lanes are open.

Thinking I'm nearly finished, it's up the tree one last time. Of course, there are a couple more branches from nearby trees that must be removed. Dropping again to the ground I remove my steps. The remaining branches are quickly out of the way and I begin with the heavy work. This means removing any sign of my somewhat drastic alteration to the neighborhood. I drag every branch and sapling eighty yards and deposit them in a deep washout. Some of the branches are so

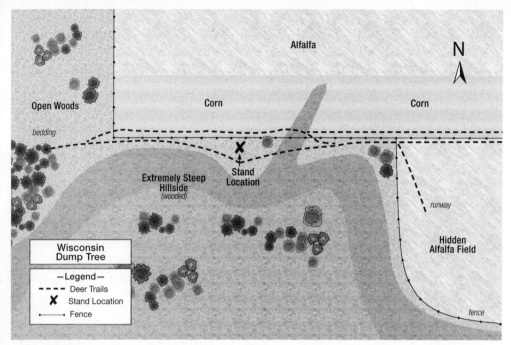

Alfalfa

Corn

Corn

N

Open Woods

bedding

Extremely Steep
Hillside
(wooded)

Stand
Location

runway

Hidden
Alfalfa Field

Wisconsin
Dump Tree

—Legend—
- - - - Deer Trails
X Stand Location
•——• Fence

fence

The dump tree is located in a narrow row of trees at the top of a very steep bluff. What a great funnel!

The maple tree ready to hunt. My saddle will be positioned in the split on the second trunk from the left. The other trunks provide great cover.

heavy that they have to be cut into sections and carried one at a time.

While finishing off the last of my water, I inspect the area one more time. Detail is a critical concept in successful bowhunting. The only visible sign remaining of my work is some scuffled leaves, a few flattened ferns, and a couple of eyeball white circles about twenty-five feet up the maple, where branches used to be. In a couple of days, no one will be able to tell that I was even here, unless they are astute observers and looking very closely. Of course, the deer will notice my work, despite my scent control efforts. This may effect the hunting this season, but this tree is now ready to serve as a stand for countless years, probably far longer

A view of my shooting lane from the top.

than I will have permission to hunt here. Four hours of hard, physical labor, a little longer than my average, is a small price for a long-term hunting spot. The work is worth it. Good primary scrape areas tend to be perennial. This maple punctuates the conclusion of my scouting on this Wisconsin farm. Hunting season here opens in three days, but I have other plans for the opener.

What To Do

- Strict attention to scent control is critical to successful, short-term hunting and scouting.
- In addition, critical to successful short-term hunts is thorough scouting. Take the time to scout!
- Internet topographic photos can help pinpoint your scouting, reduce your impact on new areas, and help you be a more successful, traveling deer hunter.
- A tree saddle is a perfect tool for short-term hunts; it increases your mobility tremendously over traditional treestands.
- When preparing your stand sights, make them as inconspicious to other hunters as possible.
- Washing your clothes and re-activating your activated carbon clothing are critical steps in reducing scent.
- Know all the regulations for where you're hunting and plan accordingly. In Wisconsin, many areas are what is called Earn-A-Buck zones, where you have to tag and register a doe before you may harvest a buck.

Chapter 3

North Dakota: Early Season Magic

I awaken at daybreak between cornfields in Wisconsin. A glance southeast reveals red clear skies, perfect weather for traveling. Without procrastinating, I jump into the driver's seat. The first stretch of road is short, ending at the nearby highway truck stop where I tank up and grab a cheap breakfast sandwich. The price of gas is excruciating. Gas prices are now thirty percent higher than a year ago. Sixty dollars worth quenches my van's thirst. The high price of gas has me concerned about my budget. As it is, about half of my money is earmarked for fuel, and I pray the price doesn't rise even higher. Another quarter dollar increase could cut my trip short. Just driving from central Michigan to western Wisconsin has already cost more than two-thirds the price of my Wisconsin, non-resident license. Upon completion of my hunting season I will have spent far more on fuel than on my various licenses. This puts non-resident license fees into perspective. They are still a good deal, in most cases. It's going to be a long day on the superslab, I-94 west. North Dakota, here I come.

Crossing the St. Croix, I burst into more suburban, and then urban chaos. As early as it is, this passes quickly behind me. The drive around Minneapolis isn't nearly as uncomfortable as the drive around Chicago. On the west side of the city the highway opens up fast, as does the landscape. The sprawl fades to farms, and the fields grow bigger the closer I get to the state line. In a few hours I cross the Minnesota-Dakota line into Fargo. Taking advantage of a highway-side sporting goods store, I stop to purchase a few items. While in Wisconsin my scouting rubber boots suffered a blowout in the form of a rip just above the ankle. Rubber boots are of little use when they have a hole in them. I have no choice but to cough up the cash for a new pair. As luck would have it, my favorite brand of boots are on sale — LaCrosse Alpha Burly's for only seventy-nine dollars.

The prairie begins where Fargo ends, literally. Coming from the deep green of Michigan the great wide open can be somewhat overwhelming, if not appear downright desolate. I'm aware that there is more to the view than meets the eye at first glance, but the huge expanse makes me a little uncomfortable. While driving I continually, and almost compulsively, search for trees, and the only ones seem to be windbreaks around farmhouses. There are miles and miles of fields as far as the eye can see. Where could all the deer possibly live? The complete lack of woods has me a touch worried. This is a completely blind trip. My hunting permission was gained as a matter of coincidence.

Access Can Come from Anywhere

While visiting good friends of mine, Hans and Corinna, I mentioned my propensity for bowhunting whitetails in September, and that the earliest opener closest to Michigan was in North Dakota. Immediately, Corinna countered that her former exchange student's brother lives in North Dakota, and that she thinks he hunts. One thing led to another, and a few weeks later I was talking to Dan on the telephone, who simply said, "If you are a friend of Corinna's, you are a friend of mine, and you are welcome to hunt." Dan told me he had access to about two thousand acres of private land I could hunt, with huge amounts of public land nearby. This all sounded so good that I had to take the chance. I ordered my license, and planned the trip. You never know where your next hunting permission might come from, especially if you are willing to travel.

Just outside Fargo, I call Dan to let him know my location. According to his estimation, my arrival at his place should be in the early evening. All the way to Bismarck I stare out the window hoping for better-looking, or at least more huntable, whitetail habitat. In Bismarck I turn north and within an hour ride into Dan's small prairie town. It isn't much; a gas station, a few small stores, an old downtown of sorts, all surrounded by a narrow ring of houses. Though anxious to finally meet Dan face to face, I have some reservations. Dan is the pastor at the local church. Though I have nothing against religious types (there are several ministers and pastors in my close circle of friends), I don't appreciate overzealous *holier than though* proselytizing. Having

Typical road on my drive through rural North Dakota.

only spoken to Dan briefly on a couple occasions, I'm not sure what to expect. Dan is in the front yard with his two young boys as I pull into his driveway. My fears turn out to be unfounded. He greets me with a big smile, and a dinner of grilled venison. We get along great.

After dinner we decide to go for a drive. Dan wants to show me some deer, and I'm quite willing to take a look at the area. Still somewhat dazed from the long ride through the great wide open, I would like to see a few cervids to ease my concerns. We shoot straight out of town on a wide gravel road across what looks likes a vast expanse of sun-charred picked wheat field, light brown for miles on both sides of the road. Still, I'm wondering where the deer could be. After ten miles of gravel we top a slight rise, and below us is a wide wooded river bottom sweeping like a narrow green oasis from north to south. In an hour it will be dark. To my pleasant surprise we get to look at about thirty deer, including a couple of yearling bucks. Now, at least I have proof there are indeed whitetails in North Dakota. Back at his house, Dan and I sit up late into the night talking hunting, and sharing stories.

The night is very short, and my alarm clock rudely sounds at 6:00 a.m. The area I will be hunting is another hour drive west. The early start should allow me to get in a solid day of scouting. Dan gives me directions and keys to his cabin. This is already way more than I had asked for. But as they say, *never look a gift horse in the mouth*, so I take the keys and listen carefully to his instructions about how to turn on the electricity and water. By 7:30, after breakfast and some more hunting talk, I'm on my way. The drive takes me across the green oasis of the Missouri River and back into the great wide open. My apprehension increases the farther from the river I drive. There sure isn't much of what I would call traditional whitetail cover. Along the way I stop to ogle a couple groups of pronghorns and snap a few photos. Pronghorns aren't animals I encounter every day.

A little after nine o'clock, I arrive at the cabin. The cabin turns out to be far more than I expected. In fact, I stop, back up, and re-read the name on the mailbox to make sure I'm at the right place before rolling up the driveway. Now I understand what Dan meant when he somewhat ironically said, "You'll like the cabin!". The cabin is a brand new house built in chalet style. I unlock the door and am met on the inside by some serious quality; wooden and tile floors, stonework, and large windows, with great views in every direction. There is a mounted pronghorn and a couple of deer on the wall. I would find out later that this is not really a cabin, but rather Dan's retirement home, built mostly by his own hard work and the help of an unexpected inheritance.

The house sits on the side of a long slope that they call a mountain in North Dakota; its really not much more than a hill. The front yard is a thin alfalfa field (which means it's more prairie grass than alfalfa) and is situated between two badland-style earthen bluffs. Beyond the front yard is light brown prairie grazing land to the horizon. The backyard is grass prairie with various sized patches of buffalo berry, and a larger alfalfa field. A wooded draw cuts down the mountain and around the west end of the field. From the house I can see more wooded draws across the road and up the mountain. The sight of trees lifts my spirits. Though I've never hunted an area

Pronghorns along the road on the way west.

quite like this before, wooded draws are at least something familiar. Dotting the mountain are giant single boulders and a few blocky rock formations. Numerous black cattle are grazing the cow-burnt slope between the rocks.

Moving into my temporary digs, I stack my four rubber tubs containing all of my hunting equipment just inside the sliding glass door, along with my two bows, a duffle bag and my selection of boots. Next to the kitchen counter is a place for my food cooler. There isn't any perishable food in the cooler, but I always take it along in the event I happen to kill a deer and have to keep the venison cold. The electricity is running with the flip of a switch, and I turn my attention to the water and water heater. This takes me a few minutes to figure out. Dan told me to sleep in the guest bedroom in the basement, so I walk down and make the bed. As far as hunting accommodations go, I don't think I've ever had it better than this, even while hunting at home. Hopefully the hunting is as good as the living standard.

Let's Get Going

Itching to get started, I take a ride to superficially investigate the area. My hunting permission includes Dan's land and some ranch property across the road. There is also a huge block of public land a couple miles north. Turning out of the driveway, I head north and then west onto the ranchland. A short lane ends in a small wheat stubble field where cattle are grazing. The property has numerous woody draws that from a distance appear to have some potential. The Badlands begin right here. Earthen bluffs extend to the horizon to the west. There isn't a cloud in the sky, and the temperature is already in the 80's. Just looking out there at those bone-dry dirt ravines gives me a parched uneasy feeling. The desert, sun, and extreme heat have never been that attractive to me, and therefore most of my outdoor experience has centered around northern boreal forest, or northwestern rainforest, rain, snow and ice. This is indeed a completely new terrain type for me. While I'm standing there glassing, a conservation officer in a gray truck idles by and into the bordering ranch. He doesn't seem to take any interest in me and is soon around the bend. With the CO out of sight, I jump back into my van and roll north towards the public land.

The land belonging to the ranches along the way look as though they should hold deer, at least the hills are laced with draws and wooded ridges. In between there is grass, grazed English garden short by too many cattle. There are also some crops, mostly wheat stubble, but a few thin alfalfa fields. Arriving at the public ground I find the terrain remains quite the same, brushy draws, a few fields, and badlands dirt buttes to the west. Rounding a curve I am shocked to discover a cornfield, with brown stalks over my head. How do they get corn to grow out here,

The little cabin on the prairie was more than I expected.

where the native prairie grass is only shin high and sun burnt? There doesn't seem to be nearly enough water for a crop like that. This has to be some new modified strain that must be crossed with cactus in order to survive without any irrigation. In about an hour I cover all the official roads, stopping here and there to glass for potential hunting spots and to study the hard packed ground for tracks around any water holes I stumble across. Starting back to the cabin I again meet the gray truck containing the conservation officer. I pull off to one side to let him pass. As he revs closer, I raise my hand in greeting. The officer stops his truck next to my van.

A man with a red sun burnt face under the brim of a soiled cowboy hat leans slightly out the window. He talks through a bulge of chewing tobacco under his lip. We exchange information for a few minutes, first about who I am; what I am doing right now; and what I'm hunting. I offer freely the information about my staying at my new friend Dan's cabin, and the rancher who is allowing me to hunt his land. Playing a little dumb, I ask questions about the deer and the local hunting. The cowboy warden is more garrulous than I expected. In short order I hear about the nearby habitat dividing line. On one side there is a majority of whitetails and on the other mule deer. He asks me if I've seen any elk yet. I haven't, and in fact, didn't even know there were any elk around here. Elk are obviously an important subject for this man. It seems the cornfields are specifically planted for the elk, to keep them out of the neighboring rancher's fields. The officer also confides that a good five by five bull is working a nearby cornfield. If I'm interested, I should post up on an overlooking butte and there is a good chance to catch a glimpse of the bull in the evening. We trade more information about hunting elk, or at least the draw chances, in our various home states. Since I've yet to hunt elk myself, there isn't much for me to say. In parting he wishes me good hunting.

The easy part is over; now I have to find some real spots to hunt. Parking along the road at the ranchland, I throw on my Scent Lok, grab my scouting pack, and three bottles of water. The sun is approaching its apex, and the temperature has risen close to 90 degrees. Up over the first mountain I go. From the peak, the draws on the other side look like they must be deer travel superhighways. I mosey down to have a look. My short look takes me from one draw to the next, and on to the next. My frustration grows in direct relation to my ever-increasing distance from my van, and my thirst. There are so many cattle in here; they have the deer sign completely trampled. Even in the best looking spots where several draws come together, I can distinguish only a few faint sets of tracks on the dusty cow paths.

Most of the trees, thick barked bur oak, are about fifteen feet tall and impossible to hunt out of, even with a saddle. Though they are small, these trees give the impression of being really old. Their trunks are knarled and crooked, with dark burn scars here and there on their thick bark. The crowning moment comes four hours into my walk when I run my shin square into a mound covered with cactus. That's right, cactus! I knew it was dry here, but I didn't really expect cactus in North Dakota. It takes me a few minutes to pick all the fine hypodermic-like needles out of my skin, and to stop swearing. In almost five hours of steady walking I've barely been able to find a deer track. By the time I arrive back at my van I am out of water, my feet hurt, my back is stiff from carrying my scouting gear, and I am drenched from sweat. I don't think I have been this physically uncomfortable in years, and mentally things aren't much better. Eighteen hours of driving and a non-resident license for this?

Returning to the cabin, I immediately drink a belly full of water; never has water tasted so good. A late lunch comes next, a can of cold Chunky soup and some bread. Sitting in the comfortable shade of the porch, I mentally weigh my options. During my walkabout, I didn't find a single obvious location to hunt. I've come too far to be able to bail out, so I have to come up with something fast, especially if I plan on hunting in the morning. For lack of a better idea I return to the public land, to an area containing a couple of water holes. As hot as it is, the deer have to drink sometime. Surrounding one of the water holes are quite a few tracks. On a slope above the water I open up a spot to sit behind a buffalo berry bush by matting the grass flat to the ground. From behind the flat green camouflage of the bush there is a twenty-five yard shot to the close side of the pond and about a forty yard shot to the other. There isn't a tree within a half-mile, and my "blind" is only about eighty yards off the main access road. This spot will have to suffice for tomorrow morning's hunt.

Disappointed with both the meager results of my scouting foray and my first impromptu blind, I return to the cabin. The sun is dropping in the west, and with it, the temperature. While physically, but not consciously, eating dinner, I stare across the prairie, wondering where the deer are. The only audible sounds are a pleasant whispering wind, and the chirping of songbirds radiating from patches of buffalo berry. Lost in my hectic pace and determination to find deer, I've failed to notice the subtle beauty of this place. In an instant the world becomes more lucid. The setting sun drapes the hills in a golden hue and a rainbow of color shimmers through the waves of undulating grass. It's time to slow down. Sipping my water, I spend an hour simply enjoying the view.

Where are the whitetails in terrain like this?

Deer-Topia

As much as I try, I just can't get over the fact that I have not seen a single deer all day, nor found much sign. In my conversations with Dan, he told me many times that there are really a lot of deer out here. Combating my rising skepticism, I climb back in my van with the intention of spending the last hour of daylight riding rubber to find some deer. Less than a half-mile from the cabin, a doe and her twin fawns are standing in the ditch next to the road. In the next hour I count more than sixty deer. They are in every field, along the road, and at the edges of draws. Mostly, I watch whitetails, but a few mule deer are among them. Just after nightfall only a few hundred yards from the cabin there are three mule deer bucks standing in the road, seemingly not at all concerned about the glare of my headlights that neatly frames them. The biggest is a tall four by four. I'm flabbergasted. This place is amazing; deer are everywhere and nowhere. Perhaps there was something I missed on my scouting walkabout today.

The next morning I'm up at 3:00 a.m. As usual, before my first hunt of the season I didn't sleep all that much. You would think with a quarter century of bow seasons under my belt, it would be possible to get some sleep before the opener; however, images of big antlered bucks doggedly keep me awake. The mounting excitement doesn't feel much different now than it did when I was a green young twelve-year-old. Though I know better than to expect too much on the first morning, I can't help myself. This feeling is probably what keeps me hunting. If there is ever a day that I'm not excited about bowhunting, that is the day I will give it up.

Out on the porch I pull on my Scent Lok BaseSlayers, and a layer of scent free (as far as my nose is concerned) long underwear. Over this comes my outer layer of Scent Lok. There is a light breeze from the west and the sky is crystal clear. The stars are amazingly bright, befitting the license plate claim of Big Sky Country from just a few miles west of here. In a hurry, though I don't need to be, I'm on my way to the public ground in a matter of minutes. After traveling across two time zones, I am uncertain about the time of daybreak, so I want to be plenty early. I park a half-mile from the water hole and walk the rest of the way. Arriving at the little patch of buffalo berry, I hunker down on my foam cushion and settle in. It only takes a half an hour for me to realize that I'm considerably under-dressed. The temperature has been in the nineties for a couple of weeks during the day, but right now it's not all that much above the freezing point. Tucking in all of my loose ends I buckle down for a hard morning. Shivering through a dark pre-dawn is something I have done often.

Two and a half miserable hours pass before daybreak. Obviously I was a little too eager to get started this morning. At first light my concentration is peaked, and I am mentally attempting to will deer in my direction, studying each wrinkle in the land as though a deer should materialize at any second. My first hunt is usually an exercise in hyper-awareness. Though I attempt to relax, it takes me a couple days to fully calm down. Suddenly a pair of headlights, glowing like Lucifer's eyes, appears in the distance and in a matter of minutes a full-sized Chevy grunts by. This first vehicle is followed in the next hour by four more trucks and two motorcycles. The guys

On my first evening drive around the area, there were deer standing everywhere, both mule deer and whitetails.

on the motorcycles have rifle cases strapped to their bikes. I might as well be sitting on I-94, as much traffic as there is out here. This sucks! Clearly I'm less than thrilled with the situation. Yesterday, I didn't see a single vehicle, except for the conservation officer, and now there are trucks everywhere.

Not having anything else to do, I decide to stick to my plan and hunt until at least 10:00 a.m. Soon the sun becomes my friend again, as the first gentle rays touch me from the west. The temperature rises noticeably and my shivering stops. The warmth brings with it something I really didn't expect. A flicker of movement catches my eye on the side of the bluff. Whoa! Antler is the next thing I see — big antler. A massively muscular mule deer buck carrying a four by four rack casually crosses the side of the hill. He strolls down, skirting the far side of the water hole, halting several times at forty yards, clueless to the fact that a human predator is lurking behind this little bush. His neck is bulging with defined muscle, that continues down into his deep barrel chest. His tines are at least a foot long. By whitetail standards this deer is a giant, and probably exactly what all these guys in the trucks are looking for. I, however, only have a whitetail license in my pocket, and must be content with just watching this fine buck. The muley slowly descends into a brushy draw and vanishes after about a half-hour. I've never hunted mule deer before, so this is a novel experience for me. The last hour of my hunt passes without incident, and shortly after 10:00, I return to my van. The motto for my first hunt is: nice buck, wrong species.

Back at the cabin, the first thing I do is delve into the North Dakota hunting regulations. Flipping a few pages, the reason for the heavy traffic this morning becomes clear. The youth rifle season is this weekend. It probably would have been wise to know this tidbit of information beforehand. Perhaps I should stick to the private land for the remainder of the weekend. Lunch and a nap fill in the next couple hours. The comatose style nap does wonders after the last couple days of continuous action and a night of little sleep. In early afternoon, I take a quick walk out in Dan's back alfalfa field and draw. In the corner where the field and the draw merge, there is sign of deer activity in the form of tracks and a few runways. Thanks to the fact that there aren't any cattle grazing here, the sign is actually visible. I select a patch of tall grass next to a buffalo berry bush to set up in. With a spot ready for my evening hunt I cruise back to the cabin and hop in my van. Moving up the mountain to the public land, I inspect a cornfield that is about a half mile off the road. There is clearly a lot of deer activity in and around the corn, but again no trees. As a consequence I open up the inside of two more buffalo berry patches to use as groundblinds. So far I haven't found a single tree I could hunt out of, at least not in a spot worth hunting. Even on short scouting forays, I find myself walking miles.

You Can't Kill a Deer Unless You are Hunting

Following a short intermezzo back at the cabin, I grab my bow and sneak out to the corner of Dan's alfalfa field. Stepping into my hiding spot, I quickly and very quietly matt down the grass, making a circle big enough to sit and have a little room to maneuver. This draw is not very wide and any deer it may contain are within a hundred yards — probably even closer. My bow lies on the ground next to me; arrow knocked. The cover around me is decent, tall grass between two buffalo berry bushes. It is just enough for a freelance hunt, as long as the deer don't come too close. Satisfied with my makeshift blind, I grab my laser range finder and select a few objects to use as range markers. The round bails in the field are obvious choices, the closest one on the left is thirty yards and the one on the right side is forty. The main runway entering the field is also about thirty yards to my left. Mentally I note these distances as reference points. If a buck comes into range, I can now estimate the shot distance in relation to a known distance to a reference point.

My expectations are very low for this evening. All I want to do is see some whitetails while hunting and relax a bit. This overall hunt is a work in progress, as I haven't found any really good locations yet. Scouting during the evening when the deer are up and moving is counterproductive, so actually I am just out to enjoy myself. But, of course, there is an unpunched tag in my pocket and a mature buck can show up anywhere, at any time. You can't kill a deer unless you're out hunting.

It is a perfect evening, with a slight breeze straight out of the west. The sun is warm but not uncomfortable. In minutes I'm settled in and totally relaxed, in a state of mind that I didn't get to this morning, shivering like I was. My eyes grow heavy in short order, so I lay down flat on the ground, on my stomach. This is an unusual experience, and I don't think I've ever hunted before while lying flat on the ground. My nest is so comfortable that I quickly doze off in a light sleep.

A wispy cough jolts me awake. Without lifting my head I open my eyes to see a deer standing about ten yards away, right on the edge of the field. The deer is still in its russet summer coat. A quick glance at its head reveals a young doe, perhaps a fawn, but without another deer present as a comparison it is hard to tell. The deer just stands there for a few seconds before taking another step or two in my direction. If it maintains its course, it will walk within a yard of me. I don't move a muscle. To my surprise the deer stops and steps into the tall grass, and beds down only eight yards away on the other end of the buffalo berry patch. I can't believe this is happening. I have had deer close before, but never this close bedded. The doe coughs again, twice; the sound is so sudden that I am startled. I can see her chest rise and fall with every breath. Her ears rotate, one at a time, and then in unison, turning to pick up sounds that I can't distinguish above the breeze. She lies there chewing her cud, at first quickly, then slower, until she stops and her head slowly drops to her chest, like a small child falling asleep. With a sudden jerk she lifts her head back up, only to lower it again. Her eyes are closed.

A wild deer is asleep only a few yards away from me. My instinct as a predator is to kill this deer, and what predator with any sense wouldn't take the opportunity this deer has given. It is as though this deer has offered itself to me. However, as a modern hunter, with only a single tag in my pocket, I content myself with watching. This is a truly incredible hunting experience. A couple of times I have been closer to wild deer, but never this close with a deer acting completely natural — totally unaware of my presence. My senses are peaked and I note every move this little doe makes. The last thing I want to do is spook her. I want to savor the moment. Though I move only very little, to shift my weight and inspect the surroundings for more deer, each movement is contemplated, slow and silent. Yet another cough-sneeze startles me. The doe raises her head and begins chewing again, shaking her head, obviously irritated by whatever is causing her cough. A few minutes later her head drops again to her chest. I feel very alive.

About forty minutes pass before the young doe suddenly stands up without any kind of warning. She stands for a minute checking her surroundings before turning and slipping down the draw. Left alone in the grass, the object of my pointed attention now gone, my thoughts begin to wander, as is normal for me while hunting. There have been hunters here for a long time, hunting much as I am right now. The Sioux resided in these hills in the 19th century after being pushed out of their earthen lodges in Missouri. They called this place Tah-kah-o-kuty, which means "the place where we kill deer," a name I find fitting under the present circumstances. Before the Sioux, this area was home to the Hidatsa. For about five hundred years they hunted deer and buffalo here, but were devastated by smallpox and other diseases brought by the Europeans. The Hidatsa believed that animal spirits were residents of the various buttes in this area of their hunting range. A nearby butte is, according to Hidatsa legend, a center of creation. Through the song of the great owl, all of the creatures of the prairie, including man, which were all spirits at the beginning of time, came into existence. It is said that if you listen, you can still here the song of the great owl.

Myself, still tucked in the tall grass, I imagine Sioux and Hidatsa hunters crouched behind this very bush, watching the wind sweep in waves through the short prairie grass, comfortable under a gentle fall sun. Their thoughts and feelings while hunting must have been quite the same as my own, though I doubt they wouldn't have accepted the offer from the young doe. I listen through whispering of the wind for the voices of these hunters past, and I listen for the song of the great owl. I imagine what this land looked like a couple hundred years ago, before roads, fences, and cattle. Though I'm sure things have changed dramatically, I am just as sure that deer lived in these oak draws. In fact, many of these knurly oaks stood witness to the Sioux and Hidatsa hunters, just as they are watching me now.

Having wild whitetails within a few yards while hunting on the ground is an amazing experience.

I hope these oaks stand for hundreds of more years, and witness the next generations of hunters. Cattle have replaced the buffalo that grazed these plains and the bears are gone. The plain's grizzly must have kept the hunters on their toes. The big cats were gone too for a long time, but have since returned to stalk the hills again. There have been hunters here for a long time, and I am honored to be able to take up the bow in this sacred land.

As the sun sinks deep to the west and the shadows grow long, more movement catches my attention to the left. A doe and two fawns are standing thirty yards away. They must have been bedded right along the side of the draw. The doe is obviously very mature; she is big and dark, with a very long nose. One of her fawns is dark and the other one far lighter in color. The darker one is a button buck. As I watch, the light colored fawn cough-sneezes a couple of times. It is the same deer that was bedded next to me. The three feed out into the field, crossing in front of me at a distance of about twenty-five yards. They aren't alone for long. Another mature doe and her two fawns step out of the draw to my right. These three also cross in front of me. At this point I have six deer feeding within thirty yards.

A few minutes behind the second group is another single deer. This one carries a pair of thick four inch spikes between its ears; a buck. This is perhaps one of the smallest antlered bucks I have ever seen, whitetail antlers don't get much smaller than the ones this guy is carrying. He feeds out amongst the other deer, careful not to get too close to the mature does. Just to see what I can get away with, I carefully ease into an upright position, as if I were going to shoot. Waiting for the right instant, with all the deer looking away from me, I slowly rise to my feet, with my bow in hand. I stand there for probably ten minutes, without being noticed. I haven't shot a deer from the ground in a very long time. It would be possible to shoot at any of the deer in the field. Satisfied that I could get a shot, I wait for the right moment and duck back into my hiding spot. The last half-hour of the evening is spent watching these deer casually feed across the field over a slight rise, and out of sight. Just before black dark a big owl silently swoops down from the oaks out of the draw behind me, right over my head, and glides across the field before vanishing into the prairie. Tah-kah-o-kuty!

The next morning I arrive at my ambush site, yet another natural ground blind tucked inside a buffalo berry bush, about two hours before daylight. The moon is full and bright, so full in fact that I don't need to use my flashlight. The sky is mostly clear, revealing the broad brilliant swath of the Milky Way, with its millions of sparkling stars. The cry of a bugling bull elk greets me. I arrange my equipment and enjoy the concert of elk. There are two bulls, one is very close, and the other towards the end of a wooded butte, to the northeast, probably about a half mile away. Their screeching cries cut sharply through the icy night air. The bull nearest me seems quite agitated and moves initially in my direction. His voice carries a deep scratchy challenge that echoes of love and fighting. He bellows and threats, and I imagine him trying to impress his harem of cows, while chasing them about. His call moves to and fro — sometimes closer, sometimes a little farther away.

On the inside of one of my makeshift buffalo berry ground blinds.

A short pause is followed by another screeching bugle not more than a hundred yards distant, in the wooded end of the draw I am hunting. Perhaps the bull will walk past me. Full of anticipation I wait, expecting to see faint moon shadows of elk crossing the draw at any second. For several minutes there is silence, and though I am not hunting elk my senses are on edge. I sure would like to have that bull walk by. My hopes though are dashed as the next bugle rings out about two hundred yards to the northeast. For the next hour I follow the sound of this lovesick bull as his course takes him up into the hills. The last hallow cry comes just at the crack of daylight; then silence. Minutes later, the first truck of the morning rumbles down the road. These hunters are late and have already missed the concert.

The black fades to gray as light seeps in from the east. It is the edge of daylight, that moment when I notice I can actually see into, and across, the draw. The blast of doe snorting only a few yards directly behind me nearly causes me to jump out of my socks. I turn to see that famous white tail bobbing straight away, and listen as the doe snorts for several minutes, letting every deer within earshot know that something isn't quite right. She must have wanted to bed in the same patch of brush as I am sitting, as close as she was to me. This is one of the principle difficulties of hunting from the ground. When deer are too close it is very difficult, and sometimes impossible, to remain undetected at eye level. And, you have to let a lot of deer pass, if you are serious about hunting mature bucks. When I set up this spot I planned for my best shot to be down in the draw, at about thirty yards. At thirty yards it is still possible to let deer pass, remain undetected, and be able to draw and shoot at deer; any closer and the difficulty of achieving this increases exponentially. The rest of the morning passes without notable event. A doe and two fawns cross the face of a distant bluff. No other deer appear.

At 10:00, I get up and walk about a quarter mile to the nearby cornfield. Along the north side of the field, I find numerous rubs and a funnel of sorts. At this point a weedy strip drops down

Two pronghorn bucks standing in the driveway to the cabin.

from the edge of the field into an extremely thick bedding area. There are fair sized rubs all along the edge. It feels good to finally discover some clear buck sign. This is actually the most buck sign I have found yet in North Dakota. Par for the course so far, there aren't any trees big enough to hunt from, so I clear out another natural ground blind inside a patch of brush. Clearing a circle down to the bare dirt on the inside requires a little work, but you have to do this to make sure that the ground is quiet. It takes me about an hour to finish the job.

Shortly before noon, I begin my drive back to Dan's cabin. At approximately the halfway mark I spy a coyote working the edge of a draw. Stopping my van to watch, I attempt to snap a couple of photos. When out hunting, a camera is always in my van. The coyote halts the second my motor is silenced; he glances in my direction, and bursts into a sudden sprint, first across a short rise and then straightaway. He doesn't hesitate for a second, and there is no opportunity to click a photo. He runs with a fair limp, perhaps from waiting too long to vacate the area after a truck stopped along the road.

Arriving at the cabin I'm met by two antelope bucks standing in the driveway. Both are young bucks. In the driveway I pull to within forty yards of them, stop and capture a couple of photos. The bucks don't seem all that concerned, and don't run away. My experience with pronghorns is basically non-existent, so I'm intrigued and grateful to have an opportunity to observe these majestic animals. Hoping to be able to observe them in a less intrusive manner, I idle up to the cabin. Perhaps there is more to see from the deck, or out one of the windows. From inside the cabin, I'm surprised to discover many more pronghorn feeding in the front alfalfa field. There are more than a dozen of these prairie speedsters out there. There are thirteen does and a single

Pronghorn in the front yard.

buck; some of the does are feeding while others are bedded at the east end of the field. The buck is cruising back and forth, constantly on the move.

Even though I admittedly know very little about pronghorns, this is a really big buck. He obviously considers these does his own. Each time a doe wanders a little too far away from the group, he trots over to gently urge her back. His fears seem founded. Around the edges there are at least four younger bucks orbiting, waiting, and hoping for a chance. While the big buck is momentarily preoccupied with a doe, one of the young bucks brazenly struts into the field. Instantly, the mature buck bolts towards his younger rival, covering the hundred yards between them in a blink. In a cloud of dust both bucks vanish over a dirt mound, completely out of sight in seconds. This is the first time I have ever seen a pronghorn really run. They are indeed very fast animals. A few minutes later, the big buck trots back over the dirt bluff to resume his duties as the dominant male. How long can he keep up this pace? This show could go on for hours, but I still have much hunting to do, so I get on with lunch.

Midday is for Practice and Scouting

After lunch, I decide to shoot my bow. It is very important to keep shooting during the hunting season. Too many hunters simply stop practicing after the season opener. From a hunting standpoint, it is critical to practice with your bow during the season for a couple of reasons. The first is simply to keep your shooting muscles in shape. Bows can be tough to draw when the weather turns cold. And the second is to always be certain that your bow is sighted in, and everything functions properly. I don't know how many times I have heard of material failures happening just as that big buck finally presented a shot. Most of the time this could have been avoided if a little more emphasis had been placed on in-season shooting.

I pull my portable Rhinehart target from its place between the front seats of my van. From the back deck I set it out at exactly thirty yards, first shooting a few groups with my field tips, and then following up with a couple arrows equipped with practice broadheads. After this I move around to the front deck. This deck is up in the air and I want to emulate hunting from a tree. Placing the target at thirty yards, I fling a few more arrows. Twenty minutes of shooting is enough. I will repeat this procedure every couple of days, all season long.

Midday is spent scouting. I explore a couple of large brushy ravines that I can see from the road, hoping to find that first premiere spot. The results of my four-hour walk are less than spectacular. Although I discover some buck sign, that one great spot where everything comes together eludes me. I know this is only my third day here, but a little frustration is beginning to set in. Though there seem to be deer everywhere, I have yet to discover any truly exceptional buck sign. The lack of scouting success weighs more in my mind than the hunting. I warn myself to be patient, if there is anything I do have, it is time, and with enough perseverance I will eventually find what I am looking for. Until that happens, I will continue hunting secondary spots reminding myself that a mature buck can show up anywhere, at any time.

A couple hours later, I find myself sneaking into the tip of a brushy draw that ends in the public land with rows of alfalfa and corn. I take my seat under a split-trunk poplar. This is yet another secondary spot. Any deer entering these fields should follow this draw. Along the edges there are several decent rubs. My best shots are out into the adjacent alfalfa field. Hunting field edges is something that I rarely do, the main reason being that while hunting field edges you almost always spook deer either in the way out in the evening, or on the way in the morning. However, since none of the spots I have found so far are what I would even call good, and you can't kill a deer if you aren't hunting, I decide to hunt this field edge.

Settled into my hiding spot, I relax and scan into the thick green of the draw. To my surprise a doe is bedded only about twenty yards away. She is in thick cover and difficult to pick out, even at such a short distance. Even so, I can't believe I didn't see her while walking to my hunting spot. On evening hunts I try to stalk the last several hundred yards to my stands. If I had been walking through she probably would have let me walk right by her. I'm sure she saw me coming from over a hundred yards away. She is staring intently in my direction, with both ears focused squarely on me. Sitting perfectly still, I return the stare. For several minutes she doesn't move a muscle, nor do I for that matter. The wind is from her to me, and I have the feeling she is either not sure what I am, or she intended to let me pass and was surprised when I stopped. Then in one calculated move she stands, and, almost crouched in an attempt to sneak, tiptoes away. She barely makes a sound. Within seconds the still green September woods swallow her. The doe leaves me with an even greater sense of awe for whitetail deer. If I had not sat down looking directly at this deer, I would probably never have known she was there.

Rubs like this catch my attention.

A half-hour later two fawns pass within ten yards of me and feed out into the field. They take turns feeding and then chasing one another around. This is fun to watch; they remind me of kids playing. Suddenly they stop and dash straight back towards the woods. In their haste they about run over me, jumping into the woods about five yards from where I'm sitting, and flying by. Barely out of sight, I hear a couple of gun shots ring out, followed by a distant barking of commands. Some bird hunters are working the ridge along the far end of the field. The remainder of my evening is spent observing these orange clad hunters from a distance, hoping that they go away before the evening is over. They are done hunting about the same time I am.

My morning hunt on day four is not much different than my other hunts so far: cold clear skies with me sitting on the ground in a secondary spot. The highlight of my morning is a howling duel between two packs of coyotes before daylight. The singing begins with a single howl followed by a chorus of yipping and chiming in of more howls reaching a raucous crescendo and crashing to a sudden halt. Almost as soon as the howling stops, a pack somewhere across a large draw begins its own primal song. A response from the first pack follows immediately. This goes on for about fifteen minutes, and then just stops. Why the coyotes end their concert is a mystery. With my set of weak human senses, I can detect no perceptible atmospheric change. Perhaps they were chanting an ancient rhythm and simply arrived at its conclusion.

Right at daylight, a single doe comes too close. We see each other at almost the same moment, at a distance of about three yards. She stops for less than a second, looks straight into a hole in the brush I cut to shoot through, and about flies out of her fur attempting to make space between the two of us. Her snorting alarm can be heard all around for several minutes. The remainder of my morning is spent watching the birds wake up, admiring the sunrise, and planning my next move. My goal for the day is to finally find some better hunting spots.

I decide to get a little farther off the beaten path. Today I don't even drive back to the cabin after hunting. I simply grab a bite to eat in my van, move about a mile north, and change into my scouting Scent-Lok. My plan is to walk at least a mile or two back to the edge of the mountains, to investigate a long wooded bluff that I had spotted while driving. I glassed a few deer near this bluff, and the woods look interesting from a distance. Parking my van at the last public land pullout, I start walking. The walk is easy as the cattle have the grass shorn short. It only takes me about fifteen minutes of steady walking to reach the bluff.

The south side doesn't have a tree on it. The north side though is covered in tall white barked poplars. Dropping down the north side of the bluff, I enter a thick aspen forest. To my surprise, many of the trees are big enough to hunt out of. These poplars must be ancient as large as they are, and considering how slow the trees grow around here. Many of them have thick black scars, an indication of age. The forest floor is laced with trails. Most of the obvious ones are cow paths, but close inspection reveals deer runways that are fairly well used. There are cattle in these woods, but not nearly as many as in some of the other areas I have scouted so far. In the poplars I get a better idea of what is happening here. The woods are about two hundred yards wide and run along the north side of this bluff for about a mile. At the west end there are some fields that are now wheat stubble, and at the east end the bluff runs into a mountain that is covered in low woods and brush.

This long narrow wood is a deer travel corridor that is obviously being used heavily. The deer movement pattern should be towards the fields in the evening and away from them in the morning. Another good thing about this spot is that it is accessible without spooking the deer, both mornings and evenings. Judging from the looks of things, this place is probably full of action during the rut. I now have to find either a tight funnel or an attraction point.

It doesn't take me long to stumble across exactly what I am looking for. Almost exactly at the middle point and right at the base of the bluff lies a little round mound. The mound rises about ten feet above the surrounding ground, and is approximately twenty yards wide by fifty yards long. It is covered with grasses and a few bushes; there isn't a single tree on top of it. It sits thirty yards from the base of the bluff, which angles slightly away from the mound towards the distant fields, creating a natural funnel between the two. This is the only opening in these entire woods, and it is crisscrossed with runways. On top of the mound I find a couple licking branches, but no ground scrapes, yet. It is probably a primary scrape area and staging area during the rut.

A few seconds is all I need to decide to clear out a tree. The question is: Which tree? There are several options, none of them particularly great. The best tree from a standpoint of ease of setting up and comfort is on the wrong side of the mound. On the better side of the mound there are two possibilities, both of them with the wrong slant, which means for a shot to some of the runways I will have to shoot across my body from my saddle. I practice shooting like this, and it is certainly possible, but not my first choice. I select the better of the two options and get to work. The big poplar is located at the base of the mound, which means that I will have to get up a little higher in order to be high enough above the deer as they cross the top. When I reach my hunting height, I am actually forty feet from the ground, but not quite thirty feet above the opening.

Sitting in my saddle, I check the shot possibilities, and indeed I will have to shoot across my body for shots to one of the main runways. As I get to work clearing shots to all the runways within shooting distance, I realize that there is even more deer activity here than I initially thought. I quickly open up shots to nine different runways, trying to leave the area as undisturbed as possible. About two hours after I started, I'm finished. Planning to hunt here within a day or two I leave my steps in the tree and continue to explore the long wooded bluff.

Turning east I follow the woods with the intention of inspecting the corner where the bluff connects with the mountain or hill. Interestingly, I notice the amount of deer sign increases in direct proportion to my distance from the public land parking spot. I am now roughly a mile and a half from my van, and there is no sign that anyone else has been here. This doesn't surprise me. Not many people are willing to get out and walk these days.

Right where the bluff and the mountain intersect is a mountain meadow. The same type of poplar forest surrounds it, but the undergrowth is much thicker. To simply say there is a lot of buck sign here is an understatement. There are rubs everywhere, and I mean some really interesting rubs that could only be made by mature bucks. An entire bush that has been reduced to sticks, and numerous rubs are completely frayed, which indicates pearling at the bases of antlers or small points. Generally, only mature bucks have this kind of antler growth. Immediately, I decide to set up a spot somewhere in this area. I slow down and attempt to solve the problem, to answer the why and the when of the deer activity.

Mixed with the deer tracks are some bigger cervid hoove prints. Clearly, elk have left them here. These are the first elk tracks I've found. As I stand there musing about these big deer, movement catches my attention across the face of the next mountain. Elk! A single cow covers about fifty yards of open grass before being swallowed by thick cover. I scour the hillside hoping to glimpse more elk, and am rewarded by the sight of a big bull. He is too far away to be able to count points with the naked eye, but I can easily see that he is a mature animal, long antlers curve over his back, rocking gently with every step. He crosses a quarter mile of open grass following the cow. His pace is steady and he never stops. A couple minutes are all I get before he too vanishes. I watch the mountain for about five minutes hoping for more elk, but none show. So I turn my attention back to Odocoilus virginianus dacotensis, a somewhat smaller deer species.

The answers to my deer movement questions come quickly. The deer seem to be bedding in the thick brush surrounding this meadow. The runways all lead to the northwest. I follow them to find their destination. Cutting through a small corridor of woods, I see immediately where the deer are going. Coming to a corner, I reach the edge of the woods, which also turns north and then back east, curving around the base of the mountain. A patch of grazed grassland borders the thick vegetation, but about a quarter mile to the north is wheat stubble field. The situation is quite clear. The deer are bedding in and around this meadow and feeding in that wheat stubble field. I am standing in an obviously well used travel route. This corridor of woods is THE SPOT for right now. The deer filter through here on their way to feed in the evening, and follow the same path returning to bed down in the morning. This is a classic setup, and one of the best for the early season, before mature bucks enter their nocturnal routine.

There aren't many trees tall enough to hunt out of, but there are a few. I select a crooked poplar along the main runway, about a ten-yard shot, and thirty yards from the edge of the grassland. This tree is a breeze to set up. I run my steps up the trunk. At the top I am only about twenty feet in the air, and there isn't much cover. This is a little low for hunting out of a saddle, but my tree choices are limited, so it will have to do. With as few trees as there are around these parts I simply hope the deer aren't accustomed to looking up, like they are in heavily hunted Michigan. I remove my steps on my way back down. My intention is to hunt this spot within a day or two. I would leave the steps in the tree, but I only brought two sets with me today, and I am not done scouting yet. There may be more trees that I need to set up. The shots are all open, and cutting a single branch to open a shot out to the edge is the only other work I have to do. It only takes me about ten minutes to complete this process. Happy with my two spots, I carefully pick my way back over the bluff, staying in the open as much as possible, trying to avoid creating any more disturbances.

On the other side I follow the base of the mountain in the other direction, initially walking south, and, turning west, exploring the sparse woods that slope gently back toward the parking spot. I've been out here for several hours and the temperature is now in the 80's and my water is just about gone. My mouth is cottony, but I resist the urge to cut a straight line back to my van. As long as I'm here, I might as well attempt to gain as much knowledge of the terrain as possible. Anything that I can discover now may save me a return trip. These long walks are a big part of the reason I exercise all year long, preparing for hunting season. The slope is variously wooded and open, a patchwork of good deer habitat. There is definitely a lot of deer activity, but not nearly as much as on the other side of that bluff, with its defined bedding and feeding areas. Here the deer movement is more random, making selecting a hunting spot far more difficult. Along the way I mentally mark several areas that could use a little more thorough investigation, but fail to find any truly exceptional locations. My roaming carries me about three more miles.

A half-mile from the parking spot, I run into the first sign of other hunters I've encountered all day. A scent drag is hanging in a bush. It's a little too early for using scent drags; I surmise that someone has fallen victim to the advertising of the hunting scent industry. Inspecting the area a little closer, I find a small cleared patch tucked between some boulders and buffalo berry bush. There are several cigarette butts crushed on the rock. Cigarettes and scent drags, what a combination! I wonder at my fellow hunter. The last portion of my walkabout is quick. It seems with every passing yard the sign of other hunters increases, until I am walking beaten down footpaths, and picking up a couple candy wrappers. Why the sudden increase in hunter activity? These woods border the parking spot, and most hunters won't walk more than a half-mile from their vehicle.

At my van, I immediately grab a plastic gallon jug and guzzle the tepid water. Hunting in the "desert" sure makes you thirsty. Slipping out of my now far-too-warm scouting Scent-Lok is like removing a hundred pound burden from my shoulders. Since I've arrived here, the weather has been the same every day. At night the mercury drops into the 30's, and during the day it climbs into the 80's, or higher. It is either too cold or too hot. A short pause is all I require to feel a lot better. It's already close to 4:00 p.m. With hunting and scouting I have been up and moving for more than twelve hours. Sipping water and snacking on wheat crackers, I drive the fifteen miles to town.

Small Towns/Big Bucks

Town is what most small towns in America used to be, and quite often wish they still were — no place for latte sipping yuppies. A couple of gas stations, a car dealer, and an elevator make up the outskirts. The wide main street, which sets on a slight rise, is lined with two short rows of old style buildings with dates like 1925 etched on them in stone. The red brick architecture is home to the kind of localities you might expect. There is a small grocery store, a hardware store, a dime store, a restaurant-slash-bar with a sign reading "Hunters Welcome", and, of course, the local attorney, among a few others. A handful of

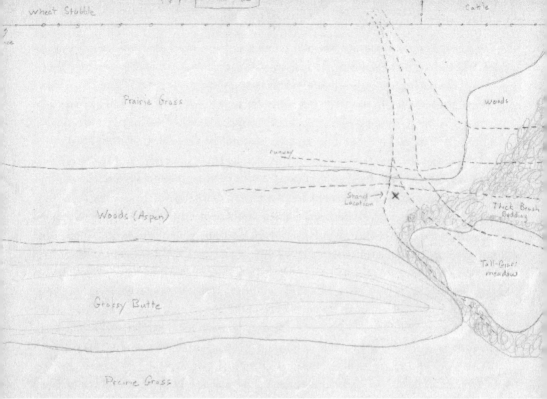

Following a mile and a half long walk out into the prairie I found a meadow and bedding area over a long grassy bluff. This is where the action was.

dusty work trucks are parked on either side of the street. At the top of the rise on the left is the local school. Radiating out from Main Street are a couple more streets decorated with small inconspicuous homes, no trophy houses in sight. I feel like I've stepped back in time, and it feels good in a nostalgic sort of way. This is how my own hometown was before the big box stores moved in. This place still has some soul.

Stepping through the doors of the grocery store, I am greeted by a woman stocking shelves. She is probably in her late fifties. This isn't a professional greeter like you find at huge shopping complexes, but rather a woman who is simply working and who sincerely acknowledges me. I greet in return and begin collecting the things I need. The grocery store is well stocked. I find everything quickly, splurging on a box of cereal and a half-gallon of milk, since there is a refrigerator at Dan's cabin. (This is a luxury I might not have for a couple of months.) At the register I meet the same woman who while scanning my things asks, "Will that be all for you today, honey?" "Yep, that's all. Thank-you" We complete the transaction, and I walk out smiling at being called honey.

Back at the cabin I relax for a while. Pleased with the results of my scouting, and having achieved the goal I set for myself today, I consider not hunting this evening. Mulling this over,

I dive right into a couple of bowls of cereal, stilling the hunger that has been gnawing at me for most of the day. An overdue shower follows dinner, while my Scent Lok is re-activating in the dryer in the basement. Sated, clean, and with my equipment all back in its designated locations, I sit down on the deck and look out across the prairie. My fondness for this area is growing daily. I decide to relax for the evening and grab a book to read.

The uncomfortable beeping of my alarm clock pulls me back to this world. Still mostly asleep and quite disoriented I stumble up the stairs and out onto the deck. The sudden shock of cold on my bare skin is enough to wake me fully. It's the coldest it's been since I arrived. The grass has doubled its diameter with a coating of white frost, and the windows on my van are decorated with an intricate white pattern of frozen water. The deer should be moving. Though I have plenty of time before daylight, I hurriedly dress in my undergarments, and toss my gear in the van. A short way up the road, a small deer zips through the beam cut by my headlights. Three big coyotes, only yards behind, follow her. Fellow hunters out for a venison breakfast. They are gone in a split second, leaving me a little uncertain as to whether I saw them at all. Mentally wishing them good hunting I drive on. I consider myself a predator and have respect for other predators, though coyotes are also occasionally my prey. Minutes later, I arrive at yesterday's parking spot.

Standing next to my van, I slip into my Scent Lok pants, and tuck the rest of my clothes in my pack. It's a long walk over that bluff to the island in the timber and I don't want to overheat. My pace is quick through the open grassland and up the bluff. Entering the woods, I slow down and carefully select my path to the tree, placing my steps gingerly where they produce the least amount of noise. I do this for two reasons. The first is that I want to give myself a chance to cool down before I start my sit. Secondly, it is wise to make every effort to remain undetected if any deer happen to be nearby. The last two hundred yards to my tree takes me almost as much time as the previous mile of walking. In the few minutes it takes me to get set up in my saddle, my body temperature has returned to normal. Retrieving my clothes from my pack, I dress while hanging forty feet up in a tree.

With the strenuous portion of the morning behind me, I rest my head against my lead strap and almost immediately fall into my hunter's trance. I am completely aware of my surroundings and register every sound, every breath of wind, every movement, and yet I have my eyes closed and my mind is at ease, resting, almost like sleep. My focus is everything and nothing at the same time — much like Zen meditation. The feeling is mostly flat, though my thoughts wander some; too much mental action is distracting. In this state I blend into the woods, and take back my place in nature, not as an observer or an outsider, but rather a real live piece of nature, holding on to what is still wild within me; the hunter. This is freedom, and something I can only experience while hunting.

There is no other way for me to reach this state. I can easily sit like this for four or five hours, and occasionally spend up to twelve hours on stand. My eyes suddenly open, and with them my concentration sharpens to a single point. Like a ghost out of the dark, an owl sweeps in to within a few feet of my face. It doesn't make a sound, and vanishes immediately in the night shadows.

How did I know this bird was there? The numinous in a hunter's world? Three more times the owl flies within a few feet of my eyes, the only part of my body that isn't camouflaged. On the last sweep it stops and hovers, flapping its wings up and down. I get the impression it is a little confused. Perhaps it mistakes my eyes for prey of its own, or perhaps there is something to the Hidatsa legend of the great owl that I should pay attention to. Suddenly thinking of razor sharp talons, I swing my arms in the air to let it know I am not food. Convinced, the owl again slips away into the inky black and doesn't return.

First light brings with it the chirping wake-up call of roosting turkeys. The feathered alarm clocks start with a few light clucks, here and there. A louder round of morning gossip follows. I listen and secretly wish I knew what they were talking about. With a firm gobble, like a call to order from the boss, a long bearded tom cuts through the chatter. His command must be clear to all. The first set of big wings glides through the trees, landing with a flurry of flapping, and the grace of a jumbo jet. A minute later, another bird drops from its roost, and then another, and another; a raucous clutter of wings and shadows all crashing down in the same general area. The confusion is cleared with a few chirps and clucks for those whose poor navigation took them a bit afield. The chatter continues, and I follow the flock with my ears until it is no longer audible.

I remain in my own roost for several more hours. No deer pass through, and by 11:00 it is downright hot. I am very uncomfortable in my cold weather gear, even after removing several layers, and decide to call it a morning. Returning to Dan's cabin I eat, and immediately hit the feathers.

Awaking from my well-deserved nap, it is already afternoon and time to get back out hunting. To avoid overheating, I slowly walk the mile and a half to the mountain meadow. It's still early as I settle into my saddle. A few hours pass before the first deer of the evening makes an appearance. A doe followed by two fawns amble out into the prairie grass about a hundred yards to the north. They turn away from me, arriving at the edge of the wheat stubble in short order. I watch through my binoculars. The mature doe pauses to assess the situation before jumping the fence. Her fawns do the same. They begin to feed, burying their noses in the short hollow straw stems. Minutes later I notice movement in the woods behind me. A group of six deer, two mature does both with twins, pass at a distance of twenty yards, eventually joining the other deer in the wheat stubble. A steady stream of does with fawns follow until there are nineteen deer in the field.

As I watch them, a buck suddenly jumps the fence, trailed by his two companions — a late summer bachelor group. All three bucks carry eight-point racks very close in stature. The lead buck is the biggest; I estimate him at around a hundred Pope & Young style inches. The other two look like twins and would come in at around eighty on the same scale. My guess is that this is a group of two-year-olds. They are about a hundred and fifty yards away and I watch them with interest, being the first decent bucks I have seen this season. A flash of brown draws my attention away from the bucks, back to the woods behind me. As I focus in that direction, a small spike ghosts out of the brush. He is alone and ambles right down the main runway past my tree. His antlers are very similar to those of the buck behind Dan's cabin, dark with heavy bases. This must be the norm for bucks around here. A few minutes later, he joins the rest of the deer in the field.

In all, I count twenty-nine deer this evening, including four bucks, nine does, and sixteen fawns. I haven't seen this many deer on a single hunt in over twenty years. I guess I've found the deer. Waiting until dark, I leave my steps in the tree and sneak out of the woods. I plan on being in this tree again tomorrow evening. Driving back to Dan's cabin I almost plow into a really nice buck, probably in the 130 class, standing in the road. Actually, slamming on the brakes and skidding to a slippery slightly sideways stop to avoid the collision.

Here We Go!

The day begins much like the previous ones; a morning hunt echoed in by the song of love-sick bull elk; turkeys dropping out of their roost; a couple of does with fawns passing within shooting range; and, a midday scouting foray. Shortly after 2:00 p.m., I make the trek back out to the meadow. It is still warm this afternoon, but the wind is really howling, straight out of the northwest. The worst possible wind direction for this tree, but putting my faith in activated carbon technology, I decide to hunt anyway. For a few hours I question my sanity. The gusts are so strong that I am bouncing against my tree, holding my bow with one hand to keep it from falling off its hook. Nothing happens until about 5:30, when a bunch of turkeys sneak out of the woods. The big, black, blue-headed birds feed in my direction until they get to within sixty yards, at which point they get spooky and veer off towards the wheat stubble. I get the feeling that their keen eyes picked me out in my hiding spot. Promptly, a doe and two fawns enter the scene about a hundred yards to the north on their way to the same field.

A half-hour later, the doe and fawns are joined by a steady stream of more does and fawns. All of them exit the woods and enter the field about a hundred yards to the north. There are fifteen deer in the field when another steps out — this time a good buck. His antlers are easy to see, even at a hundred yards. Grabbing my binoculars I take a closer look; a perfectly typical and wide eight-point rack, with even length tines on each beam. My quick guess is he would gross score around 120 inches. Behind him trail two more bucks. The second is another eight-pointer, a tad smaller than the first. The third is a big ten-pointer. He is bigger bodied than the other two bucks, and his rack is simply perfect, very dark and wide with a lot of mass. This one I estimate at somewhere over the 140 mark.

Never before, on a single hunt, have I seen three bucks of this quality. As I watch them, I second-guess my stand location. All of the nineteen deer I have seen so far tonight entered the field north of me. After watching these bucks for a few minutes, I decide to attempt to call them in. The chances are slim I know, but I have to try something. Reaching for my rattle bag, I gently roll the sticks together for a few seconds, and then turn over a *doe in estrous* call — all the time with an eye on the deer. Any early-season attempts at calling have to be very subtle in order to invoke a response. The bucks stop and look for a second, but quickly return to feeding. Judging this attempt as futile, I content myself with watching, happy to finally see a couple mature bucks.

Minutes later, I glance back into the woods and am surprised to see another nice buck moving in my direction about fifty yards away — an eight-pointer in the hundred inch category. A flash of movement a few yards in front of him alerts me to yet another deer that already crossed the fence. My view is blocked by thick foliage. I can't tell what this second deer is, but bucks are moving around in bachelor groups so I grab my bow and swing in position for a possible shot. If the bucks maintain their course, they will cut through my shooting lane at about thirty yards. Within seconds, the lead deer casually strolls out exactly where I predicted. He is larger than his companion. His antlers are bone white, outside of his ears, with a symmetrical eight-point formation. The buck stops right in my shooting lane, and even turns his head in the other direction, giving me a great look and a possible shot.

My bow is in my hands and ready to be drawn, but I hesitate, not sure if this buck meets my self-imposed standards for these hills. In a couple seconds my chance is gone, as he is now across my shooting lane and out of reach. His smaller companion trails a few yards behind. Together they join the other deer in the wheat stubble. Now there are five bucks, all over a 100 inches in that field; something I have never seen before while hunting more pressured locals. Almost immediately I am shaken by regret for not shooting. This is public land and my guess is that the buck would score probably a little over 120. I call myself a dummy, among other more harsh names; a buck in the hand is better than ten bigger ones on the hoof. In Michigan, and just about any other place east of the Mississippi, an arrow would have been flying. But this is North Dakota, a new experience, and I have the benefit of time. (I hope my decision to be more selective and not to shoot doesn't come back to haunt me.)

For the next forty minutes, I watch the deer in the field, now a count of more than twenty. I continually replay that last sequence through my mind, over and over again. So engulfed in my silent observation of the bucks and my thoughts, I am almost surprised when I notice that the wind has completely stopped. It is perfectly still. The shadows are long and darkness isn't far off. Convinced the action is over for the evening, I start mentally planning my getaway. I have to get out of here without alerting the deer in the field to my presence. As part of my habitual routine, I scan the woods behind me for deer, catching motion out of the corner of my eye. As I turn to focus, a set of antlers pass through a small opening in the foliage. This split second is all I need to decide that I will shoot this buck if presented an opportunity. There is no need to hesitate on this one, even though all I could really see were a couple of long tines. Grabbing my bow, and shifting my weight simultaneously, I move into position for a shot. The buck appears to be following the same runway the other two bucks had taken earlier, so I mentally ready myself to shoot thirty yards.

A jolt of adrenaline shoots through me followed by instant calm concentration. Simple prose is too feeble to describe with any exactness the next seconds. My concentration focuses entirely on one point. The only thing that matters right now is this deer; my self vanishes completely. I act purely on hunting instinct, completely natural, but also schooled by countless hours, and years, of training. Either I react properly or this buck, my prey, slips from my grasp. The interval between the first sighting and getting into position for a shot is perhaps two seconds, where I take my attention from the deer. Bow in hand I return to the buck. He slips through some brush and, to my favor, follows the main runway that will bring him directly under my tree, only the second deer to do so among the fifty or so I have seen from this tree. His gait is steady and he covers the forty yards to my shooting lane in seconds. Without thought, I draw and anchor. My eyes are glued to the buck, following his every move for a step or two, glancing for a split second at the large body and antlers; tall rack, narrow spread. I focus my concentration onto his chest and set my arrow free. It vanishes in the buck's ribs. He takes three short jumps and…stops.

I'm shocked! The shot looked great. He is now standing broadside in my shooting lane, at the exact spot the eight-point was standing earlier. I can clearly see blood flowing out of a hole in his chest. He stretches his neck forward, tail flicking nervously. There is ample blood pouring from is nose. "Fall over! Fall over!" I think to myself, while grabbing another arrow from my quiver. Arrow knocked, I draw again, aim, and send it squarely into the bucks chest, right into the crease. This time he bolts out into the grassland. His back legs falter once at about thirty yards. In two more leaps, he does a roll in a cloud of dust. Silence. I sit in the stillness of death, witness to the eternal deal of life for life.

The sight of the collapsing buck brings a wave of shakes and a sense of elation. Slumping in my saddle, I take a few deep breaths to regain my suddenly fragile composure. In a surge of astonished disbelief a row of questions swell to the forefront of my thoughts. Did I just shoot that buck twice? Both shots looked like perfect double lung hits! What the hell just happened?

Attempting to take my time, I lower my bow to the ground and descend the tree removing my steps as I go. With my feet on the ground, I carefully repack my backpack, consciously taking it slow, savoring the flood of emotion, while making sure I don't forget anything.

Arriving at my first arrow, I see it is buried to its middle in the ground, covered in frothy lung blood. My second arrow, which is lying flat on the ground a few yards behind where the buck was standing, also indicates a solid lung shot. A bit perplexed, I make a straight line to the buck.

What I find is an absolutely beautiful animal. His coat is short and summer red, revealing the tone of his muscular neck and shoulders. The rack is tall, heavy, and very narrow. I place my hand between his main beams as a quick measure and decide they aren't even twelve inches apart. A mature buck with such a narrow spread is quite unusual. What he misses in spread he makes up for in tine length. A great buck! I take a minute just to sit and hold my buck; I have made him my possession, to give thanks to this animal for its gift of life. No esoteric mumbo jumbo, just a real honest thank-you. My respect for these cunning deer is boundless. My elation mixes though with a twinge of sadness. If you don't feel for the animal you kill, you are not a hunter; you are simply a killer, a sort of person unfortunately all too common these days. This contradictory feeling is what I live for. It lets me know my place in the real world, and keeps me attune to the path of the hunter.

Fading light forces me to get to work faster than I would like. It's a little easier to gut a deer during daylight. Getting started, I turn the buck on his back and make the first cut, slicing into the skin around his penis and testicles. Removing these, the next cut is through some muscle along the pelvis bone. I then make an incision through the skin and stomach muscle, up to the buck's ribs; my fingers are along both sides of my knife blade to keep from puncturing the stomach or intestines. This opens up the diaphragm. I cut around it, removing the wall of muscle. The unmistakable rich smell of blood rises with the warm cloud of steam out of the deer. It fills my nostrils. Reaching my hands up to my elbows in the buck's chest cavity, I feel for the windpipe, which I cut through. This done, I pull the visceral material in its entirety out of the deer. There is blood on my hands, literally and figuratively.

Curious to know exactly what happened with my shots, I carefully inspect the lungs. The left lung has two X shaped holes in it. The right lung has one hole and a deep slice in the end. The diaphragm has a slice in it as well. Now my shots and the deer's reaction to them make sense. On my first shot, the buck was quartering towards me a little more than I thought. The arrow passed through one lung, made a slice in the second, put a hole in the diaphragm and just nicked the liver. Judging from the buck's reaction to this shot he must not have realized what happened, as he was completely unaware of my presence as he approached. I've taken other deer that didn't realize they had been shot, and they tend to take a few seconds longer to expire than normal, because there is no sudden burst of energy and thus no increased cardiovascular activity. The first shot certainly would have put the deer down in a couple more seconds. The second shot was through both lungs, and a form of insurance. He was already dead before my second shot, but just didn't realize it yet. If you ever hit a deer with an arrow and you get a second chance for a shot, take it!

Cutting the heart out from between the lungs, I lay it aside on a patch of grass. Picking up the steaming pile, I carry it about forty yards to a nearby patch of brush and toss it inside. The coyotes will have it gone by morning. Returning to my buck, I turn him over and lift his head and the antlers as high as I can to drain the blood from his chest cavity. The blood stains the brown grass and dry dusty ground, leaving a spotty black streak. Tomorrow this will be the only remaining testimony of the drama that took place here. Gutting finished; I wipe my hands clean with prairie grass. Reaching into my pack, I retrieve the plastic bag containing my tag. Punching the necessary information and attaching it to an antler takes but a minute. Slipping the deer's heart in the plastic bag I tuck it into my pack. The heart is usually the first thing I eat from the deer I kill. Perhaps this is symbolic or perhaps I just like the taste of fresh heart. Just at last light I finish. Now I can get to the work of dragging.

I'm alone with a big deer and I am about a mile and a half from my vehicle. The only way to get there is over that tall bluff. There are two choices. Either I can first walk back to my van and retrieve my dragging sled, which means walking three miles before beginning with my dragging, or I can simply grab this buck by the horns and pull him out of here. Shouldering my pack while holding my bow in my left hand, I grab the buck's antlers and pull, dragging it about ten yards. Adrenaline still shooting through my veins, I overestimate my physical prowess. That short ten yards is enough to change my mind. Adrenaline neither here nor there, getting this buck out without the help of my sled would take me all night.

The walk to my van passes quickly. I arrive shortly after dark, noticing along the way that the temperature is dropping fast. Removing most of my warm clothes at the van, I wear a single t-shirt under a thin jacket and my scouting pants for the long drag. From past experience, I know that warm clothes won't be necessary for this job. With my dragging sled in hand its back over the bluff, for the fifth time today.

Reaching the buck, I lay the sled down in front of it, then stepping into the sled I heave it over the sidewalls. To insure he remains in position and that his antlers don't hook on anything I wrap one side of the pull rope around a main beam. Now, when I pull on the handle the buck's antlers will lift up, away from the ground. Taking hold of the handle (a piece of metal tubing) I lean against the weight of the buck with both hands and begin walking. The sled slides easily over the prairie grass. About a hundred and fifty yards further along I stop, breathing heavily. I pause for about a minute and start again, most of the effort coming from my legs. This time I don't make it quite as far, clearly noticing the first slope towards the bluff. I repeat this procedure again and again. At the steepest point of the bluff, the distance between stops shortens to about ten yards, with me pulling backwards, straining against a buck that weighs more than myself. Fortunately, the hill is not so steep that the buck slides backwards when I let go of the handle. Soon I'm dripping with sweat and working so hard that I have to remove even my t-shirt in order to remain remotely comfortable. Arriving at the crest of the bluff, I pause briefly to cool down in the now chilly night air, and to put my t-shirt back on. The difficult part is behind me, and I don't want to catch cold. The rest of the way is all down hill. With gravity now working with me, my next pull covers a quarter mile in a single sweep. An hour after I started dragging I arrive at my van.

The work though isn't over. I'm faced with the task of lifting 180 pounds of dead weight into my van — thirty pounds more than myself. With the backdoors open, I lift one end of the sled and rest it on the bumper, holding the buck's antlers in one hand to keep it from sliding to the ground. Jumping into my van, I stand and pull for all I'm worth. So as not to bloody the inside of my van, the deer must remain in the sled. Initially it doesn't seem like the deer moves an inch. Again, I pull for all I'm worth, trying to use my legs. The buck moves forward, but not enough that it passes its center of gravity and flops in the van. If I let go, the buck will tumble back to the ground. Mustering all that I have left, I put my back into another heave. The sled tips forward, and the buck is finally ready for transport. Task accomplished. I really need to carry a wooden plank for such occasions. Alive with too much energy, despite the torturous drag, I race back to Dan's cabin.

Firing up Dan's satellite telephone takes me a couple of minutes. Through the crackling connection I tell him the story. He is happy with my good fortune and instantly offers to drive out in the morning to take pictures and help me with my deer. Already, he has been far more generous than I expected, and now he is going to drive over an hour in one direction just to help me out. What a nice guy! After our talk, I notice that it's after 11:00 p.m. Normally, I would be waking up in just a few short hours, but tonight I feel like I could run a marathon or two. My heart is racing with so much adrenaline as I unload the buck, leaving it in the sled on the ground, and covering it with a plastic tarp. There is already frost forming on the prairie grass, and the deer will be fine outside for the night.

Taking advantage my superfluous energy, I busy myself by washing all of my hunting clothes, re-activating my Scent-Lok, re-arranging my equipment, and cleaning the inside of my van; all before forcing myself to retire at around 3:00 a.m. The evening's events keep playing like dreams over and over again in my mind, caught in that nebulous space between sleep and waking. Breaking out of this haze just at daybreak, the time to be hunting, I wonder if I've slept at all. Although I try, I can't fall back to sleep. Climbing up the stairs, my body feels like it has been run over by a truck. With nothing planned for this morning until Dan arrives, I put the coffeemaker on the countertop to use, sit on the deck, and watch the sunrise, while writing in my journal. This is my first cup of coffee in several weeks and it sure tastes good.

The rising sun in a perfect sky transforms the frost to small drops of sparkling water that soon dissipate with the first breathes of a warm wind from the southwest. Antelope feed behind the cabin and uncountable swallows get about their daily business of hunting, gliding low across the prairie, turning, diving, swooping, stopping, and starting, all with mind boggling accuracy, plucking their prey out of the sky. Their aerial stunts are unmatched by any human created flying machine. These little winged predators on their morning hunt remind me yet again that we are surrounded by hunters everywhere, and all the time. My musing is interrupted by the sound of crunching gravel. Dan pulls into the driveway.

The sky promises temperatures in the 80's today, so we get right to business. Handing Dan my camera, he burns a roll of film while we talk about the hunt with a little more detail. The photo session lasts only a few minutes. Without any kind of cool room available, I have to get this deer skinned and quartered as quickly as possible, though normally I would let it hang for a couple days. We turn our attention to the process of turning a deer into venison.

Hanging the buck by one of its hind legs under the deck, I begin skinning. Placing the tip of my skinning knife under the skin I cut up the inside of each hind leg, all the way to the first joint. Grabbing the skin right along my first cut, I run the blade between the venison and the skin, gently cutting connective tissue until there is enough loose skin to cut around the joints on both legs. From here I carefully peel the hide off this deer, pulling and cutting, pulling and cutting; careful not to cut a hole in the hide. Keeping this hide in good shape is important for me, as I intend either to sell the cape (quality early season capes of nice sized bucks normally fetch some cash at taxidermy studios) or perhaps get this buck mounted, if I can come up with the cash. I continue peeling and cutting until I reach the base of the buck's head, at which point I cut into the muscle on either side of the neck. Having Dan hold the deer's chest, I twist the head and it falls off, right at the last joint where the vertebrae connect to the skull. Setting the skin and head aside, I begin quartering.

By cutting around the joints and twisting, I remove the lower portions of each front leg. Pulling the front shoulder away from the ribcage, I cut the connective tissue between the two, removing each of the front quarters and placing both of them in a single plastic bag. Turning my attention to the buck's neck, I cut along the vertebrae removing the muscle from both sides. Two large neck roasts are placed in another plastic bag. Starting just below the hindquarter, I cut across the backstraps and then make a shallow cut down the backbone just deep enough to get through the silver skin, which I peel off with my hand. My knife flat to the ribcage, I cut under each long muscle, using the ribs as a guide. This gives me a flat edge along the bottom of the loins that makes for a nicer cut of meat. From the inside, I remove the much smaller real tenderloins.

Turning my attention to the hindquarters, I cut through the muscle, down the outside along the pelvis bone with a half circle to the joint where the femur connects to it. On the inside of the hindquarter, I cut along the pelvis bone. Finding the joint, I slice through the cartilage that surrounds it, and the whole hindquarter falls free. This is placed in a plastic bag. I repeat this on the other side. We then place each plastic bag in Dan's basement refrigerator to firm up. Although this is my first deer of the fall, the rough butchering goes quickly.

There are countless methods and procedures to process deer, and I would do a couple things different given space, time, and a good walk-in cooler. Every hunter should at least be capable of butchering his own deer, whether he chooses to do so or not. Too many are the hunters whose knowledge of deer stops at the shot. On several occasions I have encountered hunters who didn't even know how to gut their own deer. This may be acceptable for a kid or an absolute beginner, but anyone with a few hunting seasons under his belt should be up to the task. Hunting in its total package includes every step from scouting all the way to the frying pan. Butchering my own deer is for me a celebration of the hunt, and a sign of respect to the animal. Venison is at the core of what deer hunting is about.

While Dan arranges the refrigerator and starts cleaning up, I begin caping the head of my buck. This job requires a very sharp knife that I retrieve out of my gearbox. I lay the head on a piece of cardboard on the ground and start with a straight cut through the hide about five inches below the ears, right along what would be the top of the neck. I stop about an inch and a half before I reach the base of the antlers. The next cut forms a V to each of the bases. The entire cut resembles a Y. A lot of people still cape deer by cutting all the way along the back of the neck. This is quick, and makes cutting the head off a little easier, but is mostly still practiced out of habit or ignorance of the newer method. The benefits of the Y-cut is that there is less sewing for the taxidermist to do. Without a seam, mounted animals look more realistic, and such mounts last longer.

The next step is to peel skin down through the base of the ears and around antler pedicels. I find the antler pedicels the most time consuming and difficult part of capping a buck. A trick that sometimes helps things along is a large flat-headed screwdriver — the duller the better. By placing this under the skin and using leverage against the skull, it is sometimes possible to pull the hide cleanly away from the bone. After getting around the antlers, the secret to caping is simply cutting as close to the bone as possible. As I near to the eyes, I stick my finger in the eye under the eyelids and lift the skin up, while cutting carefully towards my finger. By cutting close to the bone and towards my finger, I am making sure that I don't accidentally cut through the eyelids, a problem a lot of hunters have with caping. Of course, one has to be very careful not to cut a finger. Past the eyes, the rest of the caping job is easy. As soon as I arrive at the mouth tissue, I cut as tight to the teeth as I can to keep the deer's lips intact. About twenty minutes after starting I lay the cape on the cardboard. I roll it in a ball, starting with the nose, folding the ears on the inside, with the rest of the hide on the outside. Placing the cape in a plastic bag it goes straight in the freezer.

The last thing we do is cut the antlers off. Dan holds them while I handle my bone saw. I saw through the skull just behind the pedicels, angling slightly towards the eyes. The second cut is across what would be the buck's forehead, between the eyes and the antlers, angling in the opposite direction. The skull plate breaks free revealing milky white brain. Dan sets the antlers aside. Our work for today is mostly done. The only remaining task is to return what is left, mostly bones, some hide, a head, and a little tallow, to its proper place. Scraps all in my sled, we lift them in the back of Dan's truck and drive out to the far end of his property. There we leave the remains of the carcass near some boulders. The coyotes will have them gone in a day or two. Whenever I can, I like to return the parts of the deer I can't use to the area where that deer lived. The coyotes, fox, badgers, buzzards, and perhaps even a mountain lion, should all get their share. They continue life's cycle. (I hope someone throws my carcass to the coyotes after I die.)

Work done, Dan and I set out to get to know one another. Until now a handful of hours are all we've shared. The first project is deer. Dan is relatively new to bowhunting, with only a few years under his belt, and eager to learn as much as he can. We walk out to some of the places I selected to hunt, and I fill him in to the "why" and the "when" of each spot. We scout together some other land nearby where he has permission to hunt. While I am showing Dan what I think I know about deer, he is filling me with knowledge of the prairie. A hobby naturalist, he seems to know every plant we come across.

I am impressed with his extensive knowledge of the local ecosystem, though all the names of the different native and invasive grasses, and differentiating one from the other is a little confusing for me. Big Bluestem looks like it should rather be named Big Redstem; Dan promises me that the stems are really blue a little earlier in the year. The numerous natives like Little Bluestem, Green-Needle Grass, Blue Gama, Buffalo Grass, and Prairie Sandreed are all a mixed jumble that I'm slow to sort out. Most of the non-natives I've at least seen before, Kentucky

Bluegrass, Smooth Brome grass, and Crested Wheatgrass. And the easiest to identify are the plants that Dan considers his enemies on his land, Leafy Spurge and Canada thistle. Both of these plants choke out the natives and disrupt diversity on the prairie. He battles these two continuously. I attempt to soak up as much of Dan's insight as he offers into this beautiful land. His estimation that the area is as lush green as he has ever seen it shocks me somewhat. Coming from water-rich Michigan this place is bone dry, and for me practically desert. Obviously I have a lot to learn about the subtleties of these Great Plains and Bad Lands.

The remainder of the day flies by. We grouse hunt, unsuccessfully, watching Dan's German shorthairs work. We pay a visit to the neighbors, an anachronistic ranch family that has been out here a long time; people who remind me of late grandparents both in their ways and views. Flashes of my grandparents' century old, fieldstone house and red and white Michigan barn intertwine with my thoughts during our conversation. The smell of cattle, old wood paneling, a few old racks on the wall, and a country disarray, takes me back to my childhood out in Michigan's lost countryside, to a time, a life, and a place long gone. These ranchers are genuine; this is their place. I am privileged to be able to visit with them. As the sun sets we take a drive to look for deer out around their ranch. The place is simply enormous. We count somewhere between fifty and a hundred deer, including one really nice buck. Back at the cabin, dinner consists of fresh loin from my deer, quickly browned in a frying pan and then baked in the oven

My prairie buck.

until it is medium rare, and some bread. Having for practical purposes not slept in forty-eight hours, I find my bed shortly after dinner.

An hour before daylight, my eyes suddenly open. It's hard for me to sleep past sunrise after I start hunting in the fall. A cup of coffee and some cold venison accompanies a few minutes of filling in some of the holes in my hunting journal. Judging myself awake enough to work a knife blade, I begin the fine butchering of my deer. One at a time, each quarter is pulled from the refrigerator. The meat has firmed up since yesterday. By cutting through the connective tissue between the muscles I free each, stacking them in piles, according to how I plan to eventually cook them. Most hunters cut their venison into steaks before freezing it; I prefer to cut the various muscles into meal size portions without slicing them into steaks. This way I can be more flexible at the time I want to cook them. According to my mood and the recipe I can cut my steaks as thin or thick as I want them at the moment I toss them on the grill. Leaving the large muscles intact also reduces the amount of freezer burn and discoloration of the meat by reducing the outside surface area. I take pride in quality venison. With my cutting done, I vacuum pack all the meat, and place it in the freezer.

The rest of the day is spent with Dan, much like the previous day. We follow his dogs around and miss a few grouse, scout a couple of deep draws, shoot our bows, and enjoy fresh venison. Dan's wife Carol and his boys show up at the cabin in the evening and we finish off the day by going to dinner at the restaurant in town. On the drive back to the cabin, we stop and watch a couple of two-year-old bucks along the road.

What to do

- Hunting access can come from unexpected sources. Always follow up on offers for hunting permission.
- Arrive at your hunting locations at least an hour and a half before first light.
- Ground hunting locations should be set up for a thirty-yard shot.
- Carry a portable target with you and practice shooting while on your trip.
- Public-land hunting can be great. Always investigate public land and get far back in off the beaten path. Local DNR offices can be great sources for maps of public land. Quite often you will find land that is open to hunting that most wouldn't even find.
- While scouting, always determine what the other hunters in the area are doing. They probably have more impact on deer movement than any other factor.

Chapter 4

Wisconsin: October Lull

I rise at daylight. Like every other morning since I've been in North Dakota the air is crisp and the sky is clear, there isn't a breath of wind. In the week since my arrival my appreciation for the beauty and diversity of the great grassland has grown immensely, and I take a minute to wonder at the glowing strip of yellow and red rising to the east, my thoughts wandering to how desolate all this looked upon my arrival. Snapping out of my short bout of introspection, I fetch my cooler from my van and fill it with frozen venison, and a cape. Packed tightly, about three-fourths of the meat fits in the cooler. The remainder I leave for Dan. The venison will go to a family in Dan's congregation that is going through some tough times and could use the help.

With duct tape I seal the lid, to make sure no cold escapes. This should ensure that the meat remains frozen for at least twenty-four hours. I slide the cooler in its place behind the driver's seat, and get behind the wheel. Not quite mentally ready to leave this place, I find myself rolling along at a snail's pace, preoccupied with looking for pronghorns. Five miles of gravel crunches under my tires before I reach the pavement. Heading south through the endless brown fields and grassland it strikes me just how content I am, thankful to have had such a great hunt, and to have made a new friend, whom I understand so well. Something I didn't really expect.

Running into that concrete dividing line known as I-94 I turn east, destination Wisconsin. Today there is no time to dawdle; my cargo of fresh venison has to find space in a freezer as soon as possible. My hope is that Greg will be able of accommodate my venison.

Just short of Bismarck my van's gas gauge hits the orange stripe informing me that I need to tank up. I haven't visited a gas station in a week. The per gallon price tag of $3.15 is tough for me to swallow, but I have no other choice, so I fill up. Parting with that hundred-dollar bill hurts.

A fresh gas station coffee in my hand, I climb back into my van, and drive all the way back to Wisconsin in one sweep.

By early afternoon I arrive at the farm, and find Greg in his calf barn cleaning stalls. We chat for a few minutes while he works; as usual I feel like I am slowing him down. I show him the antlers off my buck, and relay to him the short version of the hunt. He isn't really impressed with my buck, although it is probably a four-year-old deer, and would qualify for the Pope & Young record books should I choose to enter it. An average two-year-old buck around these parts is just as large, sometimes even larger. He kindly congratulates me anyway.

It turns out that his freezer is full to the brim with a freshly slaughtered cow, meaning I have to scramble to keep my venison frozen. Greg suggests I try the local meat processor, and gives me directions.

A few minutes down the bluff I arrive at a place called Jake's, looking for the owner: Jake. Jake's is the last building in a connected row of old style architecture at the end of Main Street. Walking through the door I get the impression that Jake's father must have been named Jake as well. This place is old. The storefront is filled with unusual objects, a painted cow skull, some last century glass bottles, and a wooden wagon wheel, among empty metal meat racks. The floor is wooden and worn, and a glass display case is empty. There is obviously nothing for sale in here, and nobody in sight. I wait for a few seconds for someone to appear, nothing. A look around the corner reveals a long narrow room with stainless steel cutting tables along one side. The walls are white metal, and give away immediately the fact that behind them there must be coolers or freezers. At the last table two guys are cutting on what appears to be a side of beef. I walk back. Neither of the two is Jake, but they direct me to the right, into a large cooler.

Stepping through the long plastic strips I find the man I'm looking for. Jake is tall and thin, wearing a warm flannel, covered by a lightly bloodied butcher's apron. He too is cutting on a side of beef, tossing chunks of meat and fat into separate plastic bins. While he works I explain my predicament with my venison, and ask about the possibility of renting freezer space. No problem. The price is a case of beer for his guys when I return to pick it up. Graciously accepting the offer I retrieve my cooler, and deposit its contents in a wire basket among the rows of frozen meat. I show Jake and his guys the rack off my buck, and get nearly the same reaction as I got from Greg. Nice buck, but nothing to write home about! What qualifies as a big buck varies from region to region.

Have Secondary Spots

Back at the farm I park at the first curve. I wasn't expecting to be here in time to hunt tonight, and don't have anything planned, so I decide to spend the afternoon in my van relaxing. Five minutes is all I can take before I am pulling on my gear. It's hot and humid, with temperatures in the 80's, and not exactly the best hunting weather, but a row of dark clouds, the first clouds I've seen since my last visit here, promise a change. Sitting in the woods beats sitting in my van anytime. The only option for tonight is a secondary spot. After a quarter mile walk down the edge of the corn I settle into a groundblind I call "The Rocks".

Strewn randomly along the sides of these bluffs are blocky volcanic rock formations. Though geology isn't one of my strong points these rocks are definitely volcanic, they have a poured and layered look with small crystalline structures on the inside of what must have been bubbles in the cooling lava. At this particular spot, three huge rocks resemble a giant armchair just at the top edge of the bluff. Twenty-five yards below The Rocks is a well-used runway that parallels the side of the ridge. When I stand between the rocks they are about chest high. During my scouting trip I piled brush in the front between the rocks, completing

My ground blind was tucked between these rock formations.

an excellent natural ground blind. This is the only ground blind I have on this entire farm. It is also the epitome of a secondary hunting location. There are a few red oaks on the side of this bluff with acorns, and bedding areas in both directions, but only a single runway. This is not a true destination point, nor a funnel, as the deer have feeding areas in every direction, and several bedding areas nearby to choose from. The deer movement here is also unpredictable. A deer could use this runway anytime, morning, evening, or midday. It is a spot where anything, or nothing, can happen. I hunt spots like these when the timing and conditions aren't right for better locations.

The first thing I do is clear away all the leaves and forest clutter from the floor of the blind. If a deer does pass through I have to be able to move my feet silently. Sitting on my collapsible three-legged stool I lean back against the rocks and relax. The long drive was strenuous and I hope this hunt will clear the rigors of travel out of my head. The clouds roll in bringing with them a light misty rain. Apart from a few gray squirrels scampering about, the evening is completely quiet; a very uneventful first hunt in Wisconsin.

Back at my van I open the back door and undress, immediately returning all of my gear to its proper place, inside carbon sacks inside plastic tubs. My outer Scent Lok is wet, so placing it in a plastic bag I head for the laundromat. While I am out on the road hunting, one of my criteria for selecting areas is the proximity to a laundromat. Although I have several sets of hunting clothes for all conditions, and several sets of Scent Lok, keeping all my hunting clothing and gear dry and scent free as possible requires a washer and dryer. Strict scent control is critical to this kind of hunting. Unlike a situation near home, where scouting can be done in the spring and hunts are planned tactically according to perfect conditions and keeping disturbance to a minimum, freelance bowhunting demands that scouting and hunting take place almost simultaneously. This means hunting a very short interval between stand preparation and actual hunting, it also means hunting stands more often than normal. The only way to succeed with any regularity in this type of situation is to take every precaution to remain as scent free as possible. Bucks will tolerate some intrusion into their home ranges and core areas as long as there is little or no scent left behind. Though deer trust their eyes and ears, their sense of smell is by far their most important sense. By practicing scent control it is also possible to hunt stands more often without turning a spot sour.

The demands of scent control means washing all of my hunting clothes regularly, and re-activating my Scent Lok even more often, and this can only be done with a clothes dryer. Laundromats are a must. Most laundromats also have restrooms, and water faucets to fill up my water bottles.

While my clothes are spinning around in circles I eat my dinner in my van. The can of cold soup, crackers, and apple chased down with water are a far cry from the fresh venison of the last two days. Taking a minute, I unpack my bedding and arrange the inside of my van. The luxury of Dan's hospitality behind me, I have to settle in to my home on wheels. I bought this van with one purpose in mind, hunting. It is a mid-nineties Chevy Astro, extended model, white with pin stripes, that I picked up for $2500. Despite resembling a pinstriped refrigerator, and having the same aerodynamics, the gas mileage isn't horrible. As far as I'm concerned it is the perfect hunting machine. It's too bad that the majority of hunters think you need a new $40,000 full size truck to go bowhunting. For as little as most of these trucks actually get off-road, or carry any loads, they are overwhelmingly overkill for more pragmatic purposes, and in most cases not much more than gas guzzling status symbols. I can't even count the number of hunters I know who are so busy working to pay off their hunting truck that they don't have time to hunt. Mini vans just make perfect sense. They get better gas mileage than most trucks, you can sleep inside them, fit all your gear in them, carry several deer if you have to, and they are inconspicuous. When I need to get off-road, I like to use my own two feet, a form of travel a lot of hunters have unfortunately forgotten.

Organization is the key to hunting out of a van. The first thing I did was to remove the back seats. On the inside it is spacious enough for me and all of my equipment. There is an electric heater in the back that heats up in a hurry. It also has double back doors that swing open vertically, making loading and unloading a breeze. On the floor of the passenger's side front seat sits my electric boot dryer, which I plug into the battery outlet. The last pair of boots

I wore is always on the dryer. On the seat itself I keep my maps, journals, and reading material. Under the passenger seat I store a box of a hundred tree steps. Behind this is a small space. This is my living space, about a square yard. Then comes my bedding.

On the driver's side beginning behind the seat I have a cooler full of non-perishable food, mostly canned goods. This is followed by two duffel bags, one containing a few street clothes, and the other miscellaneous hunting gear. My dragging sled is next in line, filling in all the space to the doors. Inside the sled there are four airtight plastic tubs stacked on one another. Each of these is labeled according to contents, and everything inside of these tubs is kept as scent free as possible. The first is full of Scent Lok suits, the second with Rivers West rain gear, the third is warm clothing, and the fourth contains three hunting packs with their contents. Tucked along the side around the tubs are four pairs of rubber hunting boots. My bow, in a soft case, lies on top of the tubs. Between my duffel bags and the inside wall I store my back-up bow, and a pop-up blind in a large activated carbon sack, inside a plastic bag. Between the drivers and passenger seats is my practice target. This is home for the rest of the fall.

As soon as the dryer stops I retrieve my Scent Lok and immediately return it to its proper place. There is nothing more for me to do today, so I drive back up the bluff to the farm and pull down a two-track around the backside of a strip of corn. I listen to the radio, getting the latest on all the most recent, and approaching catastrophes, before drifting off to sleep.

Shaking gusts of howling wind, followed by torrents of rain drumming on my roof, lightning, and a concert of dramatic thunder that would put Wagner to shame, wakes me. Fumbling in the dark I find my alarm clock; in a few minutes it's time to get up.

I sit up, rubbing the sleep from my eyes, and watch nature's display of awesome power for a minute or two, before sinking back into my blankets. Hunting in the rain is one of my absolute favorites, but when the lightning starts I'm definitely done hunting, or in this case don't even go hunting.

Opening my eyes a couple hours later I'm surprised to see clear blue skies and sunshine. Except for the raindrops still clinging to my windows there is no sign of the violent storm that passed through before daylight. A rooster pheasant crows, and sounds close. Peeking through my windows reveals a brilliant ringneck, shining iridescent in the orange glow of the morning sun, not ten yards away. I try to capture the brilliance with my camera, well aware that my photos will do no justice to this bird's shimmering plumage. The rooster struts a little, and slips into the corn, leaving me alone to get on with my morning.

Groggy from too much sleep, I slide my side door open to let the stale air out of my van. Sitting in shorts and a t-shirt, I enjoy breakfast consisting of a couple of old bagels, some peanut butter, cold water and my daily multi-vitamin. There is no hurry; all of my trees are ready to go. I missed this morning's hunt, and I have the whole day until it is time to hunt this afternoon.

Just lounging, I listen to the radio, write in my journal, and read in a couple of the books. When I finally can't stand it any longer I drive to the local gas station and buy a newspaper, which I read from cover to cover.

This pheasant woke me up one morning.

This finished, I drive around a couple of the local sections (which are not square and definitely bigger than square mile sections) just looking at the land and deer habitat, before I arrive back at my parking spot. The time between hunts, all alone, is going to be the toughest part of this journey. I eat lunch, and write some more, planning my hunts in too much detail.

Do Not Disturb

Early season hunting is somewhat scoffed at by most whitetail "experts", and regarded by the majority of bowhunters as a time to bridge until things heat up during the rut. Though the rut is indeed the season when your chances of killing a mature buck are best, the early season, September and early October, is one of my absolute favorite times to hunt mature bucks. With a little thought and caution, this can be some of the best hunting of the year. Like every other time of the season, the key to successful hunting now is understanding deer behavior. In September and early October most deer are in a late summer routine that is fairly regular. This routine centers squarely around food, with deer following what most hunters consider a traditional pattern of moving towards the local food sources in the evening and returning to bedding areas in the morning. Hunts along travel routes connecting feeding and bedding areas are productive at this time, as long as the bucks, and all other deer for that matter, aren't disturbed. After mature bucks are disturbed they will often enter a nocturnal routine, and remain in that routine until the sexual urges of the rut cause them to return to a more diurnal movement. A reason a lot of bucks live through this time of season is this disturbance factor.

Hunters scouting and setting up stands in the weeks leading up to the season alert mature bucks to the coming season. Remember, deer cannot differentiate between scouting and hunting, for them unusual intrusion is unusual intrusion. The ideal is to have all of your trees ready months in advance of the opener. If this isn't possible, the other alternative is to exercise extreme scent control to minimize the repercussions of your scouting intrusion.

When hunting travel routes between bedding and feeding areas, it is important to be able to get to and from your stand undetected. This obvious little point is often simply overlooked by hunters.

Another important factor for early season success is staying off of field edges. Sitting on field edges is tempting because hunters like to see deer. However, getting to and from a stand on a field edge is almost impossible without spooking deer either before daylight on a morning hunt or after dark on an evening hunt. After a couple of hunts, such locations usually dry up.

Isolated food sources are yet another super location for early season hunting. Single isolated soft mast trees, such as apple trees, in good cover are deer magnets at this time of year. The same goes for hard mast trees, mainly oaks. The ideal is a tree located relatively close to a bedding area, where bucks may feel comfortable moving during the daylight. The fruit on these trees is a limited food source that is available on a first-come, first-served basis. Early season hunts here can be outstanding.

There is still another option for early season hunting, and that is hunting core rut areas. In late summer bucks are very true to their core areas, and don't wander much at all. They generally have an established routine. Within their core ranges there are almost always

Much of the habitat in this area looks like this. It couldn't be much better for producing big deer; they have a great combination of cover and an overabundance of food sources.

traditional rut areas, such as primary scrape areas and rut staging areas. These are also almost always in zones of heavy deer activity. Bucks incorporate these areas into their daily routine, or at least pass through regularly. At the very beginning of the season I very carefully hunt all the rut stands. The ideal is to hunt these spots once or twice, and then refrain from returning to them until the pre-rut is in full swing and the time is right. Over-hunting stands like this too early is a very common mistake bowhunters make.

The last option I sometimes employ in the early season in pressured areas is hunting escape routes. This type of hunting is for very special circumstances. In areas with very heavy hunting pressure there will be an onslaught of hunters hitting the woods on opening morning. Most of these guys get to their stands too late, and push the deer into the bedding areas in front of them. If you can find a stand along an escape route about a quarter to half mile away from where the heaviest hunting pressure will be, there is a good chance that a nice buck will pass through late in the morning on opening day. I have a couple of trees on public land that are solely for this type of situation. I hunt there once or twice per season, maximum.

› ⋙ • ⋘ ‹

By early afternoon I can't stand waiting any longer, and decide that as long as I'm doing nothing I might as well do it hanging in a tree. The corner apple tree is where I want to hunt first. Perhaps a mature buck will step out, pining for the taste of those apples.

The temperature is in the seventies as I sneak along the edge of the corn and through the old pasture. The ground under the tree is littered with apples and the forbs and grasses aren't knocked down at all. One licking branch has been chewed on recently, though there isn't a scrape on the ground. It doesn't look like there is much deer activity here. There is simply too much forage this year, apples, acorns, corn, soybeans, alfalfa, everywhere.

Quickly, I spin my steps up the tree and settle into my saddle. This is my first real planned hunt on the farm this season, and I'm optimistic. I've hunted the farm three times before, always for less than a week, and have had an encounter with a mature buck every time.

The hours fly by. Hunting is the only time I really feel alive, the only thing that is real in our virtual world of screens and metal carriages, unless you ask Sartre; he, of course, lived for something else. The diversity of life and action is endless. Sinking into the woods and becoming forgotten or unnoticed by the usual residents is a real experience, and very different from the vicarious existence most people are used to.

Three different gray squirrels scurry up the trunk of the next tree over, all stopping at arm's length to have a closer look at me before sliding back down the bole and getting on with business.

For hours uncountable small birds dart through the branches all around me, sometimes landing very close, hunting swarming black insects that fill this fencerow. A coyote crosses the pasture about a hundred yards away. The sun crosses the sky creeping slowly west. Lost in blank thought, and content to enjoy the evening, I am almost startled when a doe fawn springs out of the woods, running and kicking its feet on a short sprint, like a gangly kid happy to be up and moving. The fawn's mother is more careful. The big doe gingerly sneaks out of the cover, securing the area with her nose, tasting the air a few times before she is convinced enough to move forward. While she does this her fawn stares at her, as though she is urging her mother to hurry up. With a twitch of her tail the big doe seems to relax; immediately the fawn jogs over to the apples.

My first impression is how enormous the deer are here compared to those in the area of North Dakota I hunted. The fawn is almost as large as a mature badlands doe, and the doe is simply huge. Completely unaware of their camouflaged spectator they treat me to an interesting spectacle.

Nosing through the tall grass the doe feeds on the apples. Her technique is to select an apple and then, while pressing in to the ground, she bites it, breaking the still green and somewhat hard fruit into pieces. She then chews and swallows one piece at a time. The fawn obviously doesn't yet have very much experience eating apples. She takes one apple after another in her mouth and lifts it from the ground. With her head in the air she attempts to crush them, to no avail, the unscathed apples eventually thumping back to the earth. This goes on for at least a half-hour, and I can sense the fawn is getting frustrated. She edges close to mom, and with a subtle maneuver, attempts to snap up a piece of broken apple. For her boldness the fawn is educated with a swift blow of the hoof to her ribs. She dashes about twenty yards, stopping and staring back at mom, looking insulted for a minute or so. Having learned her lesson the fawn casually feeds back under the apple tree, and begins anew with her example of how not to feed on fresh green apples.

I watch nature's comedy with a smile on my face, silently wishing her success. Finally, after what seems like another hundred attempts, and nearly every apple under the tree tested, one of them breaks into pieces. Like a hungry child the fawn gulps down the chunks of sweet fruit. As though a light bulb turned on in her head, the fawn instantly has better luck with the apples. Her success ratio rises to about fifty percent, and she begins to imitate her mother's technique, an education in progress. Shortly before dusk the doe edges towards the woods, taking her fawn with her.

Those two barely out of sight I catch the sound of steadily approaching deer, coming from straight behind me. Probing intensely with my eyes in the fading light for the source of the sound, two raccoons cruise under the fence. Raccoons — instead of the anticipated big buck — are a solid letdown. The coons are young and still small, and obviously hungry for some of those apples, as both of them run the last fifteen yards. Wasting no time they get busy chewing, while sitting on their hind legs each holding an apple in its front paws. This entertains me until dark. Walking back to my van I am pleased with my hunt.

Two days and four hunts later bring a total of two more deer sightings. The weather has been perfect for just about everything except hunting; sunny clear skies with temperatures in the low eighties, and warm nights. I've been hunting secondary locations hoping for either cold or inclement weather to get the deer moving. The forecast is for a drop in temperature tonight, low forties or high thirties, so I plan to hunt one of my better rut spots in the morning. The extended forecast is for cold nights, and if that is indeed the case I will hunt all of my best stands in the next several mornings. I almost always hunt my best spots the first time in the morning. The chances at having a mature buck pass through are simply better in most instances in the morning than in the evening. When deer get up to feed in the afternoon they are leaving the security of their bedding area and heading towards danger. This puts them naturally on high alert. After a night of feeding undisturbed bucks are moving back towards cover, which puts them a little more at ease. Mature bucks are also more likely to be on their feet during daylight in the morning than in the evening.

True to the forecast I awake to temperatures a little under forty degrees, and perfect calm. Excited by the better hunting conditions I am up and out early.

Two hours before first light I find myself snug in my saddle thirty feet above the ground in the twelve-point tree. Two hours is a long time to wait for daylight, but I do this for a reason. The first is simply to get back to the woods ahead of the deer. Most deer spend their nights out in the fields, roaming and feeding. Before daylight most of them start their return to bedding areas. Of course, not all deer return to bed down at the same time, but mature bucks are usually the first ones to return, quite often before daylight. Other deer will pass through later in the morning. So what is the point of sitting so long in the dark if the buck is going to pass through before you can shoot him anyway? The key to early season hunting is mature buck lateral movement. Bucks will often return to the woods before daylight and then casually make their way to the bedding area through the woods. Most hunters are also arriving at, or just before, daylight. By doing so they are unwittingly pushing these bucks and other deer into the bedding areas ahead of them. You simply have to be on stand well before the deer begin their morning return.

There is also another reason to be on stand so early. Even if a mature buck passes through before daylight, there is a chance that, if undisturbed, the buck will pass by later in the morning. This is due to the fact that mature bucks, and most deer for that matter, have a period of movement in late morning through mid afternoon, between 10:00 a.m. and 2:00 p.m. to be exact. These deer will not, however, pass through later if you have spooked them with your arrival in the morning. This movement pattern is very important for hunting the pre-rut and rut, but is also relevant during the early season.

Leaning my head against the lead strap of my saddle, I do what I do on almost every morning hunt, I doze. This is not really sleep, but it is not awake either. It is somewhere in between. My intention is to conserve as much energy as possible while I hunt. This involves an extra effort both to get as much sleep as possible and to reduce mental energy by remaining as mentally flat as possible. With my head resting, I actually fall into a dreamlike state, but with my senses, particularly my hearing, on high alert. The slightest suspect noise brings me back to full awareness. I suppose this is a natural form of meditation that hunters have probably been practicing for millennia. The traditional Inuit standing perfectly still for hours at a time on the ice waiting to spear a seal must be in the same state.

A dainty double crunch of leaves causes my left eye to open, and look in the direction of the sound. It is no longer completely dark, but I can barely see the ground. The sound stops and starts again, steady. This is unmistakably the sound of deer. Squinting, I strain to see in the dark, the steps are close. Just a little more light! More steps, more searching, the sound is now practically right below me. A deer! I can see that it is a deer, but I can't tell what it is, just a moving shape in the dark. It crosses less than five yards away. This is the cusp of light, in a couple minutes I will be able to see. Right behind the first, follows a second, smaller deer. This leads me to the conclusion that the two must be a doe and fawn. A few minutes later, as light finally wins the overhand, my suspicions are confirmed as they make a small loop back, feeding along the ridge before dropping into the deep ravine. These two are very early.

I remain on stand until 1:00 p.m., all the while hoping for more action, but no more deer come my way. By the time my feet hit the ground the temperature is in the upper seventies. A quick inspection of the runways crossing near my tree reveals light but steady deer traffic. Satisfied with my morning effort I slowly, and as quietly as possible, walk back to my van. In a couple hours I will be on stand again.

Midday is time to clean up and eat lunch. Personal hygiene while nomadic bowhunting is an important topic of its own. To practice careful scent control it is vital to remain as clean as possible. This presents a few difficulties. With a little thought and planning it is possible to remain perfectly clean, while out on the road hunting. Very important to this endeavor is always having enough water. I carry five plastic gallon jugs full, which are stored in a row along the driver's wall of my van. These are refilled as necessary. There are numerous places to refill water jugs. Most rest areas have water available; laundromats, gas stations, and parks are other possibilities. If there is no place to refill your bottles, supermarkets have bottled water for about fifty cents a gallon. This water is for drinking, and washing. It can't be emphasized enough how important it is to remain clean.

The first step is what I call a half-gallon shower. I find a place with a little cover, strip down, pour water over my head and lather up, washing my whole body with scent eliminating soap; ½- to ¾-gallon is usually enough water. This only takes a minute or two, and I do this a minimum of every other day. To ease this process, I keep my hair cut very short during the fall. Less hair means less scent in the first place, and it takes less water to wash. Generally I "shower" during midday when the temperatures are the highest. During warm spells this provides a cooling effect as well, and during cold spells it is simply more comfortable.

Another portion of my hygiene plan involves a small plastic water basin, and a hand mirror. A little water in the basin is enough to shave with. While hunting I shave every day, using scent-eliminating soap as shaving cream to keep scent from facial hair to a minimum.

I also use the basin for a quick wash with a washcloth, particularly my face and armpits, on the days that I do not "shower". Scent eliminating deodorant is another vital component to this

A deer directly under my tree in very low light.

process. Keeping mouth odor to a minimum is also critical. Before every hunt I brush my teeth with a baking-soda based toothpaste.

Yet another aspect to hygiene and scent control are scent free wipes. Be careful when purchasing these, some that claim to be scent free simply stink. It took me several attempts before I found a brand that is actually scent free. I am constantly wiping my hands with baby wipes. They are also great for your bottom. All of these components simply must be followed to form the baseline of scent control that is so critical to nomadic style bowhunting. There is, however, even more to the hygiene and scent control strategy.

An often-overlooked portion of hygiene and scent control is diet. You are what you eat, and you smell like what you eat too. Garlic, onions, hot peppers, and other interesting spices are among some of my favorite tastes. The problem is, after eating any of these, your body emits a strong odor for days. We've all had the experience of standing close to someone the morning after they enjoyed a garlic-laden dinner. Imagine what this must smell like to the sensitive nose of a deer. It is simply wise practice to severely limit these and other spices during hunting season. Another common food item that causes the body to emit a strong odor is coffee. Although I drink a little coffee in the fall, I severely reduce my coffee consumption, and try never to drink it before hunting.

Diligent attention to all other sources of scent can also pay dividends. I attempt to keep the inside of my van as clean and scent free as possible. Instead of cleaning it with the usual cleaning agents I use scent-eliminating spray on all fabric and interior surfaces. This includes spraying down my sleeping mats as well. Continuing along these lines I wash my bedding, sheets, blankets, and sleeping bags weekly with scent eliminating detergent. Clean scent free bedding helps me reduce my own scent production by allowing a little scent causing bacteria build-up as possible. Any waste that collects, stored in a plastic bag inside another sealed plastic bag, should be disposed of as expediently as possible to keep any food odors to a minimum. When possible while eating, I leave the side doors and windows open to keep air flowing. Also, when I am sitting somewhere in the outdoors, I leave the doors and windows open so the interior airs out. As a final line in the cleanliness routine I always spray my hands with scent eliminating spray before I handle any of my hunting equipment, or get dressed to hunt. All this may seem a little excessive, and perhaps it is, but *after* every hunt is *before* the next hunt. Preparation and controlling variables is a key to success, and scent is an important variable to bowhunting. I use the time between hunts to prepare by going through a complete hygiene and scent control routine.

A clear hot afternoon is followed by a cloudless night, and another serious drop in temperature. I wake to find my windows painted solid white with a thick coating of frost. Another morning to hunt one of my better trees.

Having hunted daily for two weeks my routine is set, and in minutes I am dressed and walking towards my tree. This morning the dump tree is my destination. Avoiding the fields I cut into the big east woods and do a large half circle, keeping as far back from the edge as possible, following trails that the farmer's family members have cut for use during gun season. The stand is only a quarter mile from the parking spot, but I will cover about three times the distance to get there. If any deer happen to be in those fields, they should have no idea of my presence.

Walking as covertly as I can I attempt not to use a flashlight, and when I do need a flashlight I use a tiny pen style light that casts a dull beam. Super bright high beam flashlights are great for tracking, but as far as I'm concerned are overkill for walking to and from stand. Deer have eyes and notice lights bouncing through their living rooms in the middle of the night. They are more likely to spook from a dark shape moving through the woods if that shape carries a light; whereas, a deer may stand aside and let a dark object pass by if it is unable to smell it. Remaining inconspicuous as possible is the name of the game. Right in the middle of the woods I nearly step on a bedded deer. It bounds up from practically under my feet and sprints away into the woods without stopping and without any vocal complaining. I don't know who was more startled, the deer or me. Pausing, I listen for a few seconds. The deer is completely alone; the absence of an accompaniment of rustling leaves indicates a solitary animal. Pulling a couple of deep breathes through my nose I pick up a faint but distinct odor, the musky smell of rutting buck. Typical; a single buck alone two hours before daylight and already deep in the woods. His odiferous calling card convinces me that this must have been a mature buck; young bucks just don't smell that way in late September. I pick my way to the edge of the bluff, and follow it east to my tree.

Despite having already spooked a buck this morning I'm optimistic. This is a great spot. My exuberant optimism keeps me on pins and needles, and it is a struggle to relax with constant visions of giant bucks ghosting through. At daybreak a raccoon ambles out of the corn, under my tree, on to an old crooked maple right at the edge of the bluff. Nails scratching on the bark it ascends and slips into a crevice, vanishing inside a hollow trunk. The squirrels wake up, distracting me with their imitations of approaching deer. An hour after daylight a hawk darts in and alights on a branch only yards away from me. It sits and scans, eyes sharp in the morning light. I imagine just how clearly this bird must see, as it looks through me, while I stare back with my own bespectacled eyes. The hawk pays no attention to the camouflaged blob hanging in this tree, seemingly more interested in a squirrel breakfast. "Kah-kah-kah-kah-kah-kah!" The sudden cry surprises me. I've heard this call many times, but have mostly attributed it to crows, thinking the sound coming from a hawk as a longer and higher pitched sort of "kaaaaah kaaaaah." A short jump and glide brings the bird to another perch about ten yards away. He is looking into the woods. With a sudden flap, and riding on bent wings, the hawk is gone, jetting into the woods. I wonder what he saw that sent him away so quickly. Perhaps a careless young rodent a quarter mile into the trees? Everybody needs a good hearty breakfast.

At around 9:30 the soft crunch of leaves draws my attention to the west. A doe stands only twenty yards away. Right behind her are two fawns, the second a button buck. The three of them hurry through, crossing at about ten yards. These deer are heading in the wrong direction, at least the opposite from what I expected, from the bedding area towards the fields. The doe must have a clear destination in mind, because all three are moving at a very steady pace, investigating their surroundings only fleetingly. Within a couple minutes they have come and gone, never even slightly aware of the danger hanging above. It is aggrandizing to be able to observe deer so close without them being aware of any intrusion.

The next three hours pass slowly, and the only notable event is the coming of the wind. By the time my feet hit the ground it is really howling, and the temperature has risen to the high seventies.

The wind is straight out of the south, and brings heat. The mercury rises close to ninety degrees, far too hot for the last day of September. This is atrocious hunting weather, extremely windy and sweltering. Not expecting anything, I select my ground blind in the rocks as the spot to spend the evening hunt, not wanting to hunt a good stand with such poor weather.

A little after 5:00 p.m. a single young doe strolls past, right along the main runway twenty-five yards down the ridge. Just beyond my shooting lane she veers up the ridge and slips into the corn.

Right at dark I make my escape a little earlier than normal, sneaking out of my hiding spot, and cautiously stalking along the edge of the corn. The maize surrounds a small wooded peninsula that is less than a hundred yards from the road. Arriving at the tip of the point I notice a turkey buzzard sitting in the bleached white skeleton of a dead tree, just a few yards over my head. It's a scene that could be cut straight out of many a bad Hollywood western movie. The scavenger doesn't fly away; rather, it cocks its head and sizes me up as though I could be its dinner. Perhaps some day, but not right now. I'm not overly superstitious, but I sure hope this buzzard isn't a bad omen.

With that buzzard still picking at my brain, psychologically speaking, of course, I turn the last corner in the cornfield to see the shape of two big deer scoot by less than fifteen yards ahead of me, straight into the woods. This time there is no question. The dank smell of stinking, rutting buck immediately burns my nostrils. At least one of those deer was a really mature buck. Bucks just don't stink like that at end of September unless they are truly mature. A quick glance is all I need to know I made a mistake. How could I have missed this spot? Even in the twilight I can see four runways that all come together, and count a half dozen rubs. Right off the corner there is tree that is situated perfectly to cover all the shot opportunities. In my eagerness to get back into the woods I missed a great stand location less than a hundred yards from my parking spot. The only drawback is that this corner will only be good as long as the corn is standing. After the corn is cut there is no reason for the deer to pass through here during daylight. This is an area that needs to be hunted right now, and I have perhaps ruined my chance. I make it a point to clear out that tree during midday tomorrow. Maybe that buzzard was merely trying to show me where to hunt, hoping for a few scraps.

The Heat is On

October 1st, the bowhunting opener in my home state, and I'm missing it. Last night the temperature never dropped below seventy, so I slept in. By 9:30 the heat reaches into the mid eighties. Nothing like a fall heat wave to slow the hunting down.

I decide to spend the day getting some work done. The first line of business is getting that tree cleared out. A look at my Scent Lok fills me with dread, knowing just how I will roast under that stuff in these temperatures. Nonetheless, I don my scouting Scent Lok and march back to the point. The buzzard is gone. The tree itself is easy, and has a slight lean in the right direction. Running the steps to the top only takes me a couple of minutes.

The rest of the procedure turns out to be slightly more complicated than I imagined. In order to be able to shoot to one of the main runways I have to cut a hole through some upper limbs in a neighboring tree. This means running more steps up that tree, cutting several branches out of the way, and then removing the steps again on the way down.

On the point side of the tree there are two runways that are out of shooting range, so I take the time to find enough dead limbs to completely block them off in an attempt to force the deer to use the other five runways that cross within shooting distance.

Two and a half hours after beginning, I'm satisfied with my work. Though I plan on hunting this spot within the next few days, that isn't my total intention, and I know my chances of catching the same buck here from last night are very slim.

This is a tree that will always be good for early season hunting in years that corn is planted in the adjoining field. Every tree I clear out I have in mind for future seasons. You can never have enough trees prepared.

Arriving back at my van, I can't get out of my Scent Lok fast enough. Hidden behind the van I wash, cooling myself down in the process. My lightweight suit is exchanged for a pair of shorts and thin t-shirt. I already feel like I have seen more sunshine in the last few weeks than I saw all summer.

The laundromat is my next stop. Starting with a row of washing machines I wash everything I have used, including two of my backpacks, my rope for pulling my bow up, and all of my bedding. I also re-activate both my scouting Scent Lok and my hunting Scent Lok suit. While the wash cylinders and drums are spinning I eat lunch; a can of cold soup, some bread and crackers, and an apple, all washed down with cold water. Dessert is three or four fig bars, and a little chocolate. Working through my meal, I notice again that my food supplies are running low, they have been for about a week now. Since the weather is so poor for hunting I decide to drive to a nearby town to do some grocery shopping as soon as my laundry is finished.

The nearest town with a grocery store is about a forty-minute drive from the farm. I decide to take the country highway that parallels the interstate, because I have to make a couple of phone calls. It seems my cell phone only works in these parts along the highway.

My first call is to a farmer named Paul in Missouri. I've never met Paul, but he gave me permission to hunt his sixteen hundred acre farm, which I've never set foot on, nor seen. In March I ordered several plat books for different counties in northern Missouri, in areas I had driven through briefly, where I noticed the deer habitat looked promising. After comparing

The view from the top of one of my trees.

the plat maps to aerial photos from the Internet I made a list of approximately twenty-five landowners to call. Paul was number seven on my list, and the first and only to grant me permission over the telephone. Cold telephone calls are the most difficult way to gain hunting access, but I had no other choice, since I didn't know a soul in Missouri. I called Paul again in August to confirm my permission and remind him I was still coming down to hunt. Today I want to let him know I will be hunting his land in a week or so. It's lunchtime, so I hope to catch him home.

Our conversation is short. My request from Michigan to hunt his land was something new to Paul, and this got him thinking perhaps he could make a little money off his property. Nobody from outside the local area had ever asked him for hunting permission before. He tells me I can come down, but his land may be leased by the time I get there, since he is negotiating with a hunting club. After a few minutes I am told I could perhaps hunt a small corner of his land even if the lease goes through. Disappointed, but trying hard not to let it be heard, I thank him for keeping the door open for at least a chance at hunting permission.

The bad news has me scrambling a little. Although there is some decent public land nearby that I can hunt if my permission is revoked, immediately I call my old friend Chad in Michigan, whose extended family owns a large farm in the Chronic Wasting Disease management zone in southern Wisconsin. In that area, there is an Earn A Buck system in place, which means that, even if I kill a buck on the property I am hunting now, it would be possible to kill another (after taking a doe or two). We have talked about hunting that farm together a couple of times, and even once had a trip planned that fell through. I need a backup area just in case Missouri falls through. My hope is that we will be able to hunt the farm together, and in fact, the only access is with a family member. Chad wants badly to come out hunting with me, but his business is struggling, so he can't make the trip. I am left with no choice but to travel to Missouri and take my chances.

Sitting in the parking lot of a huge megastore, I finish my conversation before crossing the threshold into the hallowed halls of modern consumption. Food shopping for road hunting on a budget is foremost an exercise in frugality; however, there are a few more factors besides price that have to be taken into consideration. It is critical to eat a balanced diet. This sounds simple and self-explanatory, but becomes difficult when limited to mostly non-perishable food items. Products such as milk, meat or eggs are simply out of the question. One of the basics of a balanced diet for this type of shopping are canned goods. There is a wide variety of complete meal-style soups. Most supermarkets will have one of several brands always on sale, usually for less than $1.50 a can. To eat these soups all you need is a spoon. Another canned item I purchase is tuna fish. This is pure protein that can also be eaten with just a fork and a little bread, and can be purchased for less than $1.00 a can. For some balance I buy canned fruit as well.

Sticking with the concept of a balanced diet I always buy a bag of apples. Apples keep very well, and add a little roughage to my diet, not to mention they provide a natural pick up through their natural sugars. Five pounds of apples can be had for a couple dollars. I also always carry a couple apples with me to eat on stand. Some other essential items are bread and soda crackers. These are good fillers and sources of carbohydrates. All these items can be stored easily in my cooler.

Another serious factor in my grocery shopping plan is simple caloric intake. I prepare for hunting season like an athlete preparing for a major competition. With my on-the-spot scouting, tree preparation, walks to and from stand, climbing up and down trees, long sits in cold weather, and getting deer out of the woods, I burn calories like a distance runner. In fact, during the fall it is normal that I lose between five and ten pounds, which may not sound like much, but considering that I tip the scales at only 150 pounds in the first place, it is a substantial amount.

I have to be careful to get enough calories. For this I buy high calorie and high carbohydrate snack food. One of the most important items in this regard is bags of peanuts and mixed nuts. Nuts are high in both fat and protein. Another item I always buy are fig bars. These are really high in calories; a single two-bite bar usually has around a hundred calories. When it is cold I will eat five or six of these while I am getting up to give me enough energy to get through the morning. Six hundred calories will usually carry me through a morning hunt. The fig bars compliment a couple other high calorie snacks. I prefer, wheat crackers and cheese crackers that I munch on while driving or sitting between hunts.

The last items on my shopping list are chocolate and granola bars. These I carry with me while hunting for a quick energy boost when I need it. All this is washed down with a daily vitamin and a dietary supplement to make sure my body gets all the vitamins and minerals it needs.

This diet is a great departure from my normal health conscious eating program. The rest of the year my diet consists of large amounts of lean, low fat venison, fresh, locally grown, mostly organic vegetables and salads. For now, I'm on a mission, and forty dollars worth of food can last for more than two weeks. My budget allows that I only spend a couple dollars a day on food, and I set a personal limit of five dollars for a single day.

By the time I'm done shopping it is already afternoon and too late to even think about hunting. The temperature is close to ninety degrees anyway. Nothing left to do but relax. I return to the farm and find a parking spot in the shade, killing the afternoon by reading, writing and listening to the radio. Shortly before dark I grab my binoculars and glass a nearby soybean field. I spy two does and two fawns ambling out of the corn, where I suspect all the bucks are hiding out as well.

Returning to my van a few minutes before dark, I step over to the edge of the woods to take a leak, not really paying close attention to my surroundings. While peeing on a log, the unmistakable smell of skunk suddenly slaps my olfactory system to attention. Cautiously I peek over the log, and there, with its striped tail cocked and aimed in my direction, is indeed a skunk. One wrong move and its hasta-la-vista baby. I suppose I would be angry too, if someone so unkindly peed on my head. Moving very, very slowly I retreat, backing up while leaving a thin, wet line on the ground. That was a close call!

The next six days are pure torture. I don't think the temperature drops below seventy the entire time, not even after dark. Patience is the virtue of this long heat wave. Hunting as much as I dare, I stick to my secondary stands and manage to glimpse a deer or two per hunt. I even sleep-in a couple of mornings. Most hunters have a tendency to rush out to their best spots, which is the worst thing I could do right now. The bucks are hanging low, and I should be too, but don't have anything else to do but hunt, so I make the best of the situation. To help the time pass I read a lot, and drive around the back roads looking for deer and hunting areas. The worst part of this situation is being alone, consumed by thoughts, with no one to talk to. Normally I would leave to set up a new area with the intention of returning to hunt here later, but I want to hold on until the next cold or rain spell to hunt my good spots again. Though I haven't even seen a buck yet, in other years I never hunted this farm for more than five days without having an encounter with a mature animal. They are here, and as long as I hunt smart, it is just a matter of time until one crosses my path. Also, because of the current gas price of around three dollars a gallon I want to avoid return trips. And, for the cost of a non-resident license, I intend to make every effort to fill my tag.

Relief comes on the seventh day in the form of sudden freezing cold. During the night the temperature drops into the low thirties. This is just what I was waiting for, a couple cold days to hunt my good trees. I am up early, at about 3:30, excited to get hunting after such an unusual October heat wave, and hoping the sudden chill gets the bucks up and moving as well. It only takes me a couple minutes to dress and start walking to my stand. Shortly after 4:00 I'm sneaking through the woods close to the twelve-point tree, when my hopes for the morning are dashed. A single deer jumps up ahead of me from its bed very close to my tree, and runs off into the deep ravine. Though I can't see the deer, it sounds big, and is all alone, probably a mature buck. I stop and attempt to smell him, but can't pick up any scent. I hate it when this happens. It is more than two hours before first light, and that buck is already in the woods bedded. This behavior is one thing that keeps a lot of mature bucks alive in the fall. I call this *staging*, and this is common behavior for mature bucks, especially in pressured areas. Bucks leave the open fields and feeding areas for cover before daylight. They then bed down in staging areas. A staging area is generally a relatively open space, where a buck can see approaching danger and other approaching deer. There will normally be some cover between the staging area and the feeding area. The staging area will also provide quick and inconspicuous access to a bedding area. These areas will generally have several scrapes and rubs in them. The buck will lie in the staging area, until the other deer in the area pass through. During the pre-rut and rut this gives him the opportunity to intercept any estrous does without exposing himself to danger. If nothing interests the buck he will rise later in the morning and either move into the bedding area, or, during the rut, scent check the edge of bedding areas for hot does. The key to hunting these areas is to be there first. This morning I'm too late! I climb into my tree wondering whether I have to sit all night long in order to be here first.

As daylight slowly nears I notice the biting cold, that seems to be getting colder the closer it gets to dawn. In that short span between daylight and dark, when there is some light, but it is still too dark to really see, I hear some deer coming my way. They don't seem to be in any hurry, and it takes them nearly twenty minutes to get close. By the time they arrive to within shooting distance I can just make out their shapes on the forest floor, a doe and two fawns pass right underneath me.

I allow them to walk out of earshot before attempting a very subtle rattling sequence. Holding my rattle bag in my hands I pull the sticks apart and slap them together, trying to imitate the immediate antler contact of two bucks sparring. I then lightly grind the sticks together, not much more than tickling, with more silence spaces in my rattling than grinding antlers. Most bucks this time of year spar really casually, and all-out fighting is simply uncommon. When bucks spar in the early season it is mostly just practice, and a test of rank, nothing too serious. The does aren't even close to estrous yet, so there is nothing worth fighting for. The goal of early season rattling is simply to peak a buck's curiosity, and get him to want to join in on a little roughhousing with the boys.

A little less than a minute after starting my rattle sequence I return my rattle bag to its place in my pack. 'Less is best' should always be the motto for early season rattling.

Almost immediately I hear a deer closing in at a steady pace. The anticipation of a big buck gets my heart pounding, and I grab my bow to be ready for any eventuality. Within a few seconds a buck indeed steps into my shooting lane, a yearling five pointer. He stops and looks in every direction, and circles a couple times around my tree, obviously trying to figure out where the other bucks are. This is a nice fat young buck, though a little smaller than usual for the area as far as antler size. His antlers are about eight inches wide, with decent forks and a single brow tine. Many of the yearling bucks here approach the hundred-inch mark. The duped youngster does a couple more circles and even stops to smell the base of my tree before following the path the doe and fawns took across the point into the cornfield. This is the first buck I have seen here in two weeks of hunting.

Watching the five-point amble away brings back a sudden memory flash. It strikes me that the antler

Newly appearing sign like this big, ragged rub keeps me movitated when the hunting is slow. Notice the extra tine marks above the main rub.

configuration on his head is nearly identical to the first buck I ever shot. It was the second day of October over a quarter century ago. After a long day at school I couldn't wait to get out into the woods. It was hot and sunny as I squirreled up that giant white oak and stood on a couple of branches that made my blind. At that point I didn't even know treestands existed. It wasn't long before three young bucks fed across a fallow, grassy field under the out-sweeping canopy of the oak in search of acorns. My knees were literally knocking together as the first buck entered my one and only shooting lane. Through the convulsions of buck fever I managed to draw, aim, and release my arrow, which met its mark nearly perfect. A couple hours later, with the help of my dad, I had my very first buck. That memory is as real as stone, and definitely a defining moment in my life. Looking back, killing that buck was a coming-of-age moment for me. From that point on I was taken seriously by our hunting group.

Two more days of hunting is more of the same: very little deer activity. With the arrival of cold there is a noticeable increase in hunter activity. The next afternoon I walk out to one of my trees to find a new treestand hanging ten yards away. Suddenly, there are also several trucks parked at various spots around the farm. It's the second week of October and the other bowhunters on this farm have decided to start hunting. Having already pushed my luck as far as my own hunting pressure is concerned, I decide it is time to seek new horizons.

What to do
- Stowing your venison while on your hunt is usually possible at meat processing operations.
- Mini Vans are a pragmatic choice of vehicle for travelling deer hunters.
- Early season bowhunting shouldn't be overlooked as a possibility for good bucks.
- Personal hygiene and a sound scent control base can be achieved with just a few gallons of water.
- Be sure to scout the first 100 yards of any piece of property.
- Careful shopping can provide a somewhat balanced diet for as little as a couple dollars per day.

This is the first buck I ever killed, several decades ago.

Chapter 5

Missouri: Hunting a Heatwave and a Buck in the Rain

Before I begin my drive south the first project for this morning is to buy a case of beer. Arriving at the counter of the gas station I'm informed that the law won't allow me to buy beer at this early hour. It is so seldom that alcohol is on my shopping list that I forget you can't buy it in many states in the morning. With a couple hours to kill, I head to the laundromat and take the opportunity to wash, dry, and re-activate as required. I read the newspaper from cover to cover, noticing the extremely detailed football coverage, and splurge on a hot breakfast sandwich and a coffee, an exception on a travel day. One minute after it is legal to buy alcohol I'm walking out of the local everything-store with my case of beer. Two blocks down Main Street I deliver it to the meat-processing place. The scene is much the same as my last visit, though instead of cutting on a side of beef, the guys are butchering a hog.

Handing the beer over to Jake, he sets the case on the counter for his employees. We talk briefly of hunting. Most of the guys working are bowhunters and they chime into the conversation. The majority of them either haven't been out yet, or have been out just a few times, and claim to be waiting for the rut. I offer Jake more beer for an extension of our deal, while filling him in briefly on my plans to hunt in Missouri and then to return as soon as I can. He agrees to my offer.

Jumping in my van I finally get rolling, direction Missouri. The drive takes me west across the St. Croix, around the sprawl of the Twin Cities, and then south down Interstate 35. Slightly south of St. Paul I stop at Cabela's, mainly to use the rest room, but also to buy fuel and to take a look in the store. Filling my gas tank is financially painful, as usual. Each time I fill up, a crisp hundred-dollar bill is broken into tiny pieces, and my supply of those crisp bills is severely limited. The rest rooms are clean and I wonder at the abundance of gigantic whitetails hanging in that store; most of them would score over 200 inches, and the majority seem to have been killed in Minnesota. Browsing the book section I discover a copy of my first book, *Bowhunting Pressured Whitetails*. In twenty minutes I walk back out without having spent a dime. For now I have all the hunting equipment necessary for this trip.

Back on the highway the terrain flattens out, the rolling hills around the Twin Cities give way to agricultural prairie. This certainly is the heartland, big open fields with precious few woods. Apart from a couple narrow river bottoms there are a few tiny, wooded squares scattered here and there.

The landscape remains pretty much the same all the way to Des Moines, but south of the city things change. The land becomes hillier and is mixed with larger river bottoms, giant fields give way to pastures, and the towns seem to get smaller and farther apart. This type of terrain holds on all the way to the Missouri line, and beyond.

About a dozen miles into Missouri I pull off into the small town closest to where I will be hunting. The sign reads population three thousand and a few, the biggest town of three on my trip so far.

A few things have changed since I was here last fall. There is a brand new, highway-side motel, so fresh that the landscaping isn't yet finished. A new gas station and laundromat have taken their place just off the exit along the highway strip. Behind them, the old, early days Wal-Mart has been replaced with a newer mega sized version. I drive towards town to check on the old laundromat. It's still there, though even a little rougher around the edges than it was last year. The place was built in the seventies and nothing seems to have been repaired since: open and abused twenty-four hours a day for thirty years. The important thing though is that the dryers function, are very hot, and two quarters gets a half-hour of drying time.

Satisfied with the amenities I turn my attention to the hunting grounds. Ten miles of country highway roll by quickly. I pull onto a gravel road. True to the rural nature of this area there clearly isn't much traffic on this road, it is too narrow for two vehicles to pass each other without one of them either stopping or driving on the edge. I tour the roads around Paul's farm, and am impressed at how it looks. The deer habitat appears even better in real life than on the aerial photos; though, I somewhat expected decent hunting because I selected the general area for how it looked after driving through last year. About four miles south of this farm is a public hunting area that I hunted for a week last season.

Continuing my drive I make a quick loop around the public land. It looks good as well, some of the best public hunting ground I've ever hunted. During a week-long hunt on this public land last season I had one encounter with a mature buck, but a single error on my part saved that buck's life. I was set up on a rub and scrape line close to a bedding area on a long hunt. It started to rain in the morning, so I went out at about 11:00 a.m. with the intention of sitting until dark. About an hour before dark the buck, about an eighteen inch wide, eight-point with tall tines, traipsed out of the bedding area, but was about eighty yards away and definitely not coming in my direction. Grabbing my can-style *doe in estrous* call I turned it over three times. As if on a string, the buck walked straight to my tree. When he reached twenty yards he was facing me, and right at that point he hesitated briefly. He was standing at a split in the runway. If he turned left I would have to shoot within two steps or he would drop down a bank and be out of reach. If he kept on his path he would move a couple yards closer, giving me a broadside, twelve yard shot that I would have to turn a little in my sling to take.

The buck dropped his head down, and I drew. Unfortunately, he noticed the movement and looked right at me; and I mean stared right through me. I held as long as I could, but the buck didn't like the situation and in a single swift move swung around and hightailed it straight away from me. He didn't hesitate even for a split second. That was that.

› ➤➤➤ · ◂◂◂‹ ›

Parking at one of the public land pullouts, I grab some dinner while playing last year's mistake over and over again through my mind. That hunt will haunt me for a long time

Dinner is the usual fair; a can of cold soup, some bread, an apple, and some crackers. Following dinner I drive back to Paul's farm to introduce myself. It is early evening so the chances are good that he will be home.

A tough looking St. Bernard meets me in the driveway. His name turns out to be Buck, go figure. Someone in the family must have read Jack London's "Call of the Wild" or at least watched the film.

The house is a simple ranch style and the barns are new and efficient looking, somewhat out of place when compared to the other barns in the neighborhood. Ignoring the barking hound I knock on the door and am greeted by Paul's wife, Janet. I introduce myself and am immediately invited to sit at the kitchen table. Paul is out harvesting corn somewhere.

Although I just knocked on the door unannounced, Janet offers me a piece of fresh apple pie, which, after a month of my lean diet is certainly appreciated.

We sit down and talk for awhile. Janet's family has been on this farm for four generations; her father actually owned the land that now belongs to Paul. The new barns are the end result of a tornado that destroyed the old ones just last year, and are only about a month old. That twister literally missed their house by mere inches.

Janet has been on this land all of her life, though she has made three trips to Europe. Since I've had the opportunity to spend some time in Europe myself, we have something in common. We talk about her children and grandchildren, looking at photos on the wall. And, of course, we get to the subject of hunting permission. Janet informs me that Paul is thinking about leasing their land, which she is absolutely against. For more than an hour we converse at the kitchen table. I drive away with the instruction from Janet to return tomorrow morning at 8:00 a.m. to talk about hunting permission with Paul. I have a feeling that my chances of landing permission to hunt their land just improved dramatically.

I spend the night at a pullout in the public hunting area and rise with the sun. It is going to be hot again today. Anxious to get my hunting permission dilemma cleared up I eat quickly, dress in the one set of nice clothes I brought along, and begin my drive back towards the farm. Because I am too early for my appointment I alter my route, extending my morning drive to look for deer. Circling the public land, a doe and two fawns cross the road in front of me; other than that nothing. A single truck is parked along the south side of the public tract. The two-tone Ford is plastered with various bowhunting equipment stickers and advertising; it is clear that this guy is in the woods bowhunting. Mentally noting where he is parked I drive on, circling sections, getting ever closer to Paul's farm.

The countryside here is not stunningly beautiful at first glance, however it is attractive in its own right. This used to be rolling, tall grass prairie, laced with draws, creeks, and small rivers. The open spaces are now soybeans or corn, but the ridges and draws are still full of mature oaks, many of them several hundred years old.

The fields are much larger than in the bluffs of Wisconsin, and the farming is on a larger scale, though not nearly as neat. The woods are dryer and have a yellow brown, sunburnt hue. Many of the country roads are little more than lanes, with strips of weeds growing up the middle, that only see use during planting and harvest time. The area reminds me of rural northern Michigan in my childhood, before the building explosion ate up a lot of what used to be the country.

Arriving at Paul's place, I knock on the door at exactly one minute before eight. Janet invites me in, and offers me a cup of coffee at the kitchen table. Paul is already sitting there with his coffee mug in hand. I introduce myself and we shake hands. Paul is in his late sixties, perhaps even in his early seventies. He's not a big man, about my height with round face, and wears a pair of jean coveralls and a light flannel shirt. He looks like the classic Midwest farmer, that indeed he is.

Our conversation is very honest and interesting. I start out with who I am and what I'm doing. He tells me that he doesn't hunt, but his kids do. However, they all own their own farms now.

He never considered leasing his land until I called for permission from out-of-state, and shortly after my call a letter arrived in the mail from some kind of hunting club offering to lease his land. He shows me the letter, and the follow-up contract the company sent him. The letter begins with "Make up to $25 thousand dollars a year off your land" and the contract ends with an offer of $1500 for 1600 acres. The contract basically restricts Paul's use of his own land to farming, while the year-round hunting, and fishing rights go to the club. It is obvious that he wants me to make a counter offer. I don't.

We talk about the problems he has had with hunters on his land. Namely, poor hunter behavior, giving one person permission and then finding ten guys hunting his farm, hunters leaving gates open, riding quads and trucks across fields, and finding beer cans and trash on his farm. Until now, he has allowed nearly anyone who asked to hunt his land. I understand his concerns, and promise that I'm completely alone, and will be respectful of his property. It strikes me in the middle of our conversation that I am experiencing the end of an era. Nearly the last thing that could be had for free in the United States was hunting permission. This is slipping away fast. With good property escalating in price in some parts of the country we are headed straight for a European system of hunting, namely those with money will be able to hunt, those without, well?

Paul is clearly in a bit of a conflict. He already gave me hunting permission for the season, but he wants the extra cash. His wife doesn't want him to lease the land at all, mostly because their grandchildren hunt occasionally. I don't attempt any kind of hard sell; rather I talk politely and honestly about the situation of leasing hunting land, and understand his position completely. There is really no reason for him to give me permission, except for the fact that I asked. I even tell him of the enormous leasing prices in Michigan, Illinois, and Wisconsin. In the end, with some gentle prodding from Janet, Paul grants me permission to hunt his entire property. Relieved and grateful, I thank him, walking out the door at about 10:00 a.m.

Relieved to finally have the hunting permission my plans were based on I hop into my van and spin back to town, this time passing through the highway strip to the old downtown. There is some business I have to take care of. Compared to the gas station strip, there isn't much commercial activity. This may be the official center of town, but it has long since lost its position as the center of the community. A beautiful town square is surrounded by a few municipal buildings of white granite that hint of grand schemes that didn't materialize, and run-down red brick shops. Several crooked storefronts are simply empty with 'for rent' signs in the windows. I can't help but wonder what this looked like before that big box giant moved in.

In the northwest corner of the square is what I'm looking for, the post office. Pulling up to the drive-up blue mailbox I drop my envelopes. Bills certainly don't stop rolling in just because one happens to be out on the road hunting.

On the south side of the square I find the second destination for this trip to town, an old-fashioned barbershop. Very short hair is a must to remain scent free, particularly considering my washing facilities. The place is pragmatically decorated to say the least. Blank walls, two barber chairs, and a row of wooden stools to sit on. There is a knee-high coffee table holding a few magazines, with *Outdoor Life* and *Field and Stream* dominating the stack. On the counter across from the barber chairs is a television with a complete collection of hunting videos piled next to it. A bear hunting video is playing as I walk in.

The barber is a young man, probably in his early thirties. I sit down and pick up a magazine. I like this sort of place, it has the feel of real America, no fancy decoration or advertising, no weird haircuts, just the real deal.

The guy in the chair is a local farmer and is talking about this year's harvest and how dry it has been. Busy eavesdropping while browsing the pages of a recent edition of *Outdoor Life,* I only get through half a magazine before it is my turn in the chair.

"How do you want your cut?"

"Short."

The barber gets to business without hesitation, turning on the clippers immediately. I attempt to strike up a conversation about hunting, but am unable to get much of anything going. That he has been out bowhunting a couple of times is all the information I can coax. A certain wariness of strangers is obvious in his overt lack of interest.

The cut only takes a few minutes. Parting with six dollars I'm out the door. It's good to know places like this still exist.

Back to "work"

Now there is work to do: sixteen hundred acres of Missouri farmland to scout. For months I've studied aerial photos of the farm and I know exactly where to start. According to my maps, on the southernmost portion of the farm there are two areas that could be natural funnels. The

Small towns like this are the best to base a hunt out of, and get a haircut.

heat though is my enemy. The temperature has been in the high seventies to high eighties during the day every day for the last month, and today is no exception. I've seen more sunshine already this fall than I saw all summer. This is perhaps an exaggeration, but not by much.

Parking at the southwest corner of the farm I slip into my Scent Lok and peruse my maps one more time. Straight east across the road is a rectangle of corn that is a mile and half wide by two miles long. A few long, narrow fingers of woods stretch into that field, extensions of some slight ridges that cross Paul's land. According to my map, three of those fingers merge about a quarter mile onto his property. This convergence is my first destination.

Jumping over the fence into a small alfalfa field, that happens to contain more grass than alfalfa, I follow the overgrown, south fenceline of the property. The ten-acre field sits on the top of a rise that is wooded on three sides, a ridge on the north and a creek bottom on the south and east. The only wooded areas around here are ridges and creek bottoms, places that would be difficult or impossible to farm. All the more level terrain is either under plow, or is left fallow as CRP land.

Arriving at the east end of the field I stop and peer down a slight ridge into the open woods. In the dried out undergrowth, a network of deer runways is easy to distinguish. Already satisfied with the looks of things, I take a couple more steps down the ridge. In an explosion of action at least seven or eight deer burst out of their beds and fly off that ridge in different directions. In the sudden blur of activity I am only able to make out does and fawns.

The sightings only a few minutes into my walk catch me somewhat by surprise. The bad news is: I just spooked a bunch of deer. But the good news is: These deer were bedded in an open area, which probably means they haven't been disturbed much yet this season. Things are looking good. At the least, I am certain that there is decent deer population here.

Cruising down to where the deer were, I immediately encounter a good hunting location. A fencerow, a creek bottom, and a ridge all come together, and there are alfalfa fields on three sides.

A typical looking area on the Missouri farm.

However, since I just set out on my scouting foray, and have to walk back through here anyway, I decide to save the tree-clearing for my return.

Pressing on, I follow the dry creek bed. It takes me to the edge of a long, steep ridge and then curves around the backside of a second hay field to yet another finger of woods. At the base of the finger I discover a second good location. A smaller creek bed runs the length of the narrow woods, converging with the larger creek bed. To the north there is a small cornfield and several runways trace the finger to the corn. They are being used heavily. Noting the spot as one where it is necessary to prepare a tree, I direct my attention to the woods on the other side of the larger creek bed.

Things get interesting. The woods turns out to be a bedding area, crisscrossed with runways and littered with shredded rubs. Skirting the edge of the bedding area I circle back, arriving again at the base of the steep ridge. There is a lot of activity here!

Turning east I investigate the base of the ridge. Several large scrapes and more rubs dot a major runway that parallels the base of the ridge. A hundred yards further along I run into the creek bed again, its banks are sandy and literally plowed with deer tracks. Walking silently in the sand I reach a point where both the ridge and the creek make a ninety-degree turn straight north. Right in the corner glistens a small pool of water, the first water I have seen anywhere around, and the ground surrounding it resembles freshly tilled garden soil from all the deer activity.

Pausing on the sandy bank to look for a suitable tree I glance across the creek, and can't believe my eyes. For a split second the buck lies there staring at me. He is about fifteen yards away and tucked just in the brush on the other bank.

As he stands he turns sideways, giving me a profile view of a set of very large antlers, a perfectly typical, ten-point rack with long staggered tines, in the 150 category. With a single bound he is gone over the edge of the bank, leaving me staring at the now empty spot where he was just bedded.

Inspecting a fresh rub.

This young four-pointer came close to me
several times, even bedding down within easy
shooting range.

The contents of a freelance hunting fanny pack.

Sometimes you find hidden treasure in the woods.

A couple of fawns that meandered in real close.

A tree fully set up for my saddle provides awesome cover; the middle trunk of the three trunks growing together.

Where do the whitetails hide in terrain like this?

A patch of aspens at the base of a butte, way out in the prairie.

Finding this brushy draw would prove to be a stroke of luck.

Diverse terrain at the edge of the badlands.

105

The versatility of a tree saddle is unmatched by any other type of stand.

When using a tree saddle your tree steps as foot rests
should be placed around the tree like this.

Incredible Wisconsin whitetail habitat in bluff country.

Thick bluffs and abundant crops allow some Wisconsin whitetails to grow big.

A patch of thick bedding I discovered on Ohio public land.

The bedding was surrounded by miles of open rolling woods like this.

Deer bedded in the snow in a suburb.

A little hunting "cabin" out on the prairie.

I haven't seen too many bucks in my life as big as this one. Bucks in this class may be more common in a lot of areas around the Midwest and West, but in Michigan they are very few and very far between. With a million or so hunters it's very seldom to find bucks that big.

I'm amazed at what this buck just did. He was only fifteen yards away from me, and if I hadn't stopped and looked right at him he would have let me pass, none the wiser of his presence. I wonder how many deer I've walked right by already today, and how many eyes, and ears are studying my every move right now?

Marking the water hole as an area that definitely has to have a tree prepped I follow the creek north, the same direction the buck just departed, now circling around the eastern edge of the bedding area.

Rubs like this line the creek.

The creek runs north for two hundred yards before making a sharp turn back east. At the curve the ridge flattens. Here is a bench of sorts that is laced with runways.

A fence hanging above my head across the creek bed marks the boundary of Paul's property. The fence also marks the centerline of the section, which means now I'm exactly a half-mile from the road. Although the farm is over two miles long from east to west the south boundary isn't a straight line. There are squares cut out of it. In this case, the neighbor's property extends about two hundred yards north. This line is as far as I want to walk from the road where my van is parked. To scout the other half of the section I will start from the road bordering the other side.

It's time to start working backwards. I inspect the situation on the bench a little closer. Located right in the middle of the section, is a simple crossing point. To the north there is a huge chunk of CRP, to the south there is an oak laden ridge, to the east is more ridge and more CRP, and to the west is the thick bedding area I just walked around. There are only a few rubs and no scrapes at all, but the ten runways that cross here convince me that this is a good spot.

It takes me a few minutes to select a tree. The best one is covered in poison ivy, like so many of the trees I've seen on this property. Not wanting to mess with the treacherous vine I search

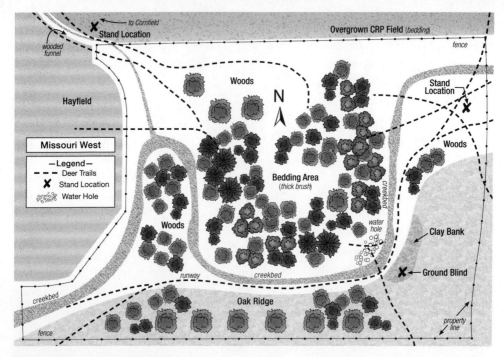

The western end of the Missouri farm property is dominated by a large bedding area lying at the bottom of a long ridge.

for another suitable option, but can't find one. With no other choice, I decide to tackle the three leaved monster, hoping to come away without the dreaded rash that unfortunately I seem to pick up a couple of times every year.

From my pack I retrieve a pair of cheap rubberized gloves, and a Zip-loc bag that I carry just for this situation. I make sure my jacket is zipped all the way up before I saw through the vines at the base of the tree and very carefully ease them off the trunk with the blade of my saw. As they fall away from the tree I watch with a keen eye. The last thing I want is for the vine to accidentally touch my face. There are three vines, and as each comes down it is immediately dragged away.

In just a few minutes the vines are gone, and with them, hopefully, all the urushiol. Urushiol is the oil in poison ivy that causes that famous blistery rash, and is it ever potent. An once of pure urushiol is enough to give a rash to the entire population on earth, and the amount that covers the tip of a pin is enough for a single sensitive person. About eighty percent of all people show a reaction to the oil, including myself.

Removing one glove and then pulling the second over the first, like a surgeon would, I deposit them both back in their plastic bag. Later I will toss them in a washer, along with all the other clothes I'm wearing right now. As soon as I get out of the woods, my first task will be to wash my body completely to insure that if oil accidentally came in contact with my bare skin, the rash won't be too bad.

With the vines removed I proceed with my usual routine: placing steps, setting my saddle, climbing down, clearing lanes, opening runways, blocking runways, removing saddle, removing steps, and setting tacks. By the time I'm finished with the "bench-crossing tree" more than two hours pass, and I feel as dry as the Sahara at high noon in the summertime. The temperature is somewhere in the mid eighties again today. I still have half a bottle of water and there are three trees that have to be prepped.

My next stop is at the water hole. As dry as it is, I have high hopes for this spot. Like every other animal, deer need water every day. From the looks of things so far this is the only water in this entire section, which is three miles long and a mile wide. Every creek and river I've encountered so far in Missouri has been reduced to dry ground. Finding the only water around can be a big shortcut to arrowing an early season hot weather buck. Hunting water holes is a tactic that has proved successful for me.

When it's really hot, water holes can be your best bet. The important thing to remember when hunting water holes is that deer often like to drink when the day is at its hottest, midday through early afternoon, which means long, scorching, uncomfortable hours on stand. Deer also prefer to drink from waterholes that are surrounded by cover.

This pool of water is tucked next to, and under, a steep dirt washout. Two well-worn runways cross within feet of the water, one above it, cut into the steep bank, and the other further below, in the creek bed.

Scanning the trees I search for one large enough to hunt out of that will also allow a shot to the water. Nothing.

Since there isn't a suitable tree I turn my attention to the dirt bank. About three quarters of the way up there is a row of four short junipers, and right behind them nothing but a dirt washout that culminates in a ten foot earthen cliff. The junipers are actually about twenty feet above the water. From the creek bed it looks as though it would be possible to tuck in behind the small conifers. I clamber up the bank, using miniature saplings and weeds as handholds, to get a closer look.

The washout butts right up to the junipers; however, the dirt is soft. There is only one possibility. Perhaps? A couple yards to my left lays a bleached white, fallen oak branch. Using the branch like a skinny shovel I begin to dig. My progress is better than expected and within mere minutes a terrace is carved into the clay bank.

Satisfied that the floor of my hideout is flat, and that there is enough room to maneuver, I hunker down behind the junipers. The makeshift ground blind is high enough above the water, the cover is good, and the shot to the other side of the water hole is open. For the current weather conditions this should be a great spot, albeit somewhat unorthodox. Being able to adjust to ever-changing conditions is very important to becoming a skilled bowhunter. The majority of bowhunters find one technique that suits them and this is how they hunt, always, unfortunately becoming too set in their ways. Often hunters find a tree that is easy to hunt from, or easy to get to, and this is where they hunt, hoping the deer

I killed this buck next to a waterhole on a very hot day.

will come. Or a hunter will only hunt from a treestand, or from the ground, or only hunt a certain type of terrain.

Stepping into new hunting situations and attempting to think outside of the box is the best way to become a better hunter. Though my preference is to hunt from trees, if there isn't one available I have no qualms about hunting from the ground. Twenty minutes of work is all it takes to complete my water hole ground blind.

The final two trees of the day are easy work, and only consume a little more than an hour each. Four hunting spots in a single day are about the maximum I can accomplish alone. Fortunately, all these spots were relatively easy. My plan is to spend a couple days scouting and clearing trees. I've divided the farm into sections, and I plan only a single scouting foray into each. Deer will usually tolerate a single intrusion; it's multiple visits that cause them to alter their routine. I won't return to this portion of the farm until it's time to hunt here.

The sun is setting as I cross the fields on the way back to my van. My boots have turned to lead somewhere along the way, and my pack has somehow ballooned to two hundred pounds, at least that is what it feels like. This is serious physical labor.

Pausing briefly for a breather about a hundred steps from my van, a dark green knife sheath on the ground halts my fleeting glance. Kicking the sheath with my boot it flips over, and to my surprise contains a knife. I sweep up the case to find a brand new hunting knife (at least it was new when it was lost) still with blood stains on the blade. The only damage is a slightly mouse-chewed corner of the hard rubber handle. The knife is a little large to really be practical for deer hunting, but I'm pleased to have found it nonetheless. By the looks of the situation someone killed a deer last fall and gutted it along this fencerow, but forgot to take his knife with him after he was finished. Hunting permission on a good farm, four good hunting spots finished, and a new knife, makes what I consider a successful first day.

The following morning the aching of sore muscles awakens me. My stomach, shoulders, arms, and hands send sharp signals of pain with every move, letting me know I did a lot of work yesterday. It's my hands that bother me the most. Stretching my fingers and opening and closing my hand to a fist for several minutes I try to loosen them up. After a month of intense scouting and hunting you would think my body would be fully acclimated to the routine, perhaps yesterday was more strenuous than I thought.

The sun burns red while rising in the east, and a single miniscule cumulus cloud drifts to the west looking as though it is fleeing the approaching heat. Taking the opportunity to enjoy the last of the cool morning air and to ease a little lactic acid build-up I decide to go for a walk.

Leaving my van at the public land pullout I follow a nearby tractor lane nearly a half-mile to a small hill covered with short, brushy woods. It is right in the corner of the public land, and is bordered directly by two roads. Most hunters zoom right by, without giving it much consideration, just as I had for an entire week, heading deeper into the tract. What I found last fall was a hill absolutely covered with rubs, and more than a dozen scrapes, including a primary scrape area. Anticipating more of the same I make a straight line to the open woods where the majority of the scrapes were. Nothing. Not a single rub nor scrape. The difference? Last year, corn surrounded this corner; this year, the crop is soybeans. Crop rotation is crucial to deer patterns. The next time the farmers plant corn in the surrounding fields the buck sign will probably reappear.

There is a lot of scouting to do today. The square of woods just south of Paul's house reveals itself to be just as good as the southwest corner. The three main components of the woods are a shallow draw, an oak and hickory covered ridge, and a deeper draw along the base of the ridge with a dry creek bed running through it. All this is bordered on the north and west sides by a late soybean field that is still green.

Though the actual woods are larger than that from yesterday, there is less variation and I only select two trees to clear out. The first is at a natural funnel in the deeper draw at the base of the ridge next to the creek. This draw extends in both directions for more than a mile and is simply a natural deer movement corridor. The second is in the shallow draw. This location is subtler, but nonetheless an excellent site to catch deer moving from feeding to bedding, and vice versa, and to catch a cruising buck. The first tree is tall and straight without much cover, which means I get up about thirty-five feet. The second is an old Osage orange tree. Osage orange is one tough customer. The wood is about as hard as iron, and the tree has abundant, but inconspicuous, needle-like thorns that sometimes even puncture leather gloves. To top this off, if a softball-sized Osage orange fruit drops on your head it would probably knock you out. Due to the cover and multiple trunks of the tree my set-up is only about twenty feet up. About six hours after beginning my trek I'm back at my van.

A brief respite, with a little water and food, is all I allow myself before jumping across the road into a large tract of CRP. About half of Paul's farm is CRP. There are two defining terrain features that cross the entire south end of this farm. The first is the ridge that runs east to west for about two miles, and the second is the now completely dried up creek that meanders along the base of the ridge, with its numerous small feeder creeks that stretch out like tentacles across the farm. The creek, along with all of its smaller arms, is lined with a narrow buffer of woods. This buffer provides cover as well as travel corridors for deer moving from the oak ridge out into the tall grass of the CRP, and beyond to neighboring crop fields. The grass in much of the CRP area is very tall, providing natural bedding. This is great deer habitat. The CRP has been mowed in an irregular fashion to remove the young saplings that had sprung up. If you looked at the land from the air it would look like someone went for a drunken joyride with a mower.

Following a small creek bed I arrive at the spot that peaked my interest in the first place. The main creek bed angles in from the north, meets the base of the ridge, and follows it to the west. Right in the corner at the base of the ridge sits an impressive white oak, still dropping acorns. Cutting down across the ridge is an overgrown lane that splits the forest growth. The forest on the east side of the lane is mostly mature oaks and open woods, but on the west side there has been a clear-cut within the last ten years. The mature oaks are gone, but there is thick undergrowth. A narrow point of mowed CRP runs right into the corner.

This is another natural crossing zone. A runway follows the base of the ridge, with a second paralleling it thirty yards up the slope. Another often-frequented runway drops right down the overgrown lane, and yet a fourth follows the creek bed right under the oak. There are four deep scrapes in the corner under some low overhanging branches. And, six rubs are visible while just standing under the tree, putting an exclamation point on this spot. That I need to hunt this oak is evident, but I still want to inspect the area more thoroughly. Investigating further I cross the dry creek and walk another two hundred yards. Discovering one of the principle runways feeding the bench tree I cleared out yesterday, I turn around. The corner white oak is the best tree for this area of the farm.

Returning to the oak, I begin placing tree steps, running them up to twenty-five feet. At that height, a few feet above a split in the trunk, is an excellent location for my saddle. There is so much cover from the two large trunks and other horizontal branches that there is no need to climb any higher. There are also open shots to all of the runways without having to remove a single branch or sapling.

The entire job of prepping this tree takes me fifteen minutes. This is a premiere stand, one that has the benefit of being huntable during both mornings and evenings, with an access route that is both short and mowed. Very pleased with my find, I sneak back to my van, hoping to hunt here within a day or two. Less than an hour has passed.

Two miles down the road at the far east end of the farm I park and take a break, eat lunch, and cool down by pouring water over my head. Rested, I resume my business.

Along the east end of the farm is another wooded ridge, and from my aerial photos I know there is almost a square mile of wooded terrain connected to it, and several large cornfields about a half mile to the north. The only problem I can foresee is the fact that the entire east half of the farm is used as a cow pasture, and the grass is cleanly cropped, far more thorough a job than a mower could ever do. From the looks of things there are a few more cattle out here than there should be.

Studying my map as I walk, I head for the ridge, hoping there is a fence to keep the cattle out of the woods. No fence! The undergrowth is plucked clean, and although there are plentiful acorns, I can't decipher much deer sign. At the top of the ridge I run into the property line, and a sturdy cattle fence. Tracing the perimeter I attempt to locate points where runways cross onto the property.

Almost immediately I discover a treestand hanging just across the fence. It's in a decent spot. A hundred yards farther down the fence there is a pop-up blind tucked right in the fencerow bordering a narrow alfalfa field. At the corner of the field is yet another treestand, this time with a trail camera strapped to a fencepost pointed at a couple interesting rubs a few yards away.

Trail cameras are an interesting gadget, but they ruin a lot of people's hunting, particularly in pressured areas. Unless mature bucks are otherwise completely undisturbed, and haven't experienced much hunting pressure, flash and camera sound will indeed cause them to avoid an area. And even more disturbing to mature bucks is that the cameras have to be checked regularly. Each visit to a camera leaves scent that any buck with his wits about him will eventually avoid.

From here I drop down into a draw, up a ridge, and down into a second draw. The undergrowth in the two draws is noticeably thicker than the oak dominated woods I just left, and there is clearly less bovine activity in them. There are even a couple of faint deer runways that haven't been trampled.

Standing at the bottom of the draw I notice movement up ahead. A doe and fawn are walking along the other side of the fence about sixty yards up the ridge. Instinctively I drop to a crouch and study the deer. Casually they amble in my direction, plucking a leaf here and there, seeming to be out for an afternoon walk and definitely not in a hurry.

At fifteen yards the doe notices me, although I haven't moved a muscle. Without a warning sound she jumps up the draw, tail waving, taking her surprised offspring with her.

Continuing on, I climb to the top the ridge to a narrow opening that extends across both sides of the fence. On my side of the fence the growth is grazed short, but the other is planted with some kind wildlife foodplot plant mix. Right across the fence is a two-story black tarpapered box blind with sliding glass windows and camouflage curtains. It reminds me of an outhouse. Two, fluorescent orange, "No Trespassing" signs decorate the fence; the message is intended for anyone on this side of the wire barrier. The funny thing is; there is a window to shoot out of on this side of the outhouse as well. I guess "No Trespassing" is meant for one direction only.

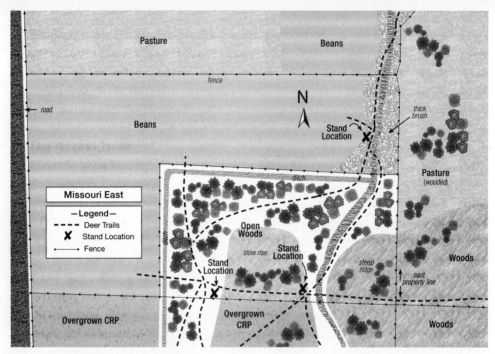

The east end of the Missouri farm property contains three good spots.

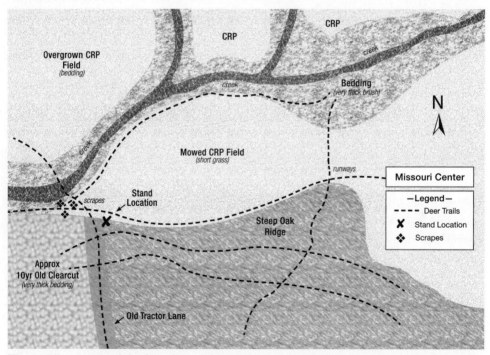

The middle section of the farm has one premiere hunting location, located at the base of the ridge along the edge of a CRP field.

Small, dry creekbeds crisscross this property, converging at the ridge in the background.

As I stand there, a hunter walks up through the middle of the food plot. He's so intent on looking off to the side, into the woods, he doesn't even notice me, although I'm out in the open. I wait for him to get to within about twenty yards before clearing my throat to get his attention. He is an old guy, probably in his seventies with most of his teeth missing, and is carrying both a shotgun and a crossbow. He is obviously a little startled by my sudden appearance.

We talk for a few minutes across the fence. The man nervously volunteers the fact that the shotgun is for turkeys. Though I don't comment, I'm not certain of the legality of either one of his weapon choices. To his credit, turkey season is indeed open. He informs me he's had no luck yet, and I tell him of my hunting permission. Wishing him good luck I depart, marching across the clearing straight away from his blind.

My walk takes me to the far southeast corner of the farm and then back west along the border fence. Along the fence I find three more treestands, bringing the afternoons total up to seven. There is a lot of hunting pressure along this edge of the farm. Less than impressed with the results of my hike, I cut back north through the property, bumping into some cattle along the way. There are some terrain features that look like deer should be using them, and probably some deer indeed move through, but the cattle make it difficult, if not impossible, to pinpoint that movement.

The sun is just beginning to set as I reach my van, not having cleared out, or even selected a single tree, to hunt from. My legs ache as though I've walked twenty miles today, and there is still more scouting to be done tomorrow. The temperature doesn't drop below seventy all night. It's another day of the same routine. Slowly I get around in the morning and then spend most of midday scouting. Up at the north end of the property I clear out two secondary spots, but don't find anything great, just some runways along a slight, brushy ridge, amidst an ocean of overgrown fields. So far I have nine trees ready to hunt. I eat, wash, fling a couple of arrows, and take a short nap. This afternoon I plan to hunt here for the first time.

It is so hot that shorts and a t-shirt suffice as insulation under my Scent Lok, hardly perfect weather. Despite the heat wave, I'm itching to get hunting again. Most of my better trees are morning spots, and those I want to save for more appropriate weather conditions. There are two principle considerations for this first hunt: One, the tree must be an evening spot. And two, it should be in an area that wasn't disturbed much by my recent scouting. The choice is simple. The only spot that fits these criteria is the corner CRP oak.

Tiptoeing through the mowed grass I arrive at the oak slightly before 2:00 p.m. Ten more minutes is all it takes to be resting comfortably in my saddle. Finally, after all of that walking, it's time to relax.

Contrary to most people, it's easier for me to relax hanging thirty feet in a tree hunting, than sitting on the sofa in my own living room. If you are reading this, you probably know what I mean. Slowly the white background noise of civilization drifts away and I can hear the woods again. I close my eyes, resting my head on the lead strap of my saddle and dream, allowing my mind to wander without the typical daily distractions that can be so overwhelming.

For hours nothing happens, and that is perfectly okay with me. Slowness and silence are conditions that I thoroughly enjoy. It's too bad they have been largely forgotten in our fast-paced, media-driven world. There is no wind, just placid warm air. The squirrels are busy doing their squirrel things. The sun moves across a clear, blue sky turning it orange towards dark.

Just as I am convinced my hunt will be deer-free, two fawns amble out of the thick woods on the ridge above me. A few minutes behind them follow two does. The last doe is absolutely enormous, and definitely the matriarch of the small family group. Her coat is darker than that of the others, and her nose is very long. Watching her, I wonder how old she is. These old mature does are wary customers that one should never underestimate.

The composition of the group is easy to make out: the old doe, her two fawns from this year, and her fawnless daughter from last year. Together they feed down the ridge, snacking on the abundant acorns, working in my direction. The focus of my attention is on that old girl. She sets the tone for the whole group.

With the fawns directly under my tree, and the two does up the ridge about twenty yards, I enjoy the show. To have wild deer so close, acting perfectly natural, with no idea that I'm around is pleasing. Either I must be doing at least some things right, or I'm lucky.

The lead doe casually lifts her head, still chewing on an acorn, and scans down the ridge across the CRP corner. Noticing something, she stops chewing, and stares intently in that direction. Her radar ears swivel to a halt.

A second later she lets out a loud snort. The sharp "Whheww" startles me nearly as much as it does the other three deer, who all jerk their heads up and stare in the same direction. My initial thought is that there must be another hunter nearby, but the doe's reaction is unusual. She doesn't move. She simply stands still, letting out another punctuated snort. "Whhhewww!" None of the other deer budge either, nor do they raise their tails in preparation to flee.

The three young does alternate between staring at the matriarch doe, and in the direction she is looking. Ever so cautiously, I edge around to look in the same direction. My movements are painfully slow, as the deer are all literally straight underneath me, but I can't see anything unusual, just the creek bottom. Perhaps the disturbance is from something more natural, maybe a coyote, or a dog. The doe snorts three more times, followed by four stiff-legged steps, angling across the ridge. She then simply resumes feeding, while moving through the oaks with a little more haste. The other deer follow suit, though now they, too, are moving faster picking up an acorn here and there as they go.

Several minutes pass before the cause of the disturbance bursts out of the wall of dry goldenrod that lines the creek. The buck crosses the corner is seconds, and what a buck he is.

Though the sudden appearance of bone white antlers sets my heart to racing a bit, a glance is all I need to know my bow will remain hanging on its hook.

The deer is a yearling. His rack and body are impressive for such a young animal. He has an inside spread of about ten inches between a beautifully typical basket, eight-point configuration of antlers. His tines are around five inches tall and his main beams almost touch at the tips. And most interestingly, he has two extra points, one at the base of each antler that curve out and forward, each about two inches long, making him a ten-pointer.

I watch him closely as he crosses a mere ten yards from the base of my tree, intent on following the does. Two thoughts keep repeating themselves in my mind: I sure would like to see this guy's dad, or even big brother. And I certainly would like to see what he looks like in two or three years. The buck has the potential to someday grow into a real monster. He grunts several times as he follows the path the does took, leaving me in my tree smiling. I have a feeling there are some really big bucks around here.

Except for two Tom turkeys flying in to roost right over my head just before dark, the remainder of the hunt is uneventful. Back at my van I quickly stow my gear, drive to my parking spot, eat dinner, and hit the hay. The temperatures tomorrow are supposed to be in the nineties, and I have a plan. I always have a plan, even if it is different than it was five minutes ago.

Paranoid about sleeping through my alarm, I'm up early. The clock reads 2:47 a.m. However, try as I may I'm unable to drift back to sleep. Giving in to my hunting insomnia I prepare for my hunt.

By 3:30 I find myself following the edge of the woods through an overgrown CRP field, hoping not to bump any deer along the way. Scanning for indistinct black shadows in the dark, and listening for telltale snorts of spooked whitetails, I reach the dry creek bed without a hitch. Sliding down the bank into the creek bed I feel a little more certain that the remainder of my approach will go undetected. Sneaking very slowly, carefully placing each step either on a rock or in soft sand, and avoiding the fallen leaves, I manage the last several hundred yards in about twenty minutes.

Reaching the water hole, I float my dim flashlight beam across the soft sand. It looks like it has been worked over again with a rototiller, so many are the fresh deer tracks.

Today the temperature is supposed to rise into the nineties, and I plan on sitting next to the only water within a mile, all day. This is one of those special situations, where an enterprising hunter can connect with a mature buck, while most hunters aren't even in the woods. I believe it is possible to kill mature bucks in any kind of weather, if a hunter has a plan for that specific kind of situation and a little luck. A super hot day next to the only water around is a golden opportunity seldom taken advantage of. Even more excited than before, I scurry up the steep bank. Setup consists of pulling my compact folding stool from my pack and setting it in place on the ground. Knocking an arrow I lay my bow across my lap and lean back, resting against the dirt bank. Listening to the sounds of the starlit Missouri night I close my eyes and rest my head against the slope, certain that I made it to the water ahead of the deer. There are over two hours to wait until my eyes will be of service.

The pre-dawn cold creeps in causing me a few shivers and then fades in sharpness directly opposite in correlation to the slowly increasing sharpness of my vision. Daylight arrives cautiously with an eerie stillness; seldom have I experienced anything like this. There is no wind causing the trees to whisper, no coyotes howl their testimony of the night's hunting success or failure, not a single squirrel hustles about, and the small birds with their chorus of wake-up songs that usher in most mornings are strangely absent. The pure silence of daybreak is maddening, almost deafening if you listen hard enough. I scarcely dare to breath, thinking a thousand ears far more acute than my own will hear me. It is as though the woods are holding its breath as well, waiting for something to happen.

The spell is broken when a single doe materializes, suddenly standing on the bank along the creek. In the sand her steps, too, are soundless, but her entry is accompanied by the singing birds and scurrying squirrels. The forest awakens.

The doe jumps down the bank into the creek bed stopping briefly to grab an already yellow leaf off a low hanging, maple branch. Clearly thirsty she daintily steps toward the water.

Arriving at the edge of the pool she lowers her head to drink and freezes in mid motion, her eyes fixed squarely on me. Her next steps are backwards, three in a row, never removing her gaze from my location. She turns, still looking at me, jumps back up the bank, and silently, with an added haste, walks straight away in the direction from which she came. I didn't move a muscle, and am surprised by the doe's reaction. It is simply tough to get past a deer's amazingly acute senses while hunting from the ground. The good thing is that she didn't outright spook, warning other deer of my presence, but she didn't like the situation either. If a good buck shows, I will have to take the first possible shot opportunity. I wonder if other deer will react the same way?

The answer to my question comes along shortly. About twenty minutes later, a wink of an eye in bowhunting time, another deer appears on the sandy bank. A quick glance reveals antlers. It's a small buck, a four-point with about a twelve-inch inside spread. He is in no hurry, and stops to feed on some acorns, seeming to dawdle. He turns and looks back a couple of times, this clues me in that there must be another deer behind him. And indeed, within a few minutes a second buck shows himself. This one is better, probably a two year old. His rack is almost black and heavy with short stout tines and an inside spread of about fourteen inches. In a lot of other places further east, I would shoot a buck like this, but here he isn't quite what I'm looking for.

The two bucks casually munch on acorns for about ten minutes before they, too, hop down the bank into the creek bed. Moving in my direction, they stop at the same overhanging maple branch as the doe did earlier, and pluck off a couple yellow leaves. I've seen deer eat sugar maple leaves before, and it is almost always after they have turned color and usually after a frost. Natural browse makes up a major portion of most deer's diets even in the best farm country. I always try to note what the deer are eating.

The four-pointer steps to the water first, looks right and left, drops his head and begins to drink. As still as it is, I can hear him slurping up water and see ripples in the pool. The eight-pointer leaves the maple branch and steps up behind the four-pointer, standing now broadside at about twenty yards. If I had the intention to shoot, this would be my shot.

For about five seconds the situation is perfect. One deer is drinking and the other is standing at a good angle, looking in the other direction. This is what bowhunting is about. I have two deer close enough to shoot, so close in fact I can hear the sound of one of them drinking, and I can make out every twitch, every hair. I am in their natural environment and they are totally unaware of my presence, despite their almost supernatural senses, so much better than my own. My heart races and the predator inside me wants to make a kill, but the single tag in my pocket restrains my instinct and keeps my bow on my lap.

Just as I begin to feel confident in my hiding spot, the four-point lifts his head, water dripping from his chin. Like the doe earlier, he fixes his attention directly on me, seemingly startled, and silently surprised that he missed something the first time. Without hesitation he bounds back from the water, stopping two jumps up the bank to stare at me. Caught by surprise, the bigger buck spins and runs up the bank close behind, first looking at his partner and then staring in my direction as well. They know something isn't right, but don't know what.

For what seems like an eternity they stare at me, through me. I barely breathe, not wanting to give myself away. The little buck stiff-legs-it across the bank to get a better view, and stares some more, suddenly letting out a loud snort that echoes off the ridge and trees and about knocks me from my stool.

Standing there he releases another snort, and another, but doesn't run away. It's as though he is trying to get me to flinch and blow my cover. I remain motionless. The two bucks circle to my left, crossing behind the bank I am leaning against. I can't see them and I don't dare lift my head over the edge to look. They can't see me either.

For a few minutes I hear nothing, but then the snap of a single twig very close behind me on the other side of the clay bank draws my attention. As slow as I can I lean forward to peek over the edge. The instant my eyes clear to the ledge I'm met with the wondering eyes of the four-point, not five yards away and at eye level. Busted! Both bucks circled around to get a better look at whatever it is sitting on that bank. Immediately, the four-point spins away, white tail waving in a cloud of flying leaves, and dashes up and over the ridge, letting out probably a dozen insulting snorts as he goes, the bigger buck in tow. So much for this spot! Every deer within a mile now knows something isn't quite kosher in this corner. Trying to remain optimistic I sit until noon, without seeing another deer.

By the time I step out of my ambush spot the temperature has risen to ninety degrees, just like the weather forecast promised. Instead of hunting all day, I have to find a better option for this corner.

It only takes me a couple minutes to find a solution, though not the best solution. There is one tree big enough to hunt out of about sixty yards from the water hole along the base of the ridge. It has two problems though: First, it is covered in poison ivy. And second, it is slanted the wrong way, meaning I will have to sit with my back to the ridge, making for some unusual shot angles across my body. With no better options in sight I get to work with the usual step placing, cutting and clearing. Par for the course, it takes me slightly more than three hours to finish the job.

A little after 4:00 p.m., I slide the side door of my van open. I have been in the woods already today for about twelve hours. Hot, tired, hungry, with sore hands and shoulders, the first thing I do is drink about a half gallon of water. As hot as it is there will be no hunting tonight, so I busy myself with lunch, a half gallon shower, and a nap. About an hour later I feel like brand new.

With a free evening I take a drive to the public hunting area to check out a couple of spots. Nothing spectacular comes to light. The private land is simply much better. As nightfall slowly approaches I cruise back roads to look for deer.

The weather is tough. Once again the temperature doesn't drop below seventy all night, and with my water hole spot messed up I don't hunt this morning. Just running out in the woods haphazardly isn't good hunting. One must be patient, and wait for the right opportunities. For me this means opting out of a few hunts on really hot days, although there is nothing else for me to do except hunt. Each one of my trees is cleared out for a specific time and condition. Already pushing my luck with my short-term, invasive scouting I don't want to sour my best spots before there is a fair chance of killing a buck there. Self control is one of the hardest parts of good bowhunting, and an aspect that is little discussed. Timing is what separates really successful bowhunters from average bowhunters. So instead of hunting, I spend the morning reading, writing, and listening to the radio while watching the sun and wind.

Around noon I explore the last unscouted corner of the farm. It is a row of brush and trees lining the dry creek that connects the south woods to the east woods curving through the cow pasture. The walk to the creek is about a quarter mile, first through a corner of the pasture and then along the edge of the late soybean field. In the corner of the field there are four scrapes and six rubs. The sign catches my interest, but field edge sign isn't really worth too much time. The main runway feeding the corner is easy to see, so I follow it through a thick patch of brush for about ten yards. To my surprise, on the other side of the brush is a beaver dam and water. This is only the second waterhole I've found. The runway crosses directly over the top of the dam.

Adding to the mix are ten rubs scattered amongst the young willows and poplars. After the runway crosses the dam, it splits; one path leads to the beans and the other follows the edge of the creek, remaining completely in cover.

Turning around, I notice that right above me is a great tree for this spot. It has abundant cover, a good slant, and would be possible to shoot to the field as well as to the inner runway and water. Unfortunately, like most trees around here, it too is draped with the dreaded poison vine.

Not convinced that I want to test my luck with the three-leaved demon again, I follow the hidden runway for another quarter mile until it reaches a cornfield, all the time searching for a better tree and trying to determine exactly how bucks use this area. Unfortunately, there isn't another tree nearly as good as the first one.

How bucks use this area is easy to figure. The row of brush along the creek is a connector route with cover between two big woods and a cornfield. Any buck that wants to get from A to B without being seen can simply stay on the runway along the creek. That this is the case is evident by numerous rubs.

It is more of a morning spot, except there is no way to get to it without either walking across a pasture or the bean field, presenting the problem of spooking deer on the way in. The same situation presents a problem for evening hunts as well. There is no way to get out of this spot without spooking any deer that might be feeding in the beans. The only solution to the problem of a spot like this is to only hunt it once or twice a season, as a better-than-average secondary spot, while being quite aware that you will probably spook deer with your entry or exit. It would also be a good, all day spot for during the rut. I can certainly imagine an amorous buck using this route to cruise from woods to woods at high noon.

I get to work. The usual: pulling down the poison ivy, running steps, and cutting shooting lanes. While removing a sapling I am struck by a strong, peculiar, flowery smell that I recognize. Closer inspection reveals a vine of wild hops wrapped across, and through, a patch of young poplars. Picking a few of the sticky, round, green cones, I pull them apart, and inhale their fresh penetrating scent. They remind me of good ale-style beer. I don't think I have ever discovered hops growing wild before, a notable find.

I finish my work, which only takes me about an hour, and hike back to my van, happy to have yet another good tree ready to go. There is no such thing as too many options while bowhunting.

My break is short, just long enough to take another half-gallon shower, a scent eliminating and urushiol eliminating measure, grab a bite to eat, and change into my hunting gear. I haven't hunted since yesterday morning and am aching to get back into a tree.

At around 2:00 p.m. I find myself sneaking back to my big corner oak. It is still in the mid 80's, so I'm sticking to my secondary spots. Placing each step carefully and as silently as I can, I follow the woods around, sticking to the mowed CRP.

Less than sixty yards from my tree I ease up the last tiny rise and am met by the sight of a big buck spinning away from me at a distance of only twenty yards. His tail tucked between his legs, he dashes into the corner right under my big oak. The only view I get of his antlers is from straight behind. His rack is tall, wide, and light colored with long brow tines. I think I count eight points, but there may be more. If I had to put a number on him, I would guess around 130, a good buck in any case.

At the same instant, a flock of Tom turkeys burst in raucous explosion of thundering wings and cackles spreading out in all directions, adding a note of chaos to the moment. In a few seconds, the buck is gone, and so are the turkeys, leaving me a little dumbfounded. I feel like I've been caught flat-footed and red-handed, with my hand in the cookie jar. The buck was either walking the edge of the woods or was bedded in the tall CRP grass.

Moving on, I look for a bed in passing, but can't find one. My feelings are mixed. I'm glad to have seen another decent buck, the second on this farm, but a little distraught that I just spooked him from right under my tree. The only thing for me to do now is to climb into my oak and hope the buck returns. Honestly, the chances of that happening are virtually zero.

Setting up takes me a few minutes, and just as I settle into my saddle a single Tom turkey glides down into the mowed strip. Clucking softly, clearly looking for his pals, he crosses the corner twenty yards away. He even stops right out in the wide open, his beard almost dragging on the ground. With a turkey license in my pack this is tempting, it's not often you get turkeys within bow range in the fall. However, I decide to stick with deer hunting tonight.

It's obvious the Tom is aware of me, but he takes little notice as preoccupied as he is. Still clucking and chirping he slips into the wall of goldenrod and is gone.

For several hours nothing much happens apart from the usual squirrel and songbird activity. The afternoon sun is downright hot. Despite it being mid October I'm still wearing only a pair of shorts and t-shirt under my Scent Lok. The extreme heat makes for tough hunting, especially now, during the October Lull.

The October Lull is usually the couple of weeks covering mid-October and is from a hunter's perspective a notable decrease in observable daytime deer activity. The deer are still moving, but far more after dark than in the early season, particularly the mature bucks. The decreased daytime movement is both a natural and human caused phenomenon. It is natural in the sense that the deer's world of lush green vegetation, which they have grown accustomed to during the long summer, is in a state of upheaval. The leaves begin to drop and the woods suddenly become more open. This causes many mature bucks to alter their movement patterns to a more nocturnal routine. They will remain in this routine until the sexual urges of the rut force them into a more diurnal pattern. The lull is also a direct response to increased human disturbance. As hunters suddenly hit the woods in the fall the deer notice the disturbance. Their natural tendency to become more nocturnal at this time is simply reinforced by hunting pressure. Where hunting pressure is severe, any remaining mature bucks might remain nocturnal throughout the entire rut. This usually isn't the case in areas where hunting pressure is light.

A lot of bowhunters get so frustrated during mid October that they simply hang up their bows until the more intense pre-rut and rut begin. This is indeed an option that, from a tactical perspective, could be right-on, especially if a hunter has very limited property to hunt. I, however, like to hunt too much to simply skip a couple weeks of the season. And I have taken big bucks during the lull before; it is just a matter of planning. My solution is to hunt a large rotation of secondary spots where anything can happen, mostly funnels between feeding and bedding areas, being very careful not to pressure any single area too much. I also wait for special circumstances to hunt either my best spots, or spots for a particular weather condition, like extreme heat or rain. It is simply impossible to force your hand while bowhunting; you have to roll with the punches, allowing the conditions to dictate your hunting.

I dream and scheme my way through the afternoon, mentally working out my hunting plan, which can literally, and does, change with the wind. A doe and a fawn interrupt my cloud of thought and keep me occupied for over an hour as they feed under my tree and across the ridge, eventually melting into the oaks. When deer are so near I lose myself and become the moment. This is what being alive and hunting is all about.

No other deer show themselves. The moon is full and looming large in the sky well before dark, and when the sun is finally gone it is more of a gray than black night. It is so bright you could hunt all night long if it were legal to do so.

A heat wave coupled with a full moon, could there be worse conditions? During a full moon, bucks simply move less than normal, and when they are up on their feet it is usually in the middle of the night, or during midday. Of course, immediate weather conditions are more important to deer movement than moon phase will ever be. Throw in a little inclement, or cold, weather and movement changes, no matter what moon phase it happens to be.

Leaving my bow and saddle in the tree I descend and make my getaway. Leaving my bow in the tree will ensure that I wake up in the morning and return to my perch. Perhaps the buck I spooked will return tomorrow morning.

By 4:30 a.m. I find myself once again nestled into my saddle, resting my head against my lead strap. Visions of that bounding buck from yesterday afternoon kept me mostly awake all night, and now in my tree my eyes are heavy from lack of sleep. Closing them, I listen. For a long time there is nothing to hear. Then, about a half-hour before daylight a pack of coyotes howl from somewhere to the east. The serenade is short, lasting a minute or two, and then more quiet. Suddenly, there is a noise directly to my left, sort of like a stick rubbing against another. Instinctively, without moving my head, I open my left eye to look in the direction of the sound. There, sitting on dead branch not eight feet away, is a great horned owl. The bird is probably two feet tall. I stare with one eye, marveling at the opportunity to be able to observe a wild owl so close. For several minutes it swivels its head, looks at me a couple of times, before concentrating his stare on the grassy field in front of us. Then, without the slightest warning, it lets out an extremely loud hoot, which is a poor word to describe this piercing cry, that sets my heart to racing and simply shocks me with its extreme volume.

A little after daylight, the same group of two does and fawns that I watched a couple days ago from this same tree, reappear. They step out of the thick woods on the ridge, seemingly going the wrong way, at least the opposite direction I expect deer to move at this spot in the morning. They casually feed their way up over the ridge.

About an hour later I hear a tractor on the neighbor's property and some yelling at cattle, which seem to yell back with a bellowing cacophony of discordant "moos." Promptly the group of four deer retrace their steps back past my tree, obviously having decided their intended destination isn't quite free of obstacles. The big matriarch doe leads the group across the tip of the fallow field into the creek bottom where I lose track of them in the tall goldenrod.

For several hours the temperature rises steadily. At 1:00 p.m. I decide the buck isn't going to return. It's time to pack it in. Back at my van the thermometer reads eighty-six degrees.

For the next two and a half days the temperature is scorching, mid-nineties during the day and mid seventies at night. The only thing I can do is kill time while waiting for hunting conditions to improve. You could have the best hunting property in the world, but it would still be tough hunting in conditions like this. I spend two evenings at out-of-the-way spots on the public land without seeing a deer, and sleep in each morning. The laundromat keeps me busy for a few hours, but most of the time I'm parked in my van relaxing, which means a lot of reading, writing and listening to the radio.

Not being able to tolerate just sitting around, I investigate a couple of distant parcels that belong to Paul's farm, that I knew were no good before I even looked at them. A few tracks and a couple random rubs is all that I find. The weather forecast receives my utmost and constant attention; rain and cold is in the forecast for tomorrow morning.

At 3:00 a.m. my alarm clock's insensitive beeping pulls me from sleep. Opening the sliding door of my van I am met with disappointment, no rain, and definitely no cold. Closing the door I quickly drift back into a deep sleep.

Waking several hours later, the sun looms large in the sky and there is barely a cloud; so much for the weather forecast. Expecting yet another long, hot day I prepare for the boredom by driving to town and picking up a newspaper, which is about all the entertainment I can afford. Parking at the south corner of the farm I get to reading over a bland breakfast.

A Day Later ... Here Comes the Rain!

While I was reading, clouds snuck in, and to the west a bank of ominous gray thunderheads loom large. This could be the break I've been looking for. Stepping out of my van I check the weather. The temperature has dropped more than ten degrees in the last half-hour. Time to get moving. I jump behind the wheel and zip around the block. By the time I get into my hunting gear, the temperature has sunk to around fifty degrees, thirty fewer than an hour ago, and misty drizzle begins to coat the parched dusty landscape. If the rain keeps up I will hunt my better trees beginning tomorrow morning, but for today I head back out to my big corner oak. Although it is only noon, I find myself hurrying to set up. I love to hunt in the rain.

Nothing seems to get mature bucks on their feet and moving more than a steady rain, and particularly following dry conditions. And even more important, bucks tend to move during daylight while it is raining. I can only speculate at why this is. Perhaps it is simply natural behavior, or a reaction to getting wet, or perhaps it is a reaction to the fact that few hunters are out in the woods when it rains. All I know for sure is that over the years, I have seen more mature bucks, relative to time spent hunting, during rain than in any other weather condition. And the bucks I see during rain always appear to be more at ease than in most other conditions. It's interesting that tactical bowhunting in the rain hasn't made more of an appearance in popular hunting literature. I think most hunters just don't like getting wet, and therefore have simply avoided hunting in wet conditions. When it rains I attempt to get out in the woods as expediently as possible.

Of course, rain presents a few of its own problems. The first and most obvious problem for a bowhunter is staying dry, followed closely by the problem of remaining quiet. Until recently it was almost impossible to do both at the same time. The typical nylon or plastic rain suits were too noisy to wear for bowhunting in. For a long time I relied on wool, and simply got wet. Thanks, however, to advances in rainwear technology, there are several brands of hunting rainwear that will keep a hunter perfectly dry and they are quiet enough for hunting. My current favorite is Rivers West gear, for the simple fact that it is quiet and can be tossed into a clothes dryer without damage.

The second problem of rain hunting is shot selection and placement. The positive aspect of bowhunting in the rain is that the bucks are up and moving. The negative aspect is that rain quickly washes away blood trails; so it is absolutely critical that bowhunters remain patient, and only take high percentage shots. Of course, this should be every bowhunter's credo anyway. A long, thin blood trail is not what you want to be following during a steady rain.

The third situation bowhunters have to think about during a rain is where the deer are going to be moving. It is true that bucks move a lot during inclement weather, but they still don't usually go prancing around in the open either. The best places to hunt are trees situated in good cover. If I know it is going to be a slow, long, steady pour, I cut to my best spots, such as primary scrape areas, staging areas, or funnels between bedding areas, even before the pre-rut when these spots usually heat up. This is the exception to normal seasonal timing. When it rains, the time is right to hunt your best spots.

By 12:30 I'm up in my oak. Just as I hang up my bow the drizzle intensifies to a light rain. Zipping my Rivers West to the top, and making sure any loose ends are covered, I tuck in against the weather. For over three hours, raindrops are the only thing happening. After so much heat and sunshine this is a refreshing change. Completely dry under my impervious shell, I enjoy the constant pitter-patter of water drops bouncing off my boonie hat and shoulders.

At quarter to four the rain suddenly stops, like someone turned off the faucet. Almost immediately I notice two deer standing along the creek bed in the tall grass about two hundred yards across the overgrown field. They step out into the open and begin to feed, slowly working in my direction. Both of the deer are fawns and a little playful. They take turns chasing each other around, feeding, and doing a little more chasing.

As they get closer I notice one of the fawns is a button buck. It takes them forty minutes to get within bow range. Together they cross under my tree at fifteen yards and walk into the woods right over the big scrapes in the corner. The fawns are out of sight less than a minute as the rain begins anew, this time a little heavier than before.

For another two hours I tuck in against the deluge before there is another break in the rain. As if on cue, another two fawns bound out of the brush along the creek at exactly the same spot as the first two. They are followed closely by two does that I immediately recognize. This is the same group of deer I've already seen twice from this stand.

Taking the lead, the Roman nosed matriarch slowly moves in my direction, the other deer following loosely. She is cautious as usual, but this time she is acting a little different. Her chosen path is a zigzag across the field. She stops every twenty yards or so and peers into either the thick brush along the creek, or up the oak ridge. Arriving under my tree she steps past at a distance of only fifteen yards and makes a straight line for the scrapes in the corner. Stopping just a few yards short of the scrapes she once again stares into the woods for several seconds before stepping forward and marking a licking branch. First, she sniffs a licking branch or two, and then follows up by giving them a good chewing. Having left her calling card she turns around and continues with her zigzag walk, but in the other direction, ending up in the far corner of the crooked little field about two hundred yards away. The other deer follow her, not paying much attention, simply feeding back and forth. I figure she will just keep on going, but to my surprise the doe turns around again, and begins working her way back. I've seen this behavior in mature does before, and it is usually an indication that a mature buck is somewhere nearby, and she is looking for him.

Darkness is approaching fast as she gets closer and closer, the other deer still in tow. I find myself mentally repeating, "Come on girl, bring him out, bring him out." With only a few minutes of shooting light left the doe has retraced her steps and is standing broadside in the field twenty yards to my left. As though a little surprised, she jerks her head up and looks back. Understanding the hint, I scan across the field. Doe, fawn, and wow! A buck with a huge neck is standing right in my other shooting lane. His neck is so swollen I notice it first, despite the set of tall antlers above his ears. Without a second glance I reach for my bow and silently maneuver into position for a shot by moving a single step around the tree. Bow in hand I evaluate the situation more closely. It's only now I notice that sometime in the last hour, while watching that doe, the rain has stopped. There isn't a breath of wind, and the buck is standing perfectly broadside at exactly forty yards. He is standing in a patch of taller grass that I have measured with my laser range finder several times. Briefly I linger in a state of indecision. Light is fading extremely fast and it's now or never, but forty yards is a long shot. I have never knowingly shot at a deer that far away before, and have reservations about attempting it now. While I'm considering my options, one of the fawns gets a little too close to the buck and he warns it to keep some distance by swinging his antlers. The fawn jumps away causing the buck to turn his head in the other direction. A big buck broadside, looking the other direction, at a distance that I practiced shooting at almost daily all summer; the decision is made. I draw.

I spend a lot of time camping out in the shade of a couple of big cottonwoods. Considering the scorching heatwave there isn't much else to do.

Reaching my anchor point, I take a controlled breath and pick a spot along the crease of the buck's shoulder. Consciously taking my time, I draw another breath, lifting my pin up off the buck and then returning it to the same point. I glance quickly at my riser to make sure everything is lined up and adjust my grip so it is stable but loose. For a third time I center my pin on the buck's chest. Convinced my hold is steady, I let my arrow fly. As though the world instantly switches to slow motion I hear the dull thump of my bow and watch the arrow as it arcs towards the deer, still standing perfectly broadside. There is another dull thump, but in the burst of movement I can't see whether I hit the buck, or not. As he jumps away the white fletching of my arrow pops up behind him. He takes two bounds and stops, looking back to where he was standing. Immediately I think my shot must have been low and that he somehow kicked up the arrow. The buck gives no indication of being hit and stands there for about three, long seconds. The next thing I know he just tips over, kicks his legs a couple times and is still. All I can see is a big, white belly pointing skywards in tall grass. Shocked, perplexed, elated, I sit back in my saddle, letting out a couple of deep breaths to settle my rollercoaster of emotions. From the misery of an unsuccessful attempt to the elation of a killing shot in three seconds, what could be more nerve wracking? My hands are shaking.

The four other deer are still standing in the field as I lower my bow and clamber to the ground. I quietly stow my steps, saddle, and rope in my pack with the dark shadows of four deer floating in the field, their attention pointed in my direction. Certainly they, too, are perplexed at the collapsed buck and the noise exuding from behind this oak. It isn't until I take a few steps that they run away, white tails streaking though the dark cusp of night, letting out a few snorts of surprise at my sudden appearance. Ignoring them completely I walk straight to the downed buck, wondering what he has for headgear. After deciding that he was big enough, I never again looked at his rack. There is plenty of time to count points and add inches after the shooting is done.

Arriving at my deer, I'm struck again by the size of its neck and body. Kneeling next to the buck I grab his antlers, lifting them out of the grass. Eight points and a two-inch sticker at the base, bringing the total to nine. The bases are very massive, having at least six-inch circumferences, and heavily pearled. The antlers are about seventeen inches between the beams and quite dark in coloration. All this, combined with the buck's wide nose, thick neck, and deep chest immediately give me the impression that this is an old deer, perhaps even on his way downhill.

For several minutes I just sit next to the buck giving thanks, still in a minor state of shock at what just happened, the shot and deer's reaction replaying in my mind. Mature bucks always arrive unexpectedly, but tonight my plan came together. Slowly realizing that I have work to do, and wondering exactly what just happened, I turn my attention to the arrow hole in the buck's chest. The shot couldn't have been more perfect; a little less than halfway up and right in the crease of the buck's shoulder. Getting up, I pace the distance from the dead buck to the point of the shot. Twenty-one yards! There is frothy lung blood everywhere. This is the shortest distance I have ever seen a deer run that wasn't spine shot.

Now needing my flashlight, I begin to look for my arrow, but can't find it immediately. A couple circles later I come across the now red arrow lying sideways in the grass about ten yards behind where the buck was standing. Returning to the deer I snap my arrow back in my quiver, lay my bow down next to my pack and walk back to my van. Coincidentally, the buck is lying right on an old tractor lane, and it's possible to drive right to him. Not only did he not go far, but there will be no long hours of dragging tonight, though I could stand to burn a little extra adrenaline.

In the glow of my headlights I tag the buck and make short business of gutting. Still collecting evidence I examine the lungs. A hole the shape of an X passes through the front center of both lungs, a perfect pneumo-thorax. This is good, but the deer still should have gone more than twenty-one yards. Turning my attention to the inside of the ribcage I inspect the entry and exit

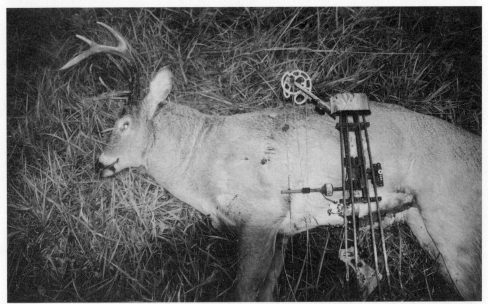

This buck had an extemely swollen neck and shoulders, despite being killed in mid-October.

holes. Both of them pass cleanly between ribs, meaning my arrow met only soft tissue on its path. Now everything becomes clear. The buck had no idea I was there, and didn't hear the shot. My arrow zipped through him so cleanly that it just kept on flying, flipping up when it met a tangle of tall grass. He didn't even know he was shot, which is why he stopped after two short bounds to look back. By then he was already dead but didn't realize it yet. A couple of seconds later he fell to the ground.

Satisfied with the evidence, and done gutting, I jerk the buck onto my dragging sled and pull him around to the back of the van. Standing outside I lift the sled up and rest it on the bumper. Climbing in my van I take hold of an antler and attempt to pull the combination sled and deer inside. It doesn't budge. I try again, and again it doesn't budge. Adding a little leverage with my legs and straining under the weight, I manage to move the deer a couple inches forward. Pulling now as hard as I can, hoping I don't get a hernia or a slipped disc, I heave for all I'm worth and ever so slowly the buck reaches the balance point and flops down into my van. I slump back thinking, once again, that I need a ramp for this job, now subjectively certain that this buck weighs over two-hundred pounds. Loaded up, I head for town.

Arriving at the first gas station along the highway strip, I stop and call Missouri's deer check system to register my buck. Listening to a computer voice and answering the questions by pressing the right buttons I get the number needed to write on my tag. The whole process takes me about a minute.

Moving up the road a little I select the cheapest looking highway-side motel and get a room for the night. Though it hurts to part with forty five dollars, plus tax, I don't want to have to sleep next to my buck for fear of becoming tick infested, and don't want to leave him lying on the ground, either. Motels are a complete luxury that I reserve for special circumstances, and this buck is such a circumstance. Inside my room I wash the remaining blood off my hands and shave, and fill up the bathtub. Sinking into the hot water I realize this is my first real bathing experience in about a month, and it sure feels good.

After cleaning up I notice my growling stomach. I haven't had a bite to eat since this morning. The fast food drive-through next to the motel is open, so I pull in and order two double cheeseburgers that cost me two dollars and twelve cents. Sitting in the parking lot I choke them down, certain that my body's fat allowance has been covered for the next two weeks. Fast food is something I avoid most of the time, preferring a more health conscious diet, high in game meat. Though the burgers sit a little heavy in my stomach the hunger pains subside immediately. It is already after 11:00 p.m., but I am still far too high on adrenaline to even think about sleeping, so I head to the laundromat and wash all of my clothes, my pack, re-activate my Scent Lok, re-arrange my equipment, and clean my van.

By 1:00 a.m. everything is clean and organized, and though completely awake mentally, I begin to feel some physical fatigue. Returning to my room I flip on the television, but after six weeks without watching a single minute of TV, I find it distracting and overwhelming. Shutting the tube off, I try to sleep.

A gas station across the road is my first stop the next morning. There are several tables inside where the local farmers gather to gossip. Grabbing a rare cup of thin coffee I ask the farmers sitting around the table where the nearest place is to get a deer processed. The answer is unanimous, and the directions are simple: six miles north, left off the highway, big building, "you can't miss it."

The directions are good as gold, and the description of the place right on, but I'm early. The doors don't open for another hour. I use the time by filling up a couple pages in my hunting journal with the events of the last twenty-four hours. Behind me, a quickening stream of cars and trucks pull behind the building the closer it gets to 8:30.

A full twenty minutes before official business hours, a guy opens the door and flips the closed sign over. He stands there for a second looking in my direction like he wants to say something. Sticking my head out the window, I'm told I can come in now. They opened the doors early because they noticed me waiting in the parking lot.

I enter a small, brightly lit room with glass door freezers and refrigerators on two sides offering a variety of custom meats. The counter takes up a full quarter of the room, behind which is an office. This transaction is painful for me for two reasons. First, I am quite particular about my venison, and take pride in butchering the animals I kill. And second, a basic butchering job costs me seventy-five dollars. That's enough money to keep hunting for probably two weeks.

With business taken care of I ask if anyone could help me by snapping a few photos. Hearing my question the boss himself steps out of the office and offers his skills. He has to hurry, though, as several customers are due to show up at the opening bell.

Together we walk out to my van. As quick as I can I jump into my Rivers West, grab my bow, and set up a photo session in a field at the edge of the parking lot. The boss snaps a couple of photos before the first cattle haulers pull in, and then excuses himself, leaving me with my deer. This isn't a problem, though, as four or five trucks pull in, one after the other. The guys waiting to unload their cattle get out to look at my buck. All of them congratulate me on a fine bow kill. The emphasis is clearly on bow kill. There seems to be large differentiation between a bow and gun-killed buck in these parts.

A farmer named Steve offers to help me with my photos. Steve is probably around fifty with blond hair, a weathered face, and thick calloused hands. We get to chatting right away. He is from Iowa, quite talkative, and full of creative, off-the-wall, conspiracy theories, most of which I have never heard before. I can certainly appreciate a good conspiracy theory when I hear one. He is here to have one of his cows slaughtered, which he seems to do begrudgingly. He claims all of his cattle are his pets. Steve owns three thousand acres in Iowa, which he calls "his country" to differentiate it from the place we are standing right now, though we are only about a dozen miles from his home. He claims bucks like the one he is photographing are too small to shoot on his land. The comment peaks my interest. The photo session is short, after which we load my deer into his cattle trailer, taking it around back.

With help from one of the employees, we hang the buck from a meat hook attached to a roller system. I want the cape, so I do the skinning myself. As I start cutting and pulling the hide down, one by one the male employees step out to inconspicuously take a look at my deer. A couple congratulate me on my fine bow kill. Steve keeps me occupied with his conversation, which varies from hunting, to politics, to ancient Indian artifact collecting, to farming, and back again. At some point along the way I ask Steve for permission to hunt his land. He tells me he would love to let me hunt, but the hunting rights to his land are leased to a couple of attorneys from Minneapolis. "Sorry, but for me hunting is purely business," are his last words on the subject. I understand his position completely.

While we are talking, a sharp pop that sounds like a .22 rifle echoes from behind the closed sliding door. Right afterward Steve dryly comments that his pet cow is dead. My buck had it a heck of a lot better than his cow did.

Reaching the actual caping part I remove the skin around the head of my buck. As the teeth are revealed Steve agrees with my assertion that this must be a really old deer. They are extremely worn. I borrow a bone saw, and while Steve holds the rack, I saw through the skull plate. Finished, I thank Steve for his help and he departs for "his country." My venison will be ready to pick up on Monday. I have four days to burn, and I'm not about to waste them.

Returning to town I swing by the local mega store and pick up a doe license for seven dollars. In Missouri hunters are allowed two bucks, however, one of them has to be taken after the gun opener in mid-November. Driving back out into the country I head straight for Paul's house to tell him, and his wife, of my good fortune, ask them if they would

I killed this old Missouri buck during a brief rain in an otherwise horrible heatwave.

I spend a couple days cruising roads like this, comparing terrain to maps, and finding landowners for the purpose of gaining new hunting permission.

like some venison, whether I should kill a doe off their land, and take a few minutes to establish a more lasting relationship.

Buck, the St. Bernard, greets me in the driveway with a few, deep-threatening barks, followed by a happy wagging tail after he notices that I don't fall for his bluff.

Paul opens the door before I even get to it, and standing in the doorway, talking quietly, informs me that my hunting permission is revoked. He has decided to lease his land to that hunting club, and the lease goes into effect on the date he chooses.

Somewhat surprised, I begin to thank him for giving me the opportunity to hunt, but am cut short when his wife, Janet, walks into the room. She immediately, and by no means subtly, reminds Paul that he already granted me permission to hunt. The two then begin to seriously argue. She clearly does not want him to lease their land. Feeling awfully uncomfortable with the situation, and not wanting to cause any more strife, I interrupt very briefly to let them know I will be gone in a couple hours after I remove some steps from some trees, and leave. Backing out, I can't get to my van fast enough. While driving away I realize that I never mentioned the deer I shot.

Time to move on

Doing as promised, I drive to a far corner of the farm and retrieve some steps. Arriving back at my van there are several messages on my cell phone. The first three are hang-ups, but the fourth is from Janet. She relates that Paul tried calling several times to apologize and that I can hunt their farm until November 1st, after which the farm will be leased. The whole deal makes me even more uncomfortable than I was a few minutes ago. I'm done hunting anyway, and if

I had told them of my buck it might have saved a little drama, but the heated argument was nothing I wanted to be a part of. However, I'm a little irritated by the situation as well. Initially I had permission, and then I didn't, and then I did again, and then I didn't, and now I do again, for a couple days anyway. The situation has nothing to do with me personally. It's simply a matter of economics and family relations. I decide the best thing to do is make a gracious exit. Tomorrow I will stop back in and show Paul and Janet my antlers, let them know I'm done hunting, and offer them some venison. That way Paul can finally lease his land. Considering how to spend the couple of days until my venison is ready I decide to make a concerted effort to gain some new hunting permission.

I busy myself during the day with driving back roads, scouring the local plat book and maps, and striking up conversations with farmers. "He hunts on me," is the phrase most farmers use in this part of the country to say someone is hunting on their land. I had never heard this farther north, and find it an interesting personal association with the land, as though the landowner is himself the land. Talking to farmers, I find myself somewhat envious of such strong identification with place. This is a far cry from the absentee-ism and floating from suburb to suburb or city-to-city that defines the lives of most modern Americans. I hear this phrase often the next couple of days.

By Monday I talk to seven different farmers. Three of them are willing to lease me their land, but simple hunting permission is out of the question. The price varies from five to fifteen dollars an acre. Two have relatives hunting their property. One has about two thousand acres that he keeps for himself. And one gives me permission to hunt about three hundred acres that consists of more than ninety-five percent cow pasture.

Since I don't have anything else to do I also "hunt" each morning and evening. With only a doe tag in my pocket, and no real intention of shooting a doe, my main focus is just to watch and perhaps snap a photograph or two. I allow myself to do this only because I am done hunting here. Normally this is not good practice if you plan to continue hunting an area. Every intrusion limits the possibility of killing a buck.

Coincidentally there is a solid drop in temperature with some frost, and the bucks are moving. I watch several bucks, including a couple of really nice two year olds.

By day three I'm more than ready to get back to real hunting. My last visit to Paul's goes off without a hitch. Everyone seems happy, and they decline my offer of venison, claiming not to like it much. I will mail them a small gift for allowing me to hunt their land after the season is over.

My first stop Monday morning is the local mega store where I purchase a new ten-dollar cooler and a role of duct tape. Driving straight to the meat-processing place I arrive at the opening of the door and pick up my venison and cape, packing my cooler tightly, the best cuts on the bottom. Apart from a couple packages of ground venison the entire deer fits inside. The remaining ground venison I donate to a "Hunters Feeding the Hungry Program". Closing the cooler lid I duct tape it shut, so no cold escapes, and load it in my van. Hitting the highway, it's straight north, back to my hunting grounds in Wisconsin, for a third time this fall.

What to do

- During hot, dry conditions always include water sources in your hunting plans. A water source will act as a magnet to drawing deer to you. This is another place where a good map comes in very handy.
- A sudden steady rain is a great opportunity to kill a mature buck, even during the October Lull in a heat wave.
- Always attempt to land new hunting permissions while travelling. Small locally-owned restaurants, gas stations with coffee shops, and any other place where you see locals gathering make great places to meet new folks and possibly gain new access.
- Never overlook church, too, as a potential place to meet new folks. Plus, getting a little help from upstairs never hurts your deer hunting chances.
- After hunting anyone's land, offer them venison if you were successful, and send a small thank you gift after the season.

This two year old eight-pointer came in real close, giving me a nice shot with my camera.

Chapter 6

Wisconsin: The Rut Is On

It's afternoon by the time I pull into Jake's meat processing. Jake is as busy as usual, reducing another hog to bacon and ham. Showing him the antlers of my Missouri buck, we extend our deal. He tells me to deposit my cooler next to the venison from my North Dakota buck. In just a few minutes I'm back out the door.

At 3:30 a.m. I open my eyes, fully alert, but something is wrong. I simply can't bring myself to crawl out from under my blankets. Lying there I consider the highs and lows of this hunting trip so far, and where I should hunt this morning. The mere thought of walking out into the woods causes me to cringe. As I debate with myself and consider my options my alarm clock makes its wake-up call.

As routine dictates I switch it off, and slide forward to start the engine of my van, turning on the heat. The motor grumbles to attention in the cold. A thick coat of frost covers the windows making it impossible to look outside. Turning on the radio as a ploy to stay awake, I slip back into my sleeping bag and wait for warmth. In minutes it is quite comfortable but my motivation unfortunately doesn't rise in correlation with the temperature.

Struggling with myself I attempt to get up and get dressed, but simply can't do it. Could I be suffering from a touch of burnout? It has been exactly seven weeks since my hunting trip began, and I have done nothing but hunt or do things related to hunting in that entire span. I feel like I've hit the wall. I simply don't feel like hunting this morning despite being well rested, with good prospects at several trees, and the fact that the rut should be just starting in this area. Succumbing to my lack of ambition I shut off my van and return to my slumber. It is times like these that a good hunting partner can be of help; it is seldom that two hunters suffer burnout simultaneously. The clock reads 9:30 a.m. when I open my eyes again. More than twelve hours of sleep!

Concerned with my mental state I immediately decide to take a short break today. It is very seldom that I'm not motivated to be out hunting when the opportunity presents itself. Spending several years in Europe without the opportunity to hunt made me hyper aware of how precious every moment of the hunt is, and how seldom the opportunity is to be able to bowhunt at all. Although it may sound cliché, a terrible day in the woods is indeed better than the best day at some dreary job. With thoughts like these playing through my mind I hit the highway and drive a half-hour to a nearby, medium-sized Wisconsin town. Busying my mind with other things for a few hours is my prescription for sinking motivation.

My first stop is a grocery store where I stock up on a few food items. Riding around town I pick up some breakfast and end up stopping at a park next to a river. For about an hour I sit on a park bench and simply stare into the current, enjoying the crisp November morning. The golden leaves and the turning of summer to fall has somehow slipped past me this year. By mere coincidence my hunting trip has coincided with one of the warmest falls on record in the Midwest, and my route has followed the heat. In all of October I saw frost only a couple times. In Missouri the leaves are mostly still green, but here they have already been swept from the branches, except for on a few stubborn oaks.

Back at the farm I park in my hidden spot, get out of my stinking town clothes, step outside, and pour lukewarm water over my head. It takes me all of about two minutes to completely wash in a lather of scent eliminating soap from head to toe. Although this kind of cleaning-up has become my routine, it is never comfortable, nor do I want anyone to see me, so I am always in a hurry. I can just imagine someone calling the police because there is a naked man standing in the woods, and then having to explain myself. Discretion is important. Clean again, and more importantly the smell of town gone, I set out for my tree.

As most of my best spots around the farm are morning stands I choose the back corner tree as a secondary option for tonight. With the cornfield now harvested, the back corner is a slightly different situation, perhaps better than before. My hope is to catch a cruising buck skirting the corner across the top of the ridge in his search for estrous does. The pre-rut should be in full swing, and the rut either already in progress or approaching fast.

Closing in on the tree my high hopes diminish. The sign hints of only slight deer activity. The scrapes in the corner don't seem to have been hit recently and the primary runway feeding the corner is clearly not being used much. The blanket of fresh fallen leaves is almost imperceptibly ruffled where the runway crosses. Deer have used it, but not many. If I didn't know the runway was there, I would probably not be able to distinguish it from the surrounding ground. Despite the lack of sign, I decide to hunt anyway.

Filling my evening are a cool breeze from the west, squirrels, two cardinals, a burning red sunset, and an owl calling from down the deep draw at dark. Conspicuously absent are the deer.

The next morning is more of the same. Comfortable in the twelve-point tree two hours before daylight, I meditate through the hunt, studying the sunrise, watching more squirrels, and feeling the first breath of wind, while attempting to will deer into view. None show.

At noon I descend, convinced something is foul. Carefully, I search for fresh sign around my tree, and there isn't much evidence of recent activity. Here too, the runways are extremely faint. Looking for answers I follow the edge of the woods, taking a circuitous route towards my van. There must be a reason for the lack of deer activity, either simply a change in deer movement patterns, or human disturbance in the form of other hunters.

Nothing changes deer movement quite like hunters. About a hundred yards from my tree I find a tree trunk that bears the marks of a climbing stand in its bark. The bark is bruised and cut in a regular pattern, and about twenty feet up there are two round, wooden eyes indicating where branches have been trimmed. That the other hunter has been here often is revealed by the fact that the cuts in the bark are numerous, sometimes only inches apart and occasionally overlapping. Every time a hunter runs a climber up a tree the length of his steps and pulls are a little different, eventually leaving bruises all the way to his chosen stand height.

Covering more ground I find two more stands, and a bait pile consisting of apples and corn; hunting pressure at its finest. Naturally there is a little more deer sign around the bait pile than otherwise, despite the fact that there is abundant food everywhere around here. Deer are indeed feeding opportunists. This portion of the farm has been getting hunted quite heavily, which is no wonder since Greg will let just about anyone who asks hunt these woods. Fortunately he is a little more selective with the other sections of his farm, which is where I now decide to concentrate my efforts.

Having seen enough, I cut straight across the fields back to my van. While repacking my gear, a red Eighties Chevy huffs past. My glance to the truck is met by countenance of two baseball cap-clad bowhunters. Their cold stares let me know they think I'm invading their space, which only reaffirms my decision to concentrate on the other end of the farm.

Lunch and an hour-long nap is all the break I take before beginning my slow walk back to the apple tree corner. My pace is slow and cautious for several reasons: For one, I don't want to overheat while walking. Secondly, it is still quite early and my sitting time will be over in six hours; there is simply no reason to hurry. Thirdly, if this area hasn't been disturbed recently the deer tend to bed in the open woods along the draw fingers that approach the field, and I try to sneak by them, hopefully undetected. And lastly, my attention is focused on reading any new buck sign that may have been recently written on the terrain.

It isn't far before the first new sign becomes apparent. Twenty yards from my van at the edge of the woods are two separate scrapes about five yards apart. I stop only for a second to investigate. Though they are both fairly large scrapes, with numerous licking branches, they are clearly nighttime scrapes with no real hunting relevance. The scrapes are about thirty yards from the road along the edge of a now cut cornfield. The positive aspect, though, is that they indicate buck activity, which is always a good thing. Before arriving at the old pasture, I count seven more scrapes and four new rubs. The pasture is still crisscrossed with runways to and from the corn. Already optimistic about my chances I arrive at the corner apple tree to find that it still holds fruit, and there are seven new scrapes; four under the apple tree itself, one under a low hanging branch from the next tree over, and two along the woods. Every scrape is pawed bare, with dirt lying on top of the grass in a couple places. As hidden from sight as this corner is, my apple tree corner is doubling as a hot, primary scrape area. This is the kind of hunting spot that dreams are made of, and it is even better looking than I had expected.

As quick as possible I run my steps back up my tree and settle into my saddle. Visions of huge, mossy-horned bucks fill my imagination while my eyes and ears scan continuously for any movement or sound.

An hour passes before the steady crunch of leaves draws my attention to the woods behind me. Turning to look, I immediately spy a single buck. The stout yearling carries a bone white, eight-point rack in the eighty-inch range, and is determined to get somewhere fast. Without stopping for more than a few seconds he marches across the corner, about fifty yards away, down the draw and straight up the steep ridge and out of sight on the neighboring property. As he strides away it dawns on me, once again, just how large the deer are around this area. A buck that size would almost have to be a two-year-old in the area I grew up hunting, and it is just a breath smaller than the two-year-old bucks I saw while in Missouri.

Something You Don't Often See

Just as I am beginning to think that the yearling buck was the only deer of the evening, the sound of a deer running grabs my focus. A single doe bursts off the ridge and bounds down in my direction. Arriving at the bottom of the draw she stops and looks back. Waiting.

She doesn't have to wait long. Sprinting over the ridge flies a buck. As he closes to within forty yards she bolts, circling back up the ridge. The buck turns and takes up chase. Together they both vanish back over the ridge.

All this happens so fast that I don't get a good look at the buck's antlers, though I know he is a yearling. However, it isn't long before there is another opportunity for a closer look. Within seconds the two hormone-crazed youngsters are back within sight.

For the next forty minutes the chase is on. The little doe darts, dashes, and circles, almost always staying within sight of the buck. She stops often, letting him come within ten yards or so before bounding away. It is as though she is teasing him.

Watching the action I can't help but compare the deer to a couple of frolicking teenagers in lust. It sure looks like they're having fun.

The corner apple tree.

At last the coquette doe circles right under my tree, and out into the pasture. As she passes she is panting heavily. The buck isn't far behind. He actually stops right under me at about fifteen yards. He is not only panting, he's drooling all over, and obviously love is on his mind. The young buck's rack tallies six points, and is about twelve-inches wide.

Out in the open the doe loops around the edge of the tall grass, sprints back towards the buck to the middle of the pasture and suddenly stops, crouching a little. The buck carefully eases his way around behind her. Realizing she is going to stand for him, he wastes no time jumping up on her back. For about ten seconds he rides her. In the wide-open and only fifty yards away I am witness to a rarely-seen event in the wild. This is the first time in my quarter century of bowhunting that I have actually seen a buck breed a doe.

With a sudden, hard thrust and deep grunt he pushes the doe forward and falls to the ground. The doe hops twice and stops about fifteen yards from the buck. Both then just stand still. The buck's tail is twitching, and he pisses down his legs over his tarsal glands, shuddering lightly. The doe also squats and urinates. For a couple of minutes they don't move; it's as though they are taking a breather.

Just as I begin to wonder if they will ever move again, the buck drops his head and takes a single step towards the doe. Immediately the chasing begins anew, up the ridge and back down, across the pasture into the cut corn, and back again. For twenty more minutes the two circle my stand, seemingly oblivious to their surroundings, before finally vanishing into the deep draw behind me.

I am completely in awe of what I just saw, and know I probably won't witness it many more times in my lifetime. It is curious that with the amount of mature bucks around this area that a doe should be bred by a yearling six-pointer. I had read somewhere that young does often are intimidated by mature bucks and prefer to be bred by younger bucks if given the opportunity. Perhaps this was the case. Seeing this also casts doubt on the old adage that mature bucks do all, or most, of the breeding; even yearlings get their chance. Or was this just an anomaly?

This hunt will be one of my most memorable ever. It's not every day a hunter gets to see a buck breed a doe, and it is a privilege to have the opportunity to witness an event that remains hidden to the vast majority of people. One thing is now certain: the rut is on!

The sun is already below the horizon when another deer slips out of the woods into the far end of the pasture. With little light remaining, I can initially only recognize it as a deer, no details.

As the deer ghosts closer I can make out a big body and thick neck. It's clearly a buck, but still too far away to see antlers in this low light. He slowly, too slowly, covers the ground between us, stopping right where the six-point bred the doe, and I still can't make out antlers, even though he is only fifty yards away.

The leftover scent must interest him as he thoroughly investigates both spots where each stood. Nose to the ground the buck cuts to the edge of the corn field taking on a standing corn stalk with his antlers. I imagine the smell of an estrous doe has his testosterone flowing

My hope is to get a quick look at an antler silhouette against the last streak of sunset, but the curve of the ground keeps this from happening. Of course, he makes a straight line to the apple tree, standing broadside for a few seconds in my shooting lane at about twenty-five yards. This has happened to me probably a hundred times, and is tough to swallow every time. Bucks come in right after shooting light, when it is light enough to tell it is a buck and to see every move the deer makes, but too dark to tell what the deer carries for antlers. I could be watching a six-pointer or a sixteen-pointer. Who knows? Just to add insult to injury the buck stops under the apple tree and works a scrape, taking his own good time, which seems to me like a form of torture. Parting the scrape, he crosses the corner of the pasture at a distance of nineteen yards, into the pitch-black woods. Following him with my ears I hear him drop down into the draw at the same place the buck and doe departed earlier. Indeed, that six-point better have enjoyed his luck; he is in for some competition soon enough.

With the buck gone, the coast is clear for me to make my getaway. The corner is hot and I hope to sneak out without the place blowing up. As furtively as possible I lower my bow and climb down, leaving my steps to hunt here again tomorrow evening. This is purely an evening spot; too many deer are out in these fields at night to hunt this tree during the morning, and there is no back door.

Hitting the ground I kneel at the base of the tree, wrapping up my rope to store in my pack. Just as I zip the pack shut, I hear the steady steps of an approaching deer across the ridge. Holding my bow I hunker down against the trunk of my tree sitting perfectly still, hoping the deer keeps its distance and doesn't notice me. As it nears I can hear a deep and regular "uhrr, uhrr, uhrr " of a grunting lovesick buck. Fortunately, he remains across the draw and steadily follows the same general route the other deer took. Now there are three bucks after that doe. She certainly is attracting a lot of attention.

As soon as the unseen buck is out of earshot I make for my van, and manage to get there without noticeably spooking any deer. This spot is as good as gold, and I can't wait to get back up that tree. However, I will have to hunt somewhere else in the morning. My decision falls upon the dump tree, which should also be seeing some action about now.

Full swing rut

Shortly before 4:00 a.m. I simply wake up, alert and ready to go. Four is quite early, but with nothing to distract me at night I end up sleeping by about 8:00 p.m., which gives me close to eight hours of sleep. Making it a point to sleep as much as I can helps keep my energy level up and my concentration focused.

Getting behind the wheel of my van, I drive the six miles from my parking spot to the main section of the farm and park at the edge of the west woods. It is clear and cold, well below freezing, so I force down about six fig bars purely for their calories; neither am I hungry, nor do they taste all that great. According to the packaging, though, each bar gives me about a hundred calories. On this trip so far I have already lost about five pounds, which is probably more than I really can afford considering my light 150-pound frame. The colder it gets, the more I have to force myself to consume high calorie food.

Slipping into my gear in a matter of minutes, I start out across the field. Normally, I would have to take a longer route through the woods to avoid spooking any deer off the fields, but the farmer has plowed both the bean and corn field that used to be here. Deer don't usually eat dirt; so straight across I go. By 4:45 a.m. I am set and ready.

Only a half-hour later I realize the cold is more piercing than I thought, so for the first time this season I make use of some adhesive body warmers, sticking one over each kidney and another one on my chest. To make sure I remain comfortable I also add a couple of mini hand warmers to my pockets. There is nothing worse than freezing out of a hunt. As well, the shooting ability of most people, including myself, sinks in direct relation to how chilled one is.

Tucking in under my Rivers West, which is windproof and very warm, I know I will be comfortable for the entire morning, and could probably hunt all day if necessary. The combination of body warmers and a warm windproof outer shell has extended my comfortable time on stand exponentially. I used to think it was normal to shiver while bowhunting; fortunately those days are over.

Slipping into my half-wake, pre-daylight hunting trance, a couple hours pass until the dull gray of breaking light, and the opportunity to begin using my eyes, snaps me to full alertness. My watch reads ten to seven. In another five minutes it is both light enough to see clearly and to shoot.

The brown flash of a deer on the move grabs my attention, cresting the ridge near the biggest dump pile, eighty yards to my right. A split second streak of antler gets me looking closer, but the buck is out of sight so fast that I'm unable to judge its size. Reaching for my *doe in estrous* can I flip it over a couple times, hoping at least to catch a confirming glimpse. To my pleasant surprise the buck turns back in my direction.

Within a few steps I've seen all I need to see, another yearling eight-point in the eighty-inch range. He stares in my direction for about a minute before losing interest and returning to his previous course. What strikes me about this buck is that he crested the ridge at nearly its steepest point; in fact, it's almost a cliff. If you were to kick a rock over the edge it might roll for a couple hundred yards. I never expected a deer to climb up right there, a mountain goat perhaps, but not a whitetail. It is interesting that a deer will walk up an almost vertical ridge, but will often walk several hundred yards out of its way to cross through a hole in a fence that it could easily jump over.

Behind the narrow row of trees in this photo is a very steep drop-off, creating a perfect ridge-top funnel. The "dump tree" is situated right in the center of the funnel.

From one instant to the next the conditions change. Out of nowhere, thick fog envelops the hilltop and woods. My view of the valley below is completely obscured, as is my view of the old farmhouse on top of the bluff. My vision is in fact limited to about sixty yards. The sudden change has an eerie touch to it, and reminds me of the Lake Michigan fogbanks that I encountered as a teenager helping out on a salmon charter boat, that seem to arise out of nowhere. Fortunately I'm not out in a boat on the big lake, and quite aware that mature bucks tend to move in foggy, wet conditions. For another two hours I sit in the hazy, gray soup, senses peaked, because if a deer indeed appears it will be on top of me by the time I see it.

A little after 9:00 a.m. the fog simply vanishes; as quickly as it came it is gone. The only detectable metrological difference is a faint breath of wind on my cheek.

A quick inspection of my surroundings reveals it devoid of deer, so with the coast clear I munch down a chocolate bar. I hadn't dared to move and make noise opening a plastic wrapper as long as I couldn't see whether any deer were on the approach. Savoring the taste, I chew slowly, enjoying every sweet morsel. Nearly the only time I ever eat chocolate is during hunting season on cold mornings when the calories are quite welcome. Chocolate bars can't taste better anywhere else.

Stuffing the plastic wrapper back in a Ziploc bag in my pack, I exchange it for my water bottle, chasing the chocolate with some ice-cold water. Sated, warm and content I adjust my saddle and settle in for at least three more hours of hunting.

As luck would have it, I don't have to wait long. A mere half-hour later I glance to my left towards the hidden alfalfa field, and standing there, on top of the ridge about seventy yards away, is a tall-tined buck. A second glance isn't necessary to know that this is the caliber of buck I'm looking for, so I immediately reach for my bow. Moving steadily he drops down into the draw.

With the buck briefly out of sight I take the opportunity to shift to my left, edging around on my treesteps, into position for a shot. Seconds later he reappears out of the draw, and without any hesitation whatsoever, foots it directly towards my shooting lane. When he is two steps from the opening, I draw and anchor.

The instant the buck's chest fills the lane I let out a short, low-toned nasal, "mmaaatt." He immediately puts on the brakes, lifts his head, but stares forward, instead of in my direction. Concentrating on a single point in the middle of his chest I let my arrow free.

My point of concentration becomes the point of impact. The buck spins and bounds three times back in the direction from which he came, and stops. He stands for a few seconds at the edge of the draw, his tail twitching and spinning in erratic circles. In an attempt to run he crosses the draw and makes it just to the other side before stopping again. For another second he stands still. He then tips to his right, leaning against a small maple. One more step and he drops to the ground, kicking his legs a few times while sliding about another fifteen yards down the bluff. The buck finally comes to rest at the base of an ancient, gnarly maple.

As the events unfold I lose awareness of myself and think of nothing. These sacred seconds that define the hunt are what it means to be alive. "Did that just happen?"

Catching my breath I work through the case of shakes that I often get after shooting deer.

Fortunately for me, my buck fever experience normally begins after the shot and not before.

I take a few minutes to savor the feeling of having just killed a magnificent deer. This feeling makes all the hard work, and time spent, worth it.

I'm astonished at how the events of the last few minutes played out. When I prepared this tree I envisioned that a mature buck would leave the hidden alfalfa field in the morning and cross the top of the bluff, following the runway right through my shooting lane. And that is exactly what happened, as though it were scripted. It is extremely rare that things work out like this. Most of the time there is a twist or turn in the story, with the big buck approaching from an unexpected direction, or at an inopportune moment. I had a stroke of luck this morning.

My arrow sticking in the dirt after the shot.

While alighting my tree I remove all of my steps. Doing my utmost to remain patient I carefully re-organize my gear in my pack. My immediate impulse is to sprint to my buck, but I also want to savor the elation of the moment, so I consciously exercise slowness. That buck is not going anywhere so I can take my time, and soak up every detail of the experience, which is quite easy in this state of hyper-awareness.

Shouldering my backpack I turn my attention to retrieving my arrow. It is stuck to its middle in the dirt twenty yards from my tree. The white and green fletching is dipped red, and the leaves behind where the buck was standing are splattered with bubbly red drops. It is obvious that my arrow cleanly sliced through the buck's lungs, but for the third time this season the deer's reaction after the hit puzzles me. Why didn't he bolt on a death run? He must have been completely unaware of my presence, or any disturbance at all, and didn't know what hit him. This buck proves to me, once again, that when deer are oblivious to lurking danger they don't necessarily take to blind flight after being shot with an arrow, even when there is a pneumothorax, and they don't travel nearly as far before expiring, as otherwise. This buck only covered sixty yards before falling

With a handful of yellow maple leaves I wipe most of the blood from the arrow and snap it back in my quiver. Although the buck is in plain sight I follow the blood trail just to see how ample it is. Ample it is indeed. Anyone could probably follow it without help. There are, in fact, three blood trails, one on each side of the path the buck took, and one up the middle coming out of his nose. At the two points where the buck briefly stopped there are actual red puddles.

Arriving at the base of the old maple I find the buck with his back against the trunk and his head hanging over a volcanic rock formation. Taking his antlers in hand I lift them up and simply admire them, an eight-point configuration with a broken brow tine. I don't jump up and down and cheer; there is no crowd, and no reason for such disrespect.

Following my ritual I sit down in the blanket of maple leaves next to the buck and give brief thanks. For several minutes I simply sit silently holding the deer that is now my possession and my responsibility that will eventually become part of me. Looking down across the bluff I let my imagination run free and envision all the hunters though the millennia who have killed deer here, and attempt to listen to their voices whispering in the light breeze, hoping to make some connection. Hunting is so very real, yet at the same time a world of dreams. As a small boy shooting a fiberglass bow in the yard I dreamed of hunting big bucks and moments just like this one, and these dreams have never left me. Occasionally, and today is one of those occasions, those dreams come true. When the dreams are gone I will stop hunting.

Realizing the work I have yet to do, I pull myself away from my buck and float with light steps back to my van. As expediently as possible I stow my gear and rearrange my van to accommodate the buck, rolling up my bedding and tucking it away in plastic bags. I also change out of my hunting clothes, replacing them with jeans and a sweater. The last thing I want to do is bloody my Scent Lok. The prospect of dragging my buck up the ridge is rather daunting, so I decide to drive to the farm and see whether Greg feels like helping. Greg helped me drag two bucks out of woods that I've taken here previously. Though he plays nonchalant about deer hunting, I think he likes it when bucks are killed off his property, and seems proud when they are nice, mature animals.

Pulling between the barns I find him outside feeding calves, busily working as usual. Parking just a few feet away I jump out and am greeted with a warm smile. He works while we chat. I tell him of the deer and the hunt, and show him the antlers from the other two bucks I killed. I can tell he wants to help me, but he is already late for some appointment, something to do with a tractor up on another section of land he farms.

In the middle of our conversation he asks me if I have noticed anyone stealing treestands off his land up where I park. I haven't. It seems five treestands have disappeared this fall. Hunters stealing from hunters is simply a sad fact that castes a long shadow on what I believe to be the moral high ground on which hunters stand. Stolen stands are one more of the reasons I hunt almost exclusively out of a sling system.

Forthcoming as usual, Greg offers that I drive right across his alfalfa field and park next to the woods, claiming he's done harvesting for this year anyway. Driving across a farmer's field is something I would never consider doing without explicit permission from the farmer himself. Driving through fields is a good way to lose permission, and one of the main complaints, along with leaving gates open, that farmers have of hunters. Thanking him for the option, and for allowing me to hunt, we part.

Driving between the barns and past two cattle pens, it's only a couple hundred yards to the edge of the woods. My buck is lying less than fifty yards down the bluff. Grabbing my sled and my gutting knife I slip down the steep hill, trying not to think about how difficult it will be getting this deer back up.

Working quickly I turn the buck on its back and get to gutting. Following a few precise cuts I am up to my elbows in hot, steaming blood as I slice the buck's windpipe. The visceral material falls onto the ground with a single pull. The entire job only takes me a couple minutes.

Turning my attention to the lungs I stick my fingers through the holes that clearly pass through each lung, high through one and in the center of the second. The shot could have been an inch or two lower. Lifting the gut pile I roll it down the hill. The coyotes, possums and coons will enjoy the feast.

Flipping the buck over so its open body cavity is towards the ground I lift its head up to drain the excess blood. With this done I step onto my dragging sled, and heave the buck over the low plastic sidewall. Positioned properly in the sled I wrap one side of the pull rope around one of the buck's antlers. This keeps the antlers from hooking in the ground, and also keeps the deer from sliding out of the sled on such a steep grade. Let the battle begin.

Try dragging a mature buck up a very steep grade. Only pure muscle gets the job done, nothing else. At least that's the way I have to do it today. In this situation I must admit that some bigger tools like a truck winch, or a quad, or even a pulley system would be of use, but since none of these things are available right now I have to pull this deer out the old-fashioned way. It would be far easier to slide the buck down to the bottom, but I would have to receive permission from the neighbors who own the lower half of this bluff and the fields on the valley floor. By the time I drive around, get permission (assuming the neighbors grant it to me,) climb the bluff, slide the buck to the bottom, and load him up, I could have it up to the top probably several times.

Taking hold of the handle, I turn the sled so that it is pointing up the hill. Turning my back to the deer I pull and immediately slip and fall, landing on my chest and face. The blanket of maple leaves is slippery. Cursing, I stand up and wipe the leaves off my sweater. Having let go of the

My Wisconsin buck taken from a great funnel.

pull rope the slack has allowed the buck to slide half out of the sled. This is going to be as difficult as I thought it would be. Fortunately, though, it's only about fifty yards to the top.

Starting over again I face the buck, dig in with my feet, and pull backwards using my legs. Five yards is all I can go before stopping. The instant there is a little slack, the buck starts sliding backwards. Reapplying tension and straining under the sudden jolt I halt the almost runaway sled.

Glancing down the bluff I wonder if the buck would slide all the way to the bottom if I simply let go. Slinging the pull rope around a maple sapling I manage a short breather. And so it goes all the way to the top; five yards at a time, and tension the whole way. The closer to the crest, the steeper the hill gets, subjectively speaking. There is nothing like a little hard work to make one appreciate the body size of a buck, and at around 170 pounds dressed this one weighs more than I do. With one last grunting effort it's over the top into the field.

My plan was to spend up to three more weeks hunting here, if necessary, but now my Wisconsin buck tag is filled, as are my tags from North Dakota and Missouri. Killing these bucks has burned up my budget faster than expected. Each buck has caused expenditures beyond the basics, food and gasoline. I have enough money left to get back to Michigan, but not enough to get this deer processed. And honestly, having other people process my deer is something I'm not keen on anyway. I also lack the funds to purchase a new non-resident license for another state, where I would have to pick a destination on a map and just drive there and hunt. My only real option is to speed back to Michigan and regroup. There are, however, a few more stops I have to make before hitting the highway.

The steps left in my tree last evening in the apple tree corner have to be retrieved, and my buck has to be checked in. Zooming around the corner I park at the middle section of the farm, and in a rush, speed-walk back to my tree. The tremendous amount of buck sign makes me wish for multiple buck tags in Wisconsin, but that is, of course, just greed on my part. The single, archery buck rule is probably one of the reasons there are so many mature bucks around here, and in Wisconsin in general.

Getting to business, I am up and back down my tree in just a couple minutes. Pausing briefly, I inspect the scrapes under the apple tree. It looks as though two of the scrapes have been worked sometime between last night and now. Right in the middle of the biggest scrape is the track of a huge deer. The corner is burning hot. Consoling myself with the words, "One in the hand is better than two in the bush," I get back to my van, already thinking about hunting this spot again next year.

At the village gas station I tank up, and purchase a final case of beer to exchange for my frozen venison, and four large bags of ice. The drive will take me at least eleven hours and it has become quite warm today, so as a precaution I want to keep my buck as cold as possible. One bag of ice is placed inside the deer's chest cavity, and a second between its hind legs. I lay the two remaining bags on top of the buck, one across its neck and shoulder and the other along its back towards the hind quarters. Since the buck is in the dragging sled the ice can melt without it being a problem.

Moving across the village I walk back into Jake's with the beer. This time Jake is standing in the main cutting room and is the first person I encounter. There are five guys knifing on what looks as though it used to be a cow. "You must have killed another one," is my greeting. Confirming Jake's suspicions I hand the beer over to the guys, who seem genuinely happy to be on the receiving end of the bargain. Although it's not quite noon the popping sound of opening beer cans immediately follows.

Jake, the guys, and I talk hunting for a couple minutes. It seems everyone in the room is a bowhunter, or at least claims to be. Cutting the conversation short with the excuse that I have to get my deer taken care of, I retrieve my venison from the freezer. Two of the younger guys volunteer to help, mainly because they want to look at my buck, and my other two racks. We load the two coolers in the van, which is now quite full. Holding both sets of antlers, one of the guys asks me how I can afford to hunt for three months straight, ending his assumptive question with, "You must be rich."

"It's all about making choices and sacrifice for the things you love to do," is my answer.

The presumption that I must be rich to spend three months hunting is nothing new to me. Most people I inform of what I'm up to assume the same thing, and rumors from distant acquaintances that I must have hidden money somewhere make it back to me occasionally. Reality, though, is quite the opposite. Saving and sacrificing for hunting season is something I do all year, starting the day hunting season is over.

There are a million different ways to save money for hunting. My method has been to eliminate nearly everything else. I've sacrificed a lot of other outdoor activities, including fishing, which for me is a big sacrifice. The money that I would have spent fishing goes into my hunting budget. Every time I think about buying something I consider it twice, and most of the time I end up placing the money I would have spent in an envelope earmarked for bowhunting.

It's amazing how much money you can save simply by eliminating small things like cola, or candy, not even to mention cigarettes and beer, from your expenses. I have several friends who always claim not to have enough money to afford a single out-of-state hunt, despite access to good hunting ground. Every time I see them they are carrying a cola in their hands. A cola a day adds up to over $500 spent in a year. $500 will presently get you a non-resident whitetail license just about anywhere. These same friends also drive new, full-sized trucks. Eliminating a single truck payment, or saving on gas by driving a smaller vehicle, generally saves more than enough money to hunt for quite some time. Bowhunting is the principle reason I drive a used vehicle instead of a new one. I also shoot my hunting bows for four or five years before replacing them. The list of possible ways to save for hunting could go on and on, but the message here is to make a commitment and stick to it.

Ducking back inside, I thank Jake again for his freezer space. "See you again next year," are his parting words.

On the other side of the street and one block down (the village is only two blocks long) I park in front of the local bar, which doubles as a deer check station. A black and orange "Hunters Welcome" sign decorates the facade above the door. Inside, the place is void of customers, but two women are at work in the kitchen, which is in plain view behind the bar. The décor is typical for a small town bar, beer signs, NASCAR memorabilia, a couple of smoke-stained whitetail mounts, some dartboards and a pool table. It looks like the kind of place where one could order a good hamburger.

The strong smell of beer and tobacco is somewhat overwhelming to my nose, which has been mostly outside for the past two months. My attention to remaining as scent free as possible has made my nose ultra sensitive, and unaccustomed to such intense and unnatural scent. The older of the two women turns in my direction, with a questioning look. Before she speaks I tell her that I have a deer to check. Stepping to the bar she reaches under the counter and hands me a small form to fill out. While I'm jotting down all the important numbers — necessary for such a transaction — including license number, telephone number, and hunting unit number, among others — she grabs a metal tag from another locked drawer in the kitchen. She waits patiently until I finish my signature before walking ahead of me out the door. Routinely she snaps the metal tag around the base of the buck's antlers.

"Nice Buck" she says.

"Thanks" I reply.

That is the extent of our conversation. She is back inside the bar before I get the doors closed on my van.

Pulling out of the village I note the time, 12:34 p.m. Six hundred miles of highway lie ahead of me.

What To Do

- Sometimes a hunting partner can be a benefit, especially when you begin to get tired. A partner can break up the monotony of the trip and help keep you motivated.
- When fatigue overcomes you, take a break for a few hours.
- Sleep early and often.
- When departing from active hunting areas, always wait until you can get out undetected, even if you have to sit around in the dark for awhile.
- As the weather turns cold adjust your diet to more high calorie food.
- Use disposable body warmers to keep your core temperature up.
- Make sure you wear water and windproof hunting gear, as it will help keep you dry and warm.
- As the rut kicks in spend more time on your best stands, and begin hunting all day.
- There are countless ways to save enough money for hunting trips. This might be as simple as cutting cola out of your diet, or packing a lunch to work.
- Make sure to be 100% respectful of the landowner when hunting on someone else's land. A tiny thing like parking your truck in the wrong spot can lead to lost permission. Ask as many questions as you can think of and always ask yourself, "Is this what I'd expect if it were my land?"

Chapter 7

Michigan: An Interlude and a Doe

According to my watch it's already after 1:00 a.m., which means that it's after 2:00 a.m. Michigan time as I pull into my brother Jon's driveway. A traffic jam in Chicago lengthened my driving time by more than an hour. Backing up to his shed I slap my van into park and silence the droning motor. The same sharp cold as last night greets me as I step outside, even though I'm several hundred miles farther east. After a warm, sunny day I'm mildly surprised by the temperature drop. To shake off the driving hypnosis caused by twelve hours on the road I stretch my back and shoulders, which ache severely from holding the wheel for so long. Though I've been awake for about twenty-two hours I'm wired on the coffee and cola-induced caffeine high that helped me through the drive. As expediently as possible I get to the reason for my endurance-driving marathon, and pull my buck from the van. It plops down on the cracked patch of cement with a dull thud. Hurriedly tossing the ice aside, and dumping the water from the bottom of the sled, I drag the buck inside.

Jon's shed is a classic workshed. Most of the year it wields tools for wrenching various automobile projects that continually keep him busy, except during deer season when it is transformed into an amateur deer processing operation. The floor is completely covered with big squares of cardboard. In the corner are two full-sized refrigerators for cooling and aging meat, when the outside temperature is too warm for such things. Along the sidewall is an eight-foot long, wooden bench that is entirely surfaced with plastic cutting block material. A magnet at one end holds a selection of knives, everything from skinning to filet knives. At the other end waits a vacuum packer. The cabinet above the bench holds a variety of plastic bags, black garbage bags and several sizes of Ziplocs. The only plastic bags that are missing are the ones for the vacuum packer, and anyone who wants their venison vacuum packed has to supply their own. There is a stack of white buckets neatly piled in the corner. These are for scrap. Hanging in the rafters are a dozen meat hooks. Four of the hooks are occupied. Two hindquarters and two front shoulders dangle off to the side, aging. Hanging from the ceiling in the middle of the shed is a pulley system, which is connected to a manual boat winch on the back wall. The winch is a convenient way to raise and lower deer. My brother and everyone in his hunting group process their own deer, and this is the place to do it. Though it is not a commercial operation it probably could be. During bow season a deer or two a week pass through this shed.

Unhooking the lower pulley from its bent nail on the back wall, I lower it to the ground. A short cut in the hide between the buck's large tendon and bone at the heel (most people would call it the deer's knee, as the whole bottom portion of a deer's leg is actually an elongated foot) allows me to slip a loop of rope through and hook onto the pulley. Several loops of rope hang at the ready from their own nail on the wall just for this purpose. Cranking the boat winch, the buck eases upward, click by click. Careful not to make a mess I slip one of the plastic buckets under his nose to catch any blood that may drain out. As soon as the buck's neck reaches a more vertical than horizontal position, a steady flow of light red, diluted liquid quickly covers the bottom of the bucket, mostly due to the ice that melted during the drive. With the deer in place for the night I switch off the light and latch the door shut.

Two coolers full of venison are my next project. One at a time I carry them onto the front porch, where a huge chest freezer waits. The level of venison in this freezer rises and falls yearly in direct relation to the proximity of deer season, full at one end and empty at the other. Popping the freezer door up I discover that there is still ample space for my venison. If it were a few weeks later I may not have been so lucky. Stripping the coolers of their duct tape seal, I open them to find the meat still frozen solid with absolutely no sign of thaw. My precious cargo has reached its destination unscathed. The packages clank together almost like the din of colliding rocks as I deposit them in the freezer.

Urgent business taken care of, I retrieve my blanket and pillow from my van. Still too awake to sleep I step inside the house and sit down at the kitchen table. Over a glass of ice cold water I ink in the activities of the last twenty-four hours on the blank pages of my hunting journal. Losing myself in the act of replaying the hunt, I scribble all the details I can muster from a still-fresh memory. Reaching a point of closure I glance up at the wall clock. Its hand's point towards 3:00 a.m. With the mere realization of the time comes a sudden feeling of exhaustion, so I wander into the living room, lie down on the sofa, and drift off into a fatigue-induced coma.

My eyes snap open at the crack of daylight and I'm filled with a sense of urgency as though I'm late for an important appointment. After a second of uncertainty I realize my whereabouts. Two solid months of morning hunting has my body accustomed to pre-dawn rising. Fully awake, mentally at least, I get up and take a look around the house. Nobody is about. It's Saturday morning and prime-time rut, and as I expected, both my brother and my uncle Bob are out bowhunting. Uncle Bob bowhunts with my brother every fall. Since the house is small, he sets up a camper at the edge of the yard. My sleep must have been deep, since I didn't hear them get up and leave. The first thing I do is put on a pot of coffee. While it brews I wash and dress. The warm running water is quite a luxury after seven weeks mostly without it.

Taking it slow I pour myself a cup of joe, sit down at the table, and fill a couple more pages in my journal. My writing this morning is more of a conversation with myself than a report of events. Having been successful more expediently than I expected, and being hit with higher gasoline prices than I had planned, almost all of my hunting money is gone. I still have four more weeks to hunt, but no new hunting area, at least until the first week of December. During the planning stages of my fall hunt I didn't make a contingency plan for the best-case scenario.

Fortunately, this is a problem I really don't mind having. It sure is better than the other way around. Working through my options I develop a possible plan.

If I can come up with a couple hundred dollars, I could drive to Southeast Ohio and hunt in the Wayne National Forest. Having hunted there once before, several years ago, I have a vague idea of some decent public land spots. Ohio's gun season doesn't open until after Thanksgiving, and there is always the possibility of getting a huge buck in those big woods. The key to this equation working, however, is the money variable. No money means no more hunting trips. Counting the few greenbacks still in my wallet I decide I need a minimum of $300 more to hunt for these last four weeks. That amount would cover an Ohio non-resident license, gas, and food. I grew up in this area of Michigan, and a couple of old friends own businesses where I might be able to work for a few days. I decide to pay them visits this afternoon.

Wanting to be ready for any eventuality I get straight to work. My van is in disarray from hauling that buck back, and from two months on the road. My first project is to re-organize my gear and clean the inside of my van. Removing all my plastic tubs I thoroughly vacuum the carpet and wipe clean the entire interior with scent eliminating spray. Leaving all the van doors open I let it air out for a couple hours while I tend to my clothes and gear.

Just as I begin to reload everything Uncle Bob rumbles into the driveway in his trademark full-sized Ford diesel. Tending to our various tasks, me to loading my van, and Bob to stowing his Scent Lok and redressing, we talk as we work. My first question is simply, "Well?" In the linguistics of our hunting group this is an all-encompassing question, which really means, "What did you see, and did you get a shot?"

"Just a couple of 'mullies.'"

Mullie is another word for doe that has been in use in my family for as long as I can remember, covering now at least four generations of hunters. Its etymology is a mystery to me. I have never heard any other hunters that we were not directly associated with ever use this term. All over America there are hunting families with their own private hunting language and personal traditions. Ours is no exception. Elaborating, Bob fills in the details of his hunt, two does and two fawns passed through at about fifteen yards an hour after daylight. Without me even asking, he helps me finish loading my van.

Moving on to my next project I ask Bob to help me with the photos of my buck. He agrees. In a few minutes we've selected a nice spot in the woods at the edge of Jon's yard and the camera is clicking away. True to the motto, take a roll of film and you'll end up with a couple pictures you like; Bob burns through thirty-six negatives. This done, we return the buck to the pulley. Chatting while cutting (and, after so many weeks alone, thoroughly enjoying the camaraderie), I skin and quarter the buck, taking the opportunity to yarn a bunch of hunting stories that have defined my fall so far. Bob helps me by holding a leg here, and opening a plastic bag there. All four quarters find their own meat hooks, while the loins and neck roasts are placed in plastic bags in one of the refrigerators, to firm up and age for at least another forty-eight hours.

There are a lot of thoughts and opinions on aging venison. Some hunters don't age their meat at all, and honestly if you enjoy your meat very well done, or you convert all your venison into hamburger or sausage, there is no reason to age it. Others go a little overboard, and sometimes ruin their venison by letting it hang too long or in temperatures too warm. The exact science of aging meat is complex but the generalities can be easily explained. All muscle cells contain glycogen, which is complex sugar that is a source of energy. As meat ages this sugar, through a natural enzymatic process, breaks down, and becomes acidic, lowering the meat's PH from near 7 to 5 or lower. The more acidic the meat becomes the more the micro structure, which contains collagen, and cell walls of the individual cells is broken down making the meat more tender and juicy. Depending on the amount of glycogen in an animal's cells most of the tenderizing effects of aging are completed within 48 hours. As long as the venison is kept at the constant and correct temperature, and is clean, the upper limit of aging is much longer, up to ten days or more. The longer meat is aged the more tender it will become, but this long aging must take place in a very controlled and clean environment. The perfect temperature for aging is 7° Celsius, or 45° Fahrenheit. Temperatures much above this mark can negatively affect the quality of venison. At lower temperatures the process takes a little longer. For practical reasons, mostly time constraints, I usually age my venison for two to four days.

My uncle Bob with a recent spike buck.

Sitting on the ground I cape the buck's head. Caping is the job that takes me the longest, about twenty minutes. Tucking in the ears and rolling the cape in a ball starting at the nose, it too is slipped into a plastic bag. Again, I can perhaps fetch a few dollars for the cape, or have this buck mounted. On my way in the house I stow the cape in the freezer, alongside the meat deposited there last night.

No news spreads faster in central Michigan than the word of who shot a nice buck. However, nice is a relative term. Though the habitat in central Michigan is decent and deer are abundant, mature bucks are seldom. In fact, any buck that tops the hundred-inch mark is considered taxidermy worthy in this area, and any buck reaching the Pope & Young minimum is for most guys the buck of a lifetime. One reason for this is hunting pressure. Michigan simply has a lot of hunters. On opening day of gun season there have been counts of up to 80 hunters per square mile in this area. Imagine more hunters than deer, and you get the picture. This is on top of the pressure applied by over 300,000 bowhunters. Another reason for the lack of mature bucks is the Michigan hunting regulations. It is a two buck state, regardless of weapon, without a check system, and a rifle season timed to coincide with the middle of the rut, where, and worst of all, baiting is legal and has become synonymous with hunting, especially bowhunting. Yearling bucks are the first killed at most bait piles. It's hard for a little buck to grow up when it's already dead. One only needs compare the number of quality bucks that come out of nearby states — Wisconsin, Ohio, or Indiana — with similar habitat, and similar hunter and deer density, to see the folly of the Michigan DNR's regulations. This isn't to say that there aren't huge bucks killed in Michigan every year, or that there are certain properties with hunting as good as anywhere in America. There are. There are always exceptions to general tendencies.

Lunch finished, and informed of all the latest hunting gossip, I proceed with my last important task for the day. My main concern is earning some cash to complete my fall hunt. Hoping for the best I pull into a small factory at the edge of town. This isn't some shot in the dark. The owner, Tom, is an old friend with whom I went to school. A quick explanation of what I'm up to is all it takes. Tom agrees to let me work, four twelve hour days, six to six. The remainder of my season is saved. The sacrifice is four days of prime rut time; the reward is three more full weeks of hunting.

Back at Jon's house I attempt a short nap but can't find peace, so I just enjoy my brother's company for about an hour. That's all the time left before he starts for his evening's hunt by jumping under the shower. Since I don't have any place of my own to hunt around here, I plan an evening of visiting old friends. My brother has only very limited access to a few small tracts of land where even two-and-a-half year old bucks are very rare. So when I'm around, I never push the hunting issue, that is unless he directly asks me if I would like to come along. Stepping out of the shower Jon asks, "Feel like shooting a doe tonight?" The question comes as a surprise. "You don't have to ask me twice."

Filling in the details, Jon tells me to hunt behind his house, back in the far corner of his property in a red oak. I am to shoot a doe, if the opportunity arises. He wants a deer to work mostly into jerky. Since I'm not doing anything in particular, he thinks I might like to do him the favor. Not only do I like to hunt for mature bucks, I simply love to hunt deer, any deer. In fact, I just plain love to hunt. Although there are very few mature bucks around there are a lot of deer, and doe permits are available over the counter.

One of the core reasons there are so few mature bucks in the area is the pattern of land ownership. There are almost forty different landowners in his section and hunting goes on in each piece of property. This section also borders a several hundred acres of heavily gunned state land. The chances of a buck surviving to three or four years of age living in an area with this much hunting pressure are practically zero. In fact, the biggest buck we've ever seen behind the house was an eighty inch eight-point, which is a typical two-year-old buck for the area. Jon is just leaving as I jump into the shower for the first real pre-hunt, scent-eliminating shower I've had in a long time.

Fishing my gear out of my now neatly packed van, I'm ready quickly, as accustomed to hunting every day as I've become. Walking past the 3-D targets in the back yard I hit the trail into the woods. Jon's property is really narrow, probably only seventy yards wide, but it is long. His seven acres stretches way back into the section, is completely wooded, and is diverse in habitat for such a small tract. The trail curves around the tip of a low, thick, spruce swale that also parallels the entire north side of his property and belongs to the neighbors, who only gun hunt occasionally every few years. Right behind the tip of swamp the land rises abruptly to a small open bench surrounded by poplars. Beyond this, and stretching to the end of

his property, is a mixed boreal forest. There are red oaks, maples, white pines, red pines, scotch pines, spruce, ash, birch, poplars, and even a few cedars, just about everything a central Michigan woods has to offer. Besides the trees and deer, the general area is also home to a few bears, bobcats, and many turkeys. There is even some pretty solid evidence that the elusive big cat of many names — Felis concolor, catamount, puma, cougar, or mountain lion — roams the area.

Even though the cougar has been officially extinct here for about a hundred years I've seen some trail camera photos from about a mile down the road, and my brother had his own personal encounter with one of those big cats one evening.

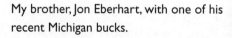

My brother, Jon Eberhart, with one of his recent Michigan bucks.

Jon was hunting deep in the public land and sitting along the edge of a thickly poplared five year old cut-over, when a glimpse of brown ghosting along the edge in his direction caught his eye. Thinking it was a deer he reached for his bow and refocused his attention towards the brown patch, which he could no longer see nor hear moving. The next thing he heard was the bark-scratching of something climbing an oak tree about fifty yards away. Thinking that a porcupine and a deer crossed paths Jon waited. The assumed deer never showed. The evening progressed without any deer activity at all. Stealthfully descending from his tree Jon hunkered briefly at the base to stow his rope in his pack when from the oak came some more scratching and the unmistakable sound of something big jumping to the ground. This was followed by a couple rapid footsteps coming his direction. Suddenly, a little unnerved, Jon grabbed his flashlight and waved it in the direction of the sound, only to hear whatever it was bound off. Cougar? Bobcat? Porcupine? Imagination? Jon is far too woods savvy for the last answer, and he has encountered enough bobcats and porcupines to know the difference. Take his encounter for what it's worth, but I am definitely convinced the big cat — Felis concolor — roams this area. Officially extinct is a bureaucratic term that is quite different from really extinct.

This tract of forest extends for a couple miles to the south, though a few roads bisect it. To the north, across the state highway, is a hundred acres of lowland marshy area. The closest crops are a mile north, but the results of local farming aren't much to speak of in the sandy soil that dominates this particular corner of the world, a couple of thin alfalfa fields. The sandy soil is probably among the reasons why it normally takes a buck in these parts three years to grow a rack that surpasses the hundred-inch mark. There is only very little farming left over here, most of the farmers around who tackled this sandy soil were blown out long ago. Beyond the open bench I tiptoe down a winding trail (created to haul firewood back to the house) through the forest to the corner of the property. The set-up is for a saddle in a double trunked, red oak. Immediately I can see why Jon sent me here. It was a good acorn year for this particular tree. There are still a few acorns on the ground. Usually by early November they are long gone. The leaves are scuffled all around, and it is clear that the two runways crossing this corner are being used. Pausing at the base of the tree I pull five steps from my pack. Even on our own hunting areas we remove the bottom five steps from our trees. This ensures that the rest of the steps will be there when we are ready to hunt. Stolen steps, just like stolen treestands, are simply a fact of life in most heavily hunted areas. Spinning the steps into their holes while climbing I hustle up the tree and settle in. It's a perfect clear, cool, November evening.

I've hunted this spot before and have always seen deer here. Two hundred yards to the southeast on the neighbor's place is a small, five-acre, natural bog. Deer in the area like to bed either around the edge of that bog or in the narrow spruce swale to the north. This oak lies in a line of oaks that extend between the two. Deer filter through the oaks while moving from bedding area to bedding area. Other than along this little funnel of sorts, the movement in the area is almost random. In years absent of acorns the deer activity drops off to nearly nothing. The old saying, "Find the food and you found the deer," is a definite truism is this case.

Finally having a chance to slow back down to hunting speed my mind takes the opportunity to work out the events of the last thirty-six hours. So much has happened so fast I haven't had time to think about, nor to notice how tired I am. Killing a big buck, driving around Chicago, little sleep, skinning and quartering a deer, and getting a short-term job; my mind is busy and my eyes are heavy. Just an hour ago I was unable to sleep. Now I find myself daydreaming with sagging eyelids, aware but not concentrating. A couple hours pass in a wink of dreamtime. I've been hunting so much I feel like I can sit ten hours without flinching. Waiting for an hour or two to pass feels like a few minutes. Hunting time is simply not the time we normally work on in our too-hectic world. Which sense of time is more real? Why do we always move so fast? I wonder...

A red fox suddenly appears, standing a mere fifteen yards away. The sight of the little red canine jolts me awake, raising my heart rate some. Where he came from is a mystery. If I had been paying attention, I would have noticed the squirrels that had been scurrying around burying acorns in the duff, have all taken flight to the trees, and are now clinging upside down to the bark, making low clucking sounds at the bushy tailed mini-predator. He stands still on the fallen bole of a dead birch for several seconds before walking atop the length of the trunk, and stopping at the end to sniff something clearly intriguing. As the fox moves closer it interests me what will happen when he crosses my track. Will he spook, or not? Three steps later and I get my answer. The instant he hits my track he halts, lifts his head, and stares in the direction in which I walked through. This reaction reaffirms my utter respect for the sense of smell that animals have. Not only did this fox detect something, his sense of smell is so keen he knows immediately what direction it was moving. The stink must, however, not be that offensive. His pause is very brief, only a second or two, before he is back to cruising for dinner, seemingly unconcerned about my scent trail; or perhaps my Scent Lok suit has reduced my stench enough that it so minimal as not to be a considered a threat. Without making a sound audible to my feeble ears the fox picks his way along the line of oaks and out of sight. As soon as he departs the squirrels return to their never-ending business. With the brief moment of excitement over I drift back into my realm of thoughts.

Wouldn't it be cool, I think, if a random, big buck just popped up out of nowhere? Stranger things have happened. Every five to ten years a 120 class buck is killed somewhere around here, usually down on the public ground where there is a big swamp, known locally as Deadman's. There is really nothing ominous about the swamp at all, just some thick cedars and a few remaining islands of hemlock surrounding a couple meandering brook trout laden creeks, so perhaps somebody died there once. I imagine there are a lot of swamps known locally as Deadman's across America. Entertaining myself with thoughts like these I bide my time, waiting. There is still about an hour until dark when a deer steps into view, not thirty yards right in front of me, and I mean right in the direction I have been staring all evening.

How do they do it? I can see all the way to the bog, and yet a deer managed to get within bow range without being detected. I didn't hear it either. Granted, neither my ears nor my eyes are the best in the world, but to get that close in these open woods is ridiculous. Once again I am humbled by a deer's ability to move so silently through the forest, and close the distance without making a sound. The real kick in the pants is, however, that the deer is a button buck, the least experienced and normally least cautious deer in the woods, not some mossy antlered old swampbuck from whom you would expect such stealth.

Ever so cautiously the young buck covers the last ten yards to the acorns under my tree, stopping three or four times for a minute or so to check the wind and look around. He appears to be really nervous, sort of like he's on his own for the first time. This could indeed be the case. Mature does run off their fawns during the rut while they are in estrus and being tended by an amorous buck. Fawns on their own can actually be a sign that the rut is in progress. His guard drops a little when he finally arrives at the acorns. Getting straight to business he lowers his nose to the ground and roots through the blanket of leaves for those delicious nuts. Every time he finds one he lifts his head to chew, and look around. I can hear the shells crunching. With each acorn his guard drops some and he becomes more at ease. It would be easy to shoot this deer, but I generally refrain from killing button bucks, especially in an area like this. Too many years of buck only hunting have skewed the population balance heavily in the does' favor. Though it is probably a quixotic cause, we leave all the button bucks and yearling bucks in the hopes that a few survive. Perhaps someday a neighbor or two will do the same, and two year old bucks will become more commonplace.

For about five minutes the button buck feeds around the base of my tree, before suddenly looking back towards the bog. My assumption is that mom will be arriving soon. Within a minute another deer is steadily following the runway towards the oak. It is indeed a doe, but not the button buck's mother, rather his sister. Immediately my bow is in my hand. To borrow a phrase from David Petersen, "Bambi must die!," or in this particular case, "Feline must die!" Biologically speaking, fawns are the deer in a herd most likely to succumb to an extreme winter or be eaten by predators. They are also the least important deer to the social structure of a deer herd, and therefore the ones hunters should kill the most.

Ever so slowly I ease into position, careful that my boots don't click on my tree-steps, anticipating the area where the fawn will give me the first close shot. Feeding on a few remaining low, yellow, maple leaves as she gets closer the young doe takes her time. She isn't nearly so cautious as her brother was on his approach, and is concentrating more on feeding than checking her surroundings for danger. A couple minutes pass before she takes up the search for acorns under the leaves, now standing about twenty yards away, which is perfect shot distance. At thirty feet up in a tree, any shot closer than fifteen yards is difficult to get the angle correct. She stops, turns broadside, and looks in the other direction while crunching an acorn, presenting me with a perfect broadside shot. I glance quickly at the button buck, which is now just two steps from the base of my tree, to make sure he is not looking in my direction.

Fortunately, his nose is buried in the leaves. The time is right. In careful motion I slowly draw, aim, and release.

The doe fawn kicks her hind legs and streaks down into the spruce swale, leaving my arrow sticking out of the ground behind where she was standing. The edge of the swale is about sixty yards from my tree and that she already covered that distance is quite a surprise to me. I listen for the sound of a crash, but hear nothing. Startled at the abrupt departure of his sister the button buck bounds three times toward the swale before stopping. He looks confused. Standing still, he alternates between staring in the direction she bolted and back at where she was standing at the shot. He lifts his nose to taste the wind several times. I can hear him pulling in deep breaths through his nostrils. This goes on for probably five minutes before he decides enough is enough and quicksteps a straight line towards the bog. Still unaware of exactly what happened he crosses within ten yards of my tree before moving out of sight. While the button buck was still in view I was cold and calculating, but now the floodgates controlling the adrenaline in my body burst open. The tremor that is buck fever begins. And it wasn't even a buck that I shot; perhaps in this case it should be called doe, or fawn, fever.

A few minutes later I'm inspecting my arrow. A glance at the abundant, bubbly, crimson blood is all I need before taking up the trail. The tracking is easy. There is almost a solid red stream clearly visible on the blanket of fallen leaves. Most of the blood is coming out of the doe's right side, which is the side my arrow exited, and the lower of the two holes. The blood leads me down to the edge of the swale, where I think she should be lying. Nothing. The blood trail curves and skirts the edge of the thick stuff towards the house. She can't be far, not bleeding like this. Expecting to find her any second I continue. After another hundred yards, and back up on the flat, I'm surprised to still be tracking. She has made it all the way to the small poplar bench. The blood trail crosses right over it and down into the corner of the swale right behind the house. There, ten yards into the spruce thicket, lies the little doe sprawled out on a bed of moss. Immediately I inspect the shot, and it looks great, a couple inches behind the shoulder. I can't believe how far she ran. This sixty or seventy pound doe fawn covered about three hundred yards, which is farther than the three big bucks I shot ran, combined.

Consciously, I pause for minute, lifting the doe's head and just looking at her. My tendency is to get caught up in the work that follows a kill, and not take as much time as I would like, to soak up the moment. This is a petite, feminine animal compared to the ones I have killed so far this year. She is just downright pretty, if you can say such a thing about a deer. It is only now in my forced state of reflection that I notice the complete and utter stillness that envelops me. There isn't a breath of air moving, and eerily I can't pick up the sound of a single bird or squirrel. My prey and I are completely alone in silence. Unsettled by the quiet I become instantly hyper-aware of the ubiquitous white noise of the nearby highway in the background, which I'd conveniently blotted out for the evening. Really it's a roar. And the very realization that it isn't silent at all distracts me. I try to get back to the wild feeling I was just having, but I can't stop hearing the cars zoom past. This small patch of wild and that highway, so close together and yet so far apart. Getting to the work portion of hunting I retrieve my knife from my pack and start gutting.

As usual I inspect the lungs thoroughly. My shot was indeed a couple inches behind the perfect mark. My arrow passed through both lungs, but at the very back of each. The far lung has only two slices in the back lobe, and the diaphragm is nicked. The wound indeed caused a pneumothorax, but not the almost instant death caused by a perfect shot through the front-center of the lungs. The difference of an inch or two right or left on a shot can mean several hundred yards more blood trailing after the shot.

Darkness is just winning the overhand as I finish gutting. The last thing I do is wipe my hands and knife clean with moss, before shouldering my pack and dragging the doe up to the house. The fortunate aspect of my shot is that the doe died less than a hundred yards from the shed, and since she only weighs probably sixty or seventy pounds dressed, I can simply pull her by a front leg without much trouble, and don't have to retrieve my dragging sled. With only a single break along the way I huff up to the shed. Leaving my doe next to the door I peel my hunting attire from my body and change into street clothes at my van. Returning to the shed I slide the doe inside and hang her from the now-vacant pulley. The shed is looking like a meat house, with a doe and eight quarters now hanging from ceiling crossbeams. Glancing at the large hindquarters from my buck, which together probably weigh as much as this entire deer, it dawns on me that this doe is my second deer in as many days.

My young doe, arrowed behind my brother's house.

Jon and Uncle Bob arrive shortly. Both of them saw deer, but nothing they wanted to draw on. Immediately they get to ribbing me for my doe. "It still has spots." "Not much meat on that one." "Which spot did you aim at when you shot?" I counter with simple answers like, "Third spot from the left". This is all in good humor, as neither of them has anything against killing does, or doe fawns for that matter. The meat is as good eating as any. The rest of the evening is spent over some more venison steaks, and conversation.

Tracking dogs

My short-term job starts the next morning. After a half an hour I'm an expert at moving plastic granulate from silo, to cardboard box, to storage hall. During breaks I talk hunting with the guys in the shop. Mostly, I wish I were actually out hunting. After a couple months of living mostly outdoors I feel shackled. With my first day of work behind me I catch a bite to eat and plop down on my brother's sofa in front of the television. While staring at the tube I feel uneasy about my quick transition into "normal" American life, silently hoping that something should happen to pull me from this killingly comfortable trap of virtual living. Suddenly my phone rings. On the other end of the line my old friend Chad asks me if I want to come along on a track? Do I ever. Just minutes later the door slams behind me. That was close.

Chad and his wife Kim are the proud owners of two Bavarian mountain hounds, a breed among the crème-de-la-crème of blood tracking dogs. In fact, Bavarians have been bred for a couple centuries for the sole purpose of blood trailing. First appearing in Bavaria in the middle of the 18th century, Bavarians were originally a cross between the large Hanover Bloodhound and the small Tyrolean Hound. The results were a mid-sized bloodhound light enough to work for long periods in tough terrain, with a damn fine nose. In Michigan blood tracking with a dog is legal as long as the dog is on a leash. Blood tracking with dogs was largely illegal in the U.S., apart from a couple of southern states, until around the turn of the century. Thanks to some dedicated souls in the Northeast doing pioneer work in the eighties and nineties, blood trailing with dogs is gaining more and more acceptance, and most importantly has been legalized in about a dozen more northerly states. Blood tracking with a trained dog on a leash simply makes good sense. Having witnessed several good tracking dogs make some amazing recoveries (that otherwise would certainly have been lost) I am all for their use, as long as they are not allowed to roam. Among the foremost blood trackers in the country is John Jeanneney of New York. John has written *Tracking Dogs for Finding Wounded Deer*, which is an absolute must-read for anyone interested in blood trailing with dogs.

Arriving at Chad and Kim's house I simply walk in the front door. Chad has been a close friend since the second grade. Inside, both of them are dressed and waiting for me. Sissy, the Bavarian bitch, is sitting in her kennel nervously shivering and whining. She has seen the thirty foot long, orange, tracking leash and knows that she is about to get to practice her specialized canine version of hunting. As soon as I walk in Kim lets Sissy out of her kennel. She is so excited she about does back flips, running around at full tilt. Sort of reminds me of myself the day before the opener. Kim scoops her up and we're back out the door, in a hurry.

A bowhunter named Mike called an hour ago to ask about the possibility of having a bloodhound attempt to find the buck he shot. He hit the big eight-point an hour after daylight this morning, and realizing his shot was a little far back, waited four hours to take up the trail. An ample blood trail faded to nothing fast after only a hundred yards. Kim, who is actually the principal dog handler in the family, decided it would be worth it to go after the buck. Sissy manages to find most of the deer she tracks that were paunch shot. For a decent bloodhound, gut-shot deer are generally among the easiest to find, if they aren't pushed. Most of these deer travel a few hundred yards to some thicker cover and bed down. Though blood visible to the eye is often quite sparse with this type of shot, there is more than enough scent for a quality hound. On the other hand, the most difficult tracking jobs are almost always the single lung shots. A deer arrowed through just one lung can cover literally miles of ground, and will sometimes survive such a wound. Pulling into the driveway of the Michigan doublewide we are met by Mike and three friends who, as it turns out, spent most of the day combing the area for the missing buck. Listening to Mike as he recounts the tracking job and ensuing attempt to scour the swamp, our spirits sink. As is usually the case, these hunters called only after they had searched for several hours. This is a noble effort, but the problem is: by walking through the blood trail and around the woods they most certainly spread a lot of scent around. This will make the job more difficult for Sissy, who will have to sort out the real scent trail from the others. The chances for a successful track increase when the hunter backs out and lets the dog make an attempt before a blanket search ensues.

Following Mike we bounce down a bumpy, two-track through a narrow woods and across an alfalfa field. In the corner of the field we park our trucks and step out. The temperature has dropped into the low thirties, and our breath clouds with every exhale. As Kim attaches the tracking leash to Sissy, Chad and I get some light burning. Chad sets ablaze the skirt of a Coleman lantern, modified with one side of the glass covered with tin foil. The thing is brighter than real daylight, will burn for hours, and is one of the best nighttime blood tracking tools there is. I carry a six battery Maglight. Kim dons a headlamp; with her hands busy controlling the tracking leash, a headlamp is the only style of light she can carry. Thus lighted up, Mike guides us into the woods to his tree. I imagine what seven lights flickering through the woods must look like from a distance. The scene could probably be confused with something out of many a frightening Hollywood production. Having so many people along on a track isn't the most optimal situation. This many human bodies can certainly distract a nervous dog, especially if the going gets tough. Fortunately, Sissy loves people and once she is vacuumed onto a good trail she is tough to pull off. At the tree Mike shows us his stand and the point of impact. Keeping our distance, we let Kim and Sissy to the front.

Kim kneels with Sissy, whispers something to her, and then calmly instructs her to, "Find the deer." Standing over the point of impact, Sissy circles for a couple seconds and then starts walking

Bavarian Mountain Bloodhound, Sissy, with one of many deer she has found in the past few years.

straight away, nose about two inches from the ground. "Sissy's got the trail," says Kim while allowing her dog to take about a ten yard lead before following, holding the leash with her right hand. Now as mere spectators, Chad and I inspect the point of impact and find a few drops of dark blood and some specks of intestinal matter. Mike affirms that Kim and Sissy are indeed right on the trail that the buck took after being wounded. As a group we all follow behind, our lights to the ground, finding here and there drops of blood that confirm the path Sissy has taken. For a hundred yards the blood trail crosses through an open woods before entering into a thick patch of autumn olives. This is where the visible blood trail ends. The patch is so thick that we have to get on our hands and knees in some places and actually crawl through. Mike and his friends claim to have searched every inch of the patch. Emerging on the other side we are suddenly standing on the edge of large marsh that is a mix of cattails, tall brome, and reedgrass, simply a killer bedding area, and a place you would expect a big buck to go after being shot. The cattails and grass are in a lot of places well over my head. Through the marsh we go for another hundred yards until Sissy arrives at a lane. About half way to the lane a single drop of blood is all we can pick up with our lights.

At the lane Sissy turns right and simply starts walking down it, nose high in the air into the light breeze. Right away Mike claims she must be off the blood. "There's nothing over there, the bedding area and the pond is to the left." Indeed everything thus far indicates that the buck is heading in that direction. Gut shot deer often head towards water. It just doesn't seem right that the buck would simply make a sharp turn away from cover. Now a little uncertain, because there hasn't been any blood visible for at least fifty yards, Kim pulls Sissy off her chosen course and returns her to the last drop of blood. Sissy responds by following the exact same route as the first time. For a third time Kim brings Sissy back and places her on the trail, with the same results. We seem to be at a standstill. Mike claims the only thing to the right is a short grass pasture that he and his friends drove right by to search the marsh already today. After a short conference, we decide that Kim will simply trust the dog, and go right, while we attempt to pick up blood with the lights in the marsh.

I busy myself backtracking a runway that veered off the one Sissy was following. With his lantern Chad takes up another split, while Mike and his friends dive off into the marsh in the direction the buck HAD to go. Not five minutes pass before Kim whistles and hollers that she's got the buck. Rushing over, we find her about eighty yards down the lane and ten yards to the side. Lying next to her is the buck that had indeed turned right, walked straight down the mowed lane and bedded ten yards from its edge in a little round patch of taller grass. Sissy is busy alternating between chewing on the deer's hindquarter and looking at us all with a look that is akin to, "I told you so." Mike had driven within yards of his dead buck a couple times today, and spent an entire afternoon stomping through a marsh looking for it. Despite some severe ground shrinkage the buck was a great find for Sissy, that otherwise would have probably rotted in that short grass. Happy, we drive back to Chad's house and celebrate by sitting around the kitchen table talking of hunting and old times until the wee hours of the morning.

I spend the next three days moving plastic granulate around, from silo, to box, to storage hall, trying real hard not to think too much about hunting. Even so, at sunrise I find myself standing in the doorway of the factory wishing I were shivering in a tree somewhere, knowing that the second week of November is prime time rut. At sunset I do the same. After work, my evenings are filled by cutting venison just the way I like it. Instead of turning the little doe entirely into jerky I make use of lesser cuts from my buck, and the lesser cuts from the doe. After three days I have all of my venison vacuum packed, and enough jerky to last for weeks. By the last day on the job I'm counting the seconds on the clock. I don't mind the work, but it's hunting season and I feel like I haven't hunted in a month. Four crisp, hundred-dollar bills in my pocket is the reward for my time. I can't get out of town fast enough. Look out Ohio; I'm on my way.

What To Do
- Aging venison can be a simple process that will increase the quality of your meat.
- Hunting for does is fun and a great way to increase the meat in your freezer. Many states have liberal doe hunting regulations even for nonresidents.
- Blood trailing hounds, if used in a controlled manner, are great for recovering deer that would perhaps otherwise be lost.

Chapter 8

Ohio:
The Late Rut in a National Forest

Flatland! The drive through far southern Michigan and northern Ohio reminds me of northern Iowa, giant table flat fields with remnant squares of woods here and there. Though the farm houses are in plain sight of one another, the distance in between might be a couple of miles. This is the far eastern end of the great American prairie. From a driving perspective it looks like the city of Columbus was placed at the very tip of America's breadbasket. Perhaps this was the original reason for its existence. As I turn southeast at Columbus the terrain wrinkles some, becoming hillier the farther away from the city I get. Soon, there is far more forest than field, and a completely different feel to the place. I've entered what is known as Appalachian Ohio. The state highway runs right into the small town that serves as my destination; a destination I selected solely for its proximity to numerous tracts of the Wayne National Forest.

The town's name carries the appendix "ville" that is so common to town names in this portion of the country. This particular "ville" sits nestled in a narrow corridor between steep hills. A low gradient sickly looking river parallels the steep ridges just south of town. It's banks — steep cut, eroding earth; and its water — milky, chocolate brown and sluggish. Like nearly every other town in the U.S. gas stations and fast food reraurants line the highway strip, but at the center of town red brick buildings tell of a different time, and here perhaps a more prosperous time. The former train station and its neighboring brick factory building have been reoccupied with outlet stores. Several more brick buildings along the tracks, that must have lain fallow too long to reclaim, lie in ruins. Century-old, Victorian style houses are tucked in between the highway and the hills, and an old square with government buildings and a conspicuous stone and granite post office make up the old downtown. Some of the small shops are boarded up, and across from the post office is a food bank. This part of town has indeed seen better days. Two blocks from downtown I find what I'm looking for; the laundromat, the most critical business locally for nomad style bowhunting. I've hunted this general area once before a couple years previously with a few friends, but we based our hunt out of another nearby town.

Done with my tour I stop at a small sporting goods shop to pick up my hunting license. Under the glass at the cash register is a reminder of why I've made the trip south. The photo of a giant non-typical is labeled with the date it was checked, the county in which it was killed, and in big black letters, "Gross score 219." For $150 I get to walk out the door with a fresh tag in my hand, and daydreams of killing a buck like the one in the photo. Honestly, I would be perfectly happy with a gross score about a hundred inches lower.

The county road south passes a row of old coal furnaces, curving into a steep draw up out of the valley, causing my old tired van to grunt and groan while dropping gears before reaching the crest. A chunk of the National Forest extends for a couple miles on both sides of the road, tall, mature, open forest as far as the eye can see. Woods like this are difficult to bowhunt. Three miles more of sharp curves through mostly private property roll quickly by, before I turn right on a smaller, somewhat paved road. It is more an asemblance of asphalt patches than actual pavement, and would definitely be smoother if it weren't paved at all. Houses stretch along both sides. The contrast is striking. Next to trophy houses, on par with the best that suburbia has to offer anywhere, are small patched-together shacks and old trailers that poverty has obviously blown through, complete with the obligatory collection of junked vehicles in the yard. I get the impression that I'm driving through two parallel worlds. Beyond the row of houses the asphalt turns to dirt as I cross through another strip of national forest.

At the end of the mile I arrive at a 'T' and turn left on the next county highway to the west. It takes me south again for a couple miles to a gravel road hidden in a curve that is both easy to miss and a dangerous corner. I pull off the highway and park about thirty yards down the track, where a gas pipeline provides convenient access to the timber. The government has

Most of the terrain in this area looks like this, open woods on rolling ridges.

recently purchased the big tracts of public land that completely surround me. They aren't yet on the official maps of the national forest, and I discovered them by visiting the ranger station and browsing through their updated maps a couple years ago. The fact that there are new areas of forest purchased by the government hasn't been lost on other hunters, but there aren't as many hunters in the unmapped areas as in the mapped ones. One key to hunting public land is finding the less treaded spots.

Don't Overlook the Obvious

This entire area is several square miles of reclaimed strip mines. The mix of habitat is tremendous. The steep ridges that were once the edge of the mines are covered with mature forest, including some ancient white oaks with trunks about five feet in diameter. The tops that were once hills have been flattened, and there is a mix of relatively open grass covered flats alternating with thick, brushy, bedding areas and young pine plantations. The bottoms almost all have creeks running though them, and are mostly natural woods, with a network of finger-like draws reaching up into the flats. The leftover mounds of mine pilings have been planted with crooked jack pines, creating more thick bedding areas. The mining also left some unusual terrain formations. For instance, extending along the top of a nearby ridge is a half mile long by forty-yard wide by thirty-foot deep hole in the ground, where I believe they must have been probing for a vein of coal. The sides of the hole are nearly vertical for almost its entire length. There are only a couple of points where deer can cross this hole, creating some unique funnels. Another ridge has been terraced into twenty-yard wide benches. The only missing ingredients are crops.

Quickly into my gear I sneak down the two-track path that marks the pipeline. My walk is short. Only 150 yards from my vehicle I arrive at the small stream that runs parallel to the gravel road. The entire streambed is covered in a milky white film. A national forest ranger informed me that the film is actually caused by acid run-off that is still leaching out of these mines. Nothing like a little long lasting ecological damage. I wonder how long it will take for the water to return to normal? With a hop, I'm across the stream and now only about fifty yards from my hunting spot for the evening. Carefully, I pick my way along the creek to my tree. My friend Knut had several encounters with a couple of really big bucks right here, including one of near Boone & Crockett proportions. This spot is less than two hundred yards from two different roads. The opposite of getting away from the crowds on public land is hunting close to the roads. Most hunters skip the first couple hundred yards of woods, and the deer seem to know this. The little bowl this tree sits in was literally full of scrapes when Knut hunted here. A quick look is all I need to see that this is not the case now; not a single scrape, and not much other sign either. The main runway, however, is lightly scuffled; an indication that it has been traversed very recently, especially considering the fact that it has rained here the last two days. Though I'm not impressed by the sign, it's too late to get out and find something else today.

Screw-in steps are forbidden in the Wayne National Forest, so I slink up the tree with strap-on steps. This is the first time this season that I have to use this style step, and it takes me a couple minutes to get used to the procedure, but by the time I arrive at the top I'm moving just as fast as I would be with the conventional version. Snug and comfortable in my saddle I notice that the sky has turned completely gray. There isn't a breath of wind, and the only sound I can hear is the gurgling brook. Forgetting for a second exactly where I'm sitting I think it will be one of those perfectly still evenings. It feels good to be hunting again, after my almost week long break. I draw a few deep breaths, slowly exhaling, consciously trying to relax and slow down my thoughts, to reach my hunting state of awareness. The week in the real world has cluttered my head with a multitude of unimportant impressions and thoughts that need to be relegated to their proper place. The sudden roaring-loud rumble of a passing semi-truck startles me. Another truck, and then a car follow it. The country highway is about two hundred yards away and actually uphill of where I'm sitting. A couple more cars blast past. So much for a quiet evening! This is the negative side of hunting so close to a well-used road. Trying to block out the noise from the intermittent stream of automobiles I concentrate on looking for approaching deer.

A couple hours pass without any activity before I hear the unmistakable sound of a quad in the distance. The sound is coming from over the ridge and moving in my direction, probably stemming from the next house up the road. ATV's are illegal to use on most tracts of the national forest, including this one, but that doesn't stop many of the locals from using them. In fact, walking seems to be out of the question nowadays. Nothing is more maddening than walking a mile or so back in a woods where the things are not allowed, only to find a well used quad track leading to someone's bait pile. If there are two things I can't stand in the woods it is quads and bait piles. Unfortunately, the two seem to go hand in hand, and baiting is legal here. If I find bait, I'll just have to hunt around it.

The first time an ATV rider ruined one of my hunts was over twenty years ago. I will never forget that cold late October morning. I was a kid who got up and walked all the way across the section where we lived to hunt a hot primary scrape area. I sat there shivering for over an hour until it finally got light enough to see. Within a few minutes a nice eight-pointer appeared across the opening coming my way. At fourteen it would have been my biggest buck by far. He made it to about fifty yards when the sound of a three-wheeler broke the silence. The buck stared briefly in the direction of the sound and bounded off. Steaming mad I watched some guy ride past about a quarter mile away with a bow hanging over his shoulder. Since then this kind of thing has happened to me more than I care to remember. I've even seen guys trying to use their camouflaged quads as blinds. What could possibly be said about that?

The puttering motor comes closer and it is easy to distinguish the minute it tops out on the ridge. Though I can't see it, the quad is only a little over a hundred yards away. I listen as it rolls down in a low spot and then back up again and stops, motor running. Expecting it to keep moving away down the pipeline I am surprised to hear it return to its initial point on the ridge.

The motor shuts off. Bang! The blast of a shotgun rings down across the forest, about causing me to flip out of my saddle. Another follows the first shot quickly. The motor starts up again and zooms to the top of the second rise, and back again. Two more shots. More quad noise. More shots from a different gun. More quad. There is a guy up there sighting in his shotguns. How smart is it to sight in your guns right on top of a gas pipeline? I sit tight hoping he will finish and leave, allowing a little time for the deer to rise and move. For over an hour, shot after shot rings out. Finally, a few minutes before dark the sputtering motor rolls back over the ridge to the house and shuts down. Leaving my steps and bow in my tree I climb down, and cursing under my breath march back to my van. Perhaps there will be fewer disturbances in the morning.

It is still two hours before first light as I settle into my saddle. Minus the shotguns, the morning isn't much different than last evening. A lot of cars, but no deer. Around 10:00 I climb down with the intention of doing a little scouting. Though I find some interesting terrain features and funnels, there just isn't that much buck sign, but contrarily many more quad trails than the last time I was here. There is even a little bowl that seems to have been converted into an ATV racetrack. It doesn't take me long to write the area off for bowhunting purposes. Within an hour I'm back at my van consulting my pile of national forest maps, comparing them to my Ohio driving atlas for directions. There is another smaller tract of public land about ten miles away that looks like it has some potential. It is only about a half mile wide, but almost three miles long, right through the middle of a huge, irregular section that is otherwise all private. According to the map the only access points are at the north and sound ends. About a mile into the public land there are several big draws that extend across the private land. This could be what I'm looking for.

The dirt back road angles north off the county highway straight up a long ridge. Breaking out of the woods I'm surprised to find alfalfa fields on both sides of the road. Crops are definitely a rarity in this vicinity. The sight of them is encouraging. The public land runs parallel to the fields to the west. As always I'm formulating a plan. If I can get back on the public land in the morning I might be able to catch deer returning from feeding. Rolling slowly on, the road becomes a series of curves through a very large tract of forest, mostly open mature hardwoods with big draws and ridges falling away from both sides. Blaze orange no trespassing and private hunting club signs are posted conspicuously on just about every tree along the way. The message is hard to misinterpret. A little over two miles into the woods there is small pullout. According to my map this is the only access point at the north end of the public property. Immediately it is clear that this parking spot sees a fair amount of hunter activity. There are fresh truck tracks, and a beaten-flat footpath into the woods. Jumping out into the woods I follow the path for about a quarter mile to where it dissipates into grassy meadow surrounded by tall poplars. At least there aren't any quad tracks. Beyond a meadow to the south is a deep draw that looks like it could be promising. A walk from here back down behind those fields would be quite the undertaking. Hoping to gain a better overview of the area I hustle back to my van and continue with my drive, first to the north and west, and then back again to the county highway.

A Rare Find!

The south end of the public land is another mile up the highway. Investigating the situation I slow down and look north into the mature forest. To the south, across the street, the terrain is completely different. A thick bedding area of red willow, brown brush, young saplings of several varieties, with a row of mature trees through the middle, borders the road. This is the only obvious bedding area I have seen in many miles of driving. A neat wire fence puts an end to the bedding area, transforming it instantly into pasture. About fifteen yards short of the fence a clear, well-used runway drops down off a high ridge, crossing the road straight into the bedding. Stopping to take a closer look at the runway I count no less than seven rubs within fifteen yards of the road. That bedding area is obviously where the action is. The runway looks like someone walked down it with a rototiller. "No Trespassing" signs posted on stakes line the border. Two hundred yards further on, on the north side of the road, an old logging road, wide enough for a single car, is the only parking spot. A metal gate across the two-track reads, "Foot traffic welcome." The small print clearly points out the fact that ATV's are illegal here, and surprisingly there isn't a quad track anywhere. There isn't nearly as much hunter sign as at the north end. Consulting my maps a last time before my planned scouting foray I am met with a pleasant surprise. According to my official national forest map the bedding area across the road is on public land! It's a small piece, probably about forty acres, shaped like a right triangle, and offset from the end of a long piece of public land, only overlapping for about fifty yards. The parking spot is approximately 150 yards from the fenceline. But what about the no trespassing signs? This must be investigated.

With my map on my lap I pull back onto the road and, while driving at a crawl, compare the map with the land. The no trespassing signs are on wooden stakes and on a couple trees clearly on the pasture side of the fence, and extend only sixty yards deep into the property. They match the signs along the pasture bordering the county highway. Either the neighbors are using the same signs, or the signs are just a slick attempt to keep hunters out of this patch of national forest. Parked at the big runway that crosses the road I double-check my map again, and again. Everything lines up. This land is indeed public! Another hundred yards up the road there is a row of three houses. On the map they are little black dots surrounded by small squares. In real life there are two old trailers and a small brown house, each yard cluttered with a collection of blown-out cars, and a variety of other stuff, to put it nicely. Strips of public brushy land extend to the road between the rectangle patches of mowed lawn. Private property signs conspicuously decorate each of the yards. These houses compare perfectly with the map as well. Without intense scrutiny it would be easy to assume that the entire south side of the road is private land.

Haling from Michigan I've seen this kind of thing on numerous occasions, people either posting public land directly, or, as in this case, placing signs in such a fashion that public land appears to be posted. There is absolutely nothing illegal about the no trespassing signs I am looking at, not a single one is actually on public property; however, there has been an obvious effort to deceive. It can be worth it to take a really close look at maps and borders. One forty-acre piece of public land I hunt in Michigan has been conveniently, and illegally, cut in half by the landowners behind the property. A row of hunter orange posted signs marks their "new" border. I went in with an official map and measured the property, finding the old border fence conveniently knocked down. Whenever I hunt that property I simply carry a map with me. There are a couple pieces of property I have hunted like this. If anyone decides to give me grief, I offer to call the conservation officer for him or her. This is usually enough to come to an understanding. Elated by my discovery, I change my plans for the afternoon. Instead of scouting I'm just going to walk in the woods and hunt, the ultimate in freelance hunting.

Busting into the local bedding area right in the middle of the rut definitely isn't proper bowhunting decorum, but on a short term hunt there is room for exceptions. Suddenly overcome with a sense of urgency I zip back to the parking spot. Stuffing my face with fig bars, bread, and an apple while dressing, I can't seem to move fast enough. Those big rubs are beckoning. In an attempt to keep a low profile I cut along the face of the tall ridge, instead of walking down the pavement, and cross into the brush at the big runway. Good public land spots are rare finds, and the last thing I want to happen is the neighbors, or anyone else for that matter, discovering that I'm hunting here. My first area of interest is the soft dirt of the runway. The black mud reveals an abundance of deer tracks, but no boot tracks. Keeping off the runway I position my own steps carefully, trying not to leave my own signature in the mud. Following the runway it parallels the fence and I emerge from thick brown brush into a strip of head high, dead golden rod, and other tall hard-stemmed forbes that I can't identify, under a powerline. This is followed by patchy brush and tall grass. Here the runway veers a ways from the fence to the west, and is intercepted by several others. Rubs of various sizes are randomly strewn all about. The brush opens up even more along a creek. The runway is crossed here by three more runways before cutting straight into the creek. The banks are steep, well over my head as far as I can see in either direction. This is the only decent crossing point within a couple hundred yards, and the deer are using it. There are at least six sets of very fresh tracks in the soft sand and gravel, deer that I may already have pushed ahead of me.

I slide down the bank into the water. The creek bottom is good solid gravel and the water is only ankle deep. The white slick of acid covers the small stones here, too. Using some thick roots as steps I clamber up the other bank. On top of the other bank towers a giant multi-trunked sycamore. The closest trunk of the sycamore would be a possibility to hunt from, but I need to look just a little more. Twenty yards from the base of the tree the runway merges with another well-worn deer trail that parallels the creek; beyond that is a wall of brown brush with small runways emerging out of tunnels under the low canopy. There have to be deer bedded nearby. Positioning each footstep with extreme care I almost still-hunt along the creek. Three scrapes and half a dozen rubs within fifty yards convince me I've seen enough. The sycamore is my tree for tonight.

Conscious of every movement and sound I work my way up the crooked trunk. Immediately it is clear that my camouflage is completely wrong for this tree. The light tan and splotchy green bark is a difficult match. My answer to the fact that I stick out like a sore thumb in my dark attire is simply to climb a little higher and hope for the best. At least there are five more trunks that provide some vertical cover. Purveying the situation from the top I almost have difficulty believing my eyes. There are six runways that cross within shooting distance, most of them converging within ten yards of my tree, three scrapes in sight, a natural funnel where the deer cross the creek, good cover in all directions, and no sign of anyone else hunting here. This spot simply has a buck "feel" about it. If this area turns out to be as good as it looks, perhaps I've hit the public land-hunting lottery. Now, if only the deer cooperate.

Settled into my saddle well above the tops of the lower brush I'm able to take a closer look at the larger picture. The sycamore is less than two hundred yards from the county highway. Between the creek and the road is a strip of thick bedding that extends all the way behind the three houses. On the other side of the road is a steep ridge dotted with mature maples and a few oaks. The ridge is crowned with a patch of dark green scotch pines. The creek extends into the neighboring pasture land in one direction and angles towards another ridge in the other. I'm sitting right in the middle of a wide valley of sorts. Behind me, the bedding covers an entire overgrown slanting hillside that was once a field and ends abruptly at the interface with a steeper ridge covered with more mature forest.

For several hours nothing much happens apart from the usual songbirds, and passing automobiles, until 4:30 when I notice a single doe across the creek. She is standing on the runway that parallels the creek about thirty yards away. Her appearance catches me by surprise. It's not that a deer suddenly standing in front of me is anything new, but particularly surprising is the direction from which she is coming. Either she strolled down off the ridge and crossed the road, following almost my exact footsteps, or she was bedded somewhere between the runway and the fence along the pasture (which for most of the way is less than thirty yards apart) and let me walk right by her. In any case, I certainly didn't expect to have deer coming from that direction tonight, not after marching right through. The doe moves slowly, nipping at browse along the way. Every few steps she stops and looks back. It is clear that she is waiting for someone. But whom? Her fawns? Old Mr. Big? She covers about sixty more yards along the creek before my question is answered.

The buck emerges from the brush at almost the exact spot where I initially spotted the doe. His antlers are bone white. He carries eight points and a spread a little wider than his ears. If I had to put a number on him, my guess would be somewhere in the 115 inch range. Decision time! In any spot I have to hunt in Michigan I would attempt to shoot this buck, but in some other states I wouldn't lift my bow. This is public land, though, and that is a really nice buck, but I'm sure there are bigger in southern Ohio. It is only the second day of a ten-day hunt. And so I argue with myself while watching the buck. His pace is slow but determined as he follows the path the doe took. As he edges closer he answers my 'to shoot or not to shoot' question for me. Instead of following her exact footsteps he cuts the corner, crossing about forty yards away through some brush. There is no way I could shoot even if I wanted to. The doe waits

This Ohio public land bedding area was a great find.

for him to get within about twenty yards of her before slowly proceeding. For the next hour the two ghost slowly along the edge making small circles. The buck is not chasing, simply following, and the doe is not running, rather walking. Imagine the rut in slow motion and you get the picture. There is absolutely no rush at all to their actions. At one point the buck stops and rakes a sapling with his antlers really getting into the effort, twisting and snapping a few branches. I wonder if things will liven up when he completes making his rub? Finished, he resumes his slow motion chasing, not even a heartbeat faster than before. Eventually the two wander off toward the point where the creek appears to reach the base of the ridge, leaving me to ponder the deer behavior I just witnessed. No other deer show themselves. Leaving my steps and saddle in the sycamore I slide out of the woods at dark.

By 5:30 a.m. I'm back in the light barked tree, this time wearing a lighter version of camouflage that still doesn't match the tree. It is, however, the lightest colored camo pattern I have with me. The weather is clear and comfortable, in the low to mid thirties. Passing time I watch the road. Well before daylight a schoolbus stops at the houses, pulls up the road and then comes back again. A steady stream of cars zip past in the dark, on their way to work I suppose. By daybreak the stream has diminished to a single automobile here and there. Usually I don't pay attention to the passing automobiles, but nothing is happening in the woods. There isn't even a squirrel to keep me guessing whether that last crunch was a deer or not. That is, until shortly before nine.

Suddenly, in the exact spot where I first saw the doe last evening stands a young buck. Moving rapidly he quicksteps towards my tree, and drops down the bank into the creek bed. Now, straight underneath me I can see that the small white antlers I thought were spikes are forked. He is one of the smallest four-pointers I have ever seen. His antlers aren't quite as long as his ears and the forks are backwards, like on a roebuck. In fact, his antlers, as small as they are, would fit well on the head of a roebuck. I surmise that he came down off the ridge crossing the road into the bedding area. Apparently in a hurry, the buck hops up out of the creek and marches straight down the runway towards the point, and is out of sight within a minute.

Nearly an hour later, movement in the direction the buck departed, catches my attention. Out of the brush steps another deer that I peg as a doe, coming my way. But as the deer closes the gap to within thirty yards I notice a glint of antler between its ears. Giving me an opportunity to get a better look the tiny buck walks right under my tree to cross the creek. His antlers are almost black, pencil thin, and are only about half the height of his ears. The left beam has a tiny fork, making him a three-point. This has to be among the smallest antlered bucks I have ever seen, not including rubbed out button bucks. Taking his time, and stopping for a drink of water, I get a really close look at this buck. Apart from his tiny rack, he looks like a healthy fair-sized yearling. Up out of the creek he proceeds towards the road, where he slips into cover and vanishes. Three bucks in my first two hunts in this spot is not a bad way to start in a new area.

It's shortly after 11:00 a.m. as I climb down, with a plan, of course. Though this creek crossing has already proven itself a good spot, the rest of this property simply must be investigated. Not wanting to carry my bow with me I hide it in a patch of brush before sneaking along the creek. The creek is a travel corridor right through this bedding area. There is a grassy strip along both sides that the deer are clearly using. The first destination I have in mind is the point where the creek meets the ridge. All four deer I have seen so far have either come or gone through that point. It's only a short walk before I discover why. The creek indeed curves towards the base of the ridge, and right at the point where they come together, an abandoned railroad grade cuts along the base of the ridge straight through the bedding area. Along the top of the grade is a well-worn runway. On the south side of the grade a draw reaches up into the big woods. Several runways come down the draw to the base of the grade, with some crossing, while others merge leading into the bedding area. This is yet another excellent pinch point. Several trees on the south side of the grade in the draw are huntable.

With the intention of returning to this spot I continue, and walk up the west edge of the draw, which borders the bedding area. All along the interface there are scattered rubs, some of them clearly made by big bucks, with shredded bark and broken branches the diameter of my thumb. Circling the south edge of the bedding I eventually arrive at the west edge of the public land. Right at the fence I discover a ladder stand, with a quad trail leading to it. The trail is from the pasture next door. Five feet from the base of the ten-foot tall ladder-stand is pile of apples. Hanging on a branch about ten yards away is a tampon that has been doused in some kind of deer scent. The sight of this set-up just makes me wonder. There is buck sign everywhere around here, along with well-used runways and pinch points, and this guy thinks he needs to use bait to get a deer close. From the looks of things he is either a kid or a very novice hunter. Actually I'm happy to know that this hunter won't be a real problem for my own hunting. Turning south I follow the old western border fence until I run into some no trespassing signs. The signs are on trees about thirty yards short of the old southern fence. I follow them back east until I hit the corner of the woods, right where it meets the draw.

Just inside the corner I discover four large scrapes around a single crabapple tree. Within forty yards I count six more scrapes. The combination travel route, cover, and bedding make this a classic primary scrape area. Fortunately, there is a perfectly sized tree twenty yards from the main scrapes. The unfortunate part is that it is a rough bark hickory. By the time I get to the height I like to hunt there is a pile of bark lying at the base of the tree that I have scraped off while on my way up. This hickory couldn't be located in a better position for this corner. There are shots to the scrapes, into the corner, into the draw, and at four different runways that cross within shooting range. Very happy with my discovery I climb back down to continue scouting.

All the deer movement in this area comes together at the base of this ridge.

Working backwards I walk down the middle of the draw. Several good runways cross from east to west, from the high ridge into the bedding, but they are all single runways that may be used one day but not the next, or the next, and are all a little too random for my taste. Clearly the base of the draw along the railroad grade is where things come together. Right at the base of the grade stands a tall river birch with a perfect slant. I run my steps up it. From the top I have a shot to the grade, across into the corner where the creek runs into the grade, and both along the west side of the draw, and up the middle. Five runways cross right here. This is simply a great spot. As soon as my feet hit the ground I make my way towards my van, picking up my bow along the way. It is a quarter to four when I finally arrive at my parking spot.

Satisfied with my day's work, but tired, hungry and late, with no good options for a quick afternoon hunt, I decide to take the evening off, which means that I have the opportunity to explore for more hunting spots. The first thing I do is attempt to get a better overview of the area by driving around the block to the south. It's a ten-mile circle in all, and apart from a small patch of brush at the far south end, as far as I can tell the entire remainder of the section is mature hardwoods with tall ridges and deep draws. The area I scouted today is the only public land in the entire section, and perhaps the only real bedding area. Of course, deer bed on the sides of ridges and in the draws as well, but this one, little, thick spot must be a real attraction. By the time I complete my tour of the north section again the sun is over the horizon. Just after dark I park at a pullout in a nearby tract of public land for the night. The forecast is for rain all night and all day tomorrow. As far as I'm concerned there isn't much better hunting weather than a steady light rain during the rut. As I fade away into a deep sleep my wish is that the forecast becomes reality.

Sometime in the night the pitter-patter of raindrops on my roof begins. Anxious to hunt my new spot I'm wide awake at 3:30. It's still a little early, but unable to sleep I get up and take my time getting ready, forcing myself to eat some breakfast; a dry bagel, some fig bars, an apple, and my daily vitamin. While eating I notice that the temperature has risen considerably during the night. My thermometer reads exactly 60 degrees, about 15 degrees warmer than when I fell asleep. It's a little too warm for mid November, but at least it's raining. Despite attempting to take my time I arrive at my little patch of public land heaven before 4:00 a.m. Dressing in Scent Lok and Rivers West, and not much else, I soon find myself sneaking along the runway towards the creek crossing. Well protected in my soft waterproof shell, I notice the rain and dripping wet weeds and brush, but don't think much of it. The fact that it has rained a little more than I thought becomes clear when I slide down the bank and step into the water. The gravel that was yesterday high and dry is now submerged. The water level has risen from ankle deep to about mid boot, and the current has picked up some momentum. Hoping that the water doesn't rise much more I climb up the bank and follow the creek to the grade. It's only a few minutes after 5:00 as I'm set-up and ready to go in my new tree at the base of the draw. My plan is to sit here all day.

Only minutes later the clouds burst and the gentle rain transforms into a deluge. And I mean it is raining hard, no wind, just a wall of water. Instinctively, I tuck in all loose ends and zip all my zippers shut to batten down against the rain. Shortly, big fat drops are rolling off my waterproof boonie hat in front of my eyes. Perfectly dry under my Rivers West I drift off into my hunting state and wait for daylight. Unlike clear days when light arrives in a slow progression, today, shooting light arrives from one minute to the next. For over two hours the rain continues with its same intensity, until about 7:30 when it slows just slightly. If I were in a house or in a vehicle I probably wouldn't even notice the change, but since I'm sitting out in the midst of the storm even the most subtle nuance is palpable. As though it were waiting for a brief respite in precipitation, a deer slides out of the bedding area into the draw behind me. Immediately I recognize the little buck as the same small four-pointer I saw yesterday. He crosses the draw and climbs straight up the ridge, moving in the opposite direction that I expected deer to move at this spot in the morning. The second the buck is out of sight, the rain resumes with its previous wrath.

For another hour and a half a wall of water is my only companion, even the birds and squirrels seem to have taken shelter. I busy myself counting drops and watching the small rivers that form on the bark, alternating their paths randomly. Scanning north across the creek for the thousandth time I'm met with the unexpected sight of a great buck. Standing a little over 100 yards away on the other side of the creek along the edge of the thick bedding is a tall tined ten-pointer. Even at that distance his rack is easy to see. His antlers are bone white, just like the eight-pointer from two days ago, but much larger. He has a row of three even length tines across each main beam. Three seconds to look is all I get before the buck steps forward out of sight. He appears to be heading right for the row of houses, behind which is a narrow patch of really thick bedding. Beyond the houses to the east is a forty-acre overgrown field. I can't imagine him crossing that field during daylight. That is the deer I'm after! With the buck out of sight my attention is drawn to the creek. Whereas yesterday I couldn't see any water between the banks from my perch, now I can see a brown, whirling torrent. Perhaps that was the reason why the buck didn't cross.

Not prone to panic I note the situation, well aware that I may have some difficulties finding a place to cross, and continue with my vigil. My only change in plans is to nix the all day sit. The last thing I want to do is attempt to cross the now-raging creek in the dark. At noon the rain suddenly stops, giving way within minutes to a mostly clear sky and sunshine. The sunshine is accompanied by strong gusts. By 2:00 p.m. the wind is howling and no more deer appear, so I decide my hunt is over. Hyper-aware of the problem I have to deal with, I cut straight to the creek. The water has risen to within a foot from the top of the banks, which means at most places the water is over five feet deep. I walk down the bank past my normal crossing point, over the fence and at least a quarter mile onto the neighbor's property, looking for a fallen tree, or a bridge, or anything else that might get me to the other side dry. Nothing! I know I'm trespassing, but I don't really want to spend the night waiting for the water to drop, or a couple of nights by the looks of things. I just hope I don't meet anyone, and if I do, I pray they understand my predicament. It's fairly obvious.

After about an hour of searching for a way across without any luck I decide I have no option but to get wet. About fifty yards into the pasture land the landowner has flattened the banks and created a gravel lane across the creek. Here the water now spans about twenty-five yards, and is therefore not nearly as deep as everywhere else. To help me with my footing I fashion a wading stick from a dead branch. With a deep breath I quick-step it right into the creek. The water is deep enough that it reaches the point where it really gets cold, if you know what I mean. A couple of even more expedient steps later, and I'm up the other bank, a little wetter and with a slightly higher voice, but none the worse for wear. Marching straight back to the public land I stop just over the fence and empty my boots. There is less water in them than I thought there would be. By the time I slosh back to my van the clock reads 3:30 p.m. Stripping out of my hunting clothes I toss them in plastic bags. There won't be any hunting tonight. My only option is to head to the laundromat.

My visit to town is brief, just long enough to get all my clothes clean, dry, and reactivated. After the sight of such a big buck my motivation is running high. Back out in the country I find a parking spot along a road named Possum Ridge. As usual I listen to the weather forecast, and it isn't good. There is a tornado watch in effect, and the temperature has risen above 70 degrees with high winds. There is supposedly a cold front moving in from the northwest. Perfect conditions for funnel clouds. My options are very limited since I can't get across the creek as long as the water is so high. The only other tree I could hunt is the one from my first day. Listening to the howling wind I drift to sleep.

A few hours later I awaken to even more wind. Trying to decide what to do, I turn on the radio to discover the tornado watch is now a tornado warning. Half a dozen funnel clouds have been sighted in this, and surrounding counties. Not exactly safe hunting weather. I roll over and fall back asleep, silently praying one of those tornadoes doesn't bounce me off this ridge.

Daylight arrives, and after a couple hours of sitting around, the winds still show no sign of residing. Now a little bored I decide to do some scouting. Perhaps I can use the gales to my advantage. My destination is the north end of the public land. My two-hour walk doesn't reveal much exceptional sign. The terrain is simply big woods, and deep draws, with nothing to focus deer movement towards any single point. This is the difficult aspect of big woods hunting. Without defined feeding and bedding areas the deer movement is often quite random. Pinpointing a general area that deer will move through is relatively easy, but in most spots a deer might move fifty, or even a hundred, yards either way with no rhyme nor reason why. This is great for shotgun or rifle hunting, but difficult with archery equipment. With more time I could probably unravel the deer movement here in more detail, but this is a short-term hunt and I have to cut to the chase. At midday I consult my maps and locate another parcel of public land a few miles up the road.

This four-pointer was the result of a previous frustrating and tough Ohio public land hunt.

On one side of the road there is a parking spot and another well-worn path into the woods, but on the other there is about a thirty-foot drop covered in brush. One thing I've learned about hunters is that they tend to take the path of least resistance. Most guys wouldn't even think of climbing down a steep bank, and it's impossible to get a quad up that hill, keeping even more hunters out of the woods. After lunch I slip down the bank with the intention of simply finding a spot and hunting. Honestly, at first glance the bottom of the bank doesn't look that promising. The only thing visible is a square of mature scotch pines planted in straight rows with nothing at all growing under them. However, according to my maps there is another deep wooded draw beyond the pines. Since the wind is still blowing I want to get down out of the gales, and perhaps I will catch a roaming buck moving up the draw. On my last trip to Ohio I was successful on my last evening with just such a maneuver. With a frustrating week of hunting behind me, where nothing really came together, I simply found a spot on a map and walked about a mile back into a draw and climbed up a tree. About a half-hour before dark a two-year-old four-point strolled by at ten yards. My arrow put him down following a seventy-yard sprint. There is no denying that sometimes luck is the deciding factor in bowhunting.

Beyond the pines the woods opens up into the typical deciduous forest of this area. About three quarters of a mile down the draw I find a narrow point with a suitable tree. The only buck sign is a rub here and there. I climb up and hope for the best. My reward is an evening watching seven different does and fawns filter through the area, the closest being about forty yards away.

After dark the first thing I do is drive to a spot where the creek that I forged yesterday crosses a road. The water has already dropped considerably. It is still too high for my boots, but not by much. I wish I had brought my waders along on this hunt. Waders are an important part of my hunting gear, which I left at home due simply to space considerations. Since I'm close by, I pull into Emma's country store. The place is a throwback to an earlier decade, and is a little bit of everything. Emma's is a hardware store, a party store, a pizza joint, a gas station, and in the summer time an ice cream parlor. The ice cream signs and coolers line the wall, obviously in storage until spring. You can also check your deer, if you would like. The restaurant portion is decorated with metal lunch boxes hanging from the ceiling. The sight of them takes me all the way back to kindergarten, and my own metal lunch box. I was pretty proud of that Godzilla lunchbox. Splurging a little I sit down and order a personal pizza and a cola. My body tells me I need some extra fat and calories to keep me going. Apart from the couple running the place I'm the only customer. Browsing the Ohio hunting regulations booklet I eat and enjoy the nostalgic feeling with my own long forgotten memories. After dinner it's back up to Possum Ridge for the night.

Up at 4:00 a.m. I'm surprised to find thick frost on all of my windows. Starting up the motor, and heater, I check my thermometer. It reads 23 degrees, about fifty degrees less than yesterday. This must be the cold front they had been talking about in the weather forecast. With a drop in temperature like this, the deer should be moving. The wind has also slowed to a very slight breeze out of the northwest. I jump in the driver's seat and cruise to where the creek crosses the road. To my surprise the water has dropped nearly as fast as it rose, and you would never guess that two days ago the creek had almost been over its banks. I know where I want to be. At my parking spot I dress, pulling on my wool underwear for the first time this season. The moon is full and so bright that I'm able to walk to my railroad grade birch without using a flashlight. By 5:00 a.m. I'm sitting comfortably.

The snow starts falling just after daybreak, at first just a couple errant flakes, but then heavily. Soon, fat white flakes dust the ground and by 9:30 the forest floor is white. Snow is sticking to all the stems and branches. Rain, wind, heat, tornados, clear cold skies, and now snow, could the weather change any more quickly? Splashing in the creek catches my attention. It sounds like a beaver slapping its tail before diving for cover, or perhaps a few ducks flew in and landed. Concentrating on where the sound came from I am surprised when a deer appears walking down the grade. The spike buck is dripping wet. That clears up the mystery of the splashing water. He passes at fifteen yards, strolling straight into the bedding area. His antlers have the same distinct, almost pure white coloration as three of the other bucks I've already seen in this area.

The buck is barely out of sight as I catch a glimpse of movement to my right. A single doe deliberately tiptoes down from the grade, past my tree, and straight up the draw. She is being extremely cautious, as though she doesn't quite trust the white stuff that is still falling from the sky. She is still within sight as a button buck pops up over the grade right in front of me. Unlike the doe he doesn't seem to have a care in the world. Interestingly, his buttons are polished and about an inch long, and his coat is russet colored, like it should be in the summer. Either he is really late with his fur change, or he simply has the reddest coloration I have ever seen. His path takes him up the west edge of the draw out of sight. Although I sit until 2:00 p.m., no other deer show themselves.

The next morning finds me sitting in the same tree. Today the temperature is even colder than yesterday, a mere 15 degrees. Huddled in my saddle I'm glad to have several body warmers positioned over my kidneys and on my thighs. Without them I would freeze, despite my wool underwear and windproof outerwear. 15 degrees is simply cold, and sitting still for hours on end doesn't help the situation. Right at daylight a yearling six-point meanders along the grade. His antlers share the light coloration of his brethren. He cuts straight into the bedding. When he is just out of sight I hear the unmistakable steady pace of another deer on the ridge. In a few seconds the same eight-pointer from my first hunt in the sycamore crosses the grade and follows the edge of the creek. He offers several good looks at his rack, and I think about attempting to call him in, but instead I decide to wait for the big guy. He selects the runway that angles towards the creek crossing and vanishes behind a wall of brush. I can't believe the quantity of bucks I've been seeing, six different bucks in only a hand full of hunts. I've actually seen more bucks than does. The action lasts less than five minutes.

I spend the next six hours shivering slightly and waiting for more activity. Just after 1:00 p.m. I glance across the grade and there is big ten-pointer a mere fifty yards in front of me, strolling out of the bedding area. Man, is he a nice buck. His rack is tall, wide and heavy. This is an awesome buck for public land, and a nice buck for anywhere in America. My guess is somewhere above 140, as a conservative estimate. He is on the same runway the button buck used this morning, and if he continues he will cross the grade at just under twenty yards. The wind is perfect. Slowly adjusting my weight I reach for my bow and swing into position for the anticipated shot.

Keeping my eyes on the buck, I watch him take a few steps towards me. He is now standing facing me at about forty yards. "Just ten more yards and I have a shot, just ten more yards," I find myself mentally willing him closer. From a frontal view I can see that his rack is about eighteen inches wide. For a long time he just stands still, obviously checking his surroundings. To my dismay, instead of following the runway he angles towards the creek, stopping to work a licking branch. Now about forty-five yards out, I watch him lift his head and chew on a branch and then rake the overhanging limb with his antlers. "Turn and come my way, just a little closer, come on:" again I attempt mental telepathy. It doesn't work.

The buck turns and walks straight away from me. He isn't spooked in the least. Reacting quickly I reach into my pack and retrieve my *doe in estrous* can and turn it over twice. The buck immediately puts on the brakes and stares in my direction. Nearly holding my breath I wait for his next move. Dropping his head he continues toward the creek. I turn the can over again, but he just keeps walking. Now about eighty yards distant, and still facing straight away, I reach back into my pack and pull out my rattle bag. Quite gently, not wanting to sound overwhelming, I tickle the sticks together for about three seconds. Tucking his tail the buck splashes across the creek and bolts into the bedding area, right behind the three houses, gone in a wink. Oops! Perhaps I made a mistake. That was clearly the proverbial straw that broke the camel's back. Either this buck has experienced this trick before, or he isn't the boss buck in the neighborhood. You can't win them all. Hopefully he isn't spooked to the extent that he turns completely nocturnal.

About an hour later I climb down and move up the draw to my hickory tree. From my saddle I can see that the scrapes have been hit recently. The chances of the big buck coming in are quite slim after me spooking him today, but perhaps there is another, or perhaps the eight-pointer will give me a close opportunity. I only have to wait about an hour before the action begins anew. Up out of the bedding area steps the same tiny three-pointer I saw crossing the creek during my initial morning hunt. He cuts a straight line to the scrapes, and after a brief inspection, proceeds to mark and chew on licking branches all the way around the crabapple tree. This done, he turns his attention to one of the scrapes. Tossing dirt behind him with his front hooves he clears the scrape of debris with gusto. Then, standing in the scrape, he urinates down his legs, before parting the scene by crossing the draw and climbing up over the ridge to the east.

Not even a half an hour passes before yet another buck ambles out of the bedding area. This time it's the four-point that I've already had within shooting range twice. Tracing the first buck's footsteps almost exactly, he too crosses directly under my tree, but instead of concentrating on the scrapes he veers to the left, stopping at a small patch of greenbrier. Oblivious to everything else he starts plucking the remaining leaves off the briars. He reminds me of a kid in a candy store, making sure to get every last remaining, sweet-as-can-be leaf. They sure must taste good. He even pushes right up inside the little patch to get at the leaves in the middle. It takes him until just about dark before he has eaten nearly every leaf from the patch. Nothing left, he casually strolls north, down the draw towards my birch tree. Just a few minutes later a doe followed closely by a fawn, ghost out of the bedding and crosses into the woods in the opposite direction. As soon as they vanish I climb down. On my way out I check the ladder stand for activity; nothing has changed except that the apples are gone. What a day! Any time you see five different bucks in a single public land outing, it is a good day hunting.

It's still cold the next morning as I climb up in my birch tree well before daylight. I've been putting a lot more pressure on this spot than I normally would, but the rut is in progress and I haven't been able to locate any other comparable locations on my afternoon jaunts in the big woods. Just after daylight, movement catches my attention on the grade and out of the bedding area walks a guy carrying a shotgun. He is at least forty and has a full gray beard. In a still-hunting fashion he soft steps it up the draw, never noticing my presence. He is only out of sight a few minutes before another shotgun toting hunter sneaks along the other side of the creek. What is going on? Are these guys rabbit hunting? At any rate I decide to bail. I slide down my tree, stopping at the base to turn my hat inside out to its hunter orange side. I also slip a two sided orange vest out from under my coat to wear as an outer, just a precaution so as not to get shot. At my parking spot I find three other cars parked next to my van. Irritated by the situation I grab the Ohio hunting regulations and have a look. The beginning of gun season is still a while off. Today is the first day of the special youth shotgun season. I guess I should have read the youth season dates earlier, but since I very, very seldom hunt with a gun I just didn't pay close attention to that part of the regulations booklet. This is the second time this season that this has happened to me. Both of the guys I saw must be awfully mature looking teenagers.

Curious about the amount of hunting pressure, I drive around the section containing the public land to the north. Ten cars are parked at various places along the route. Continuing on, I tour all the public hunting areas nearby, only to find vehicles parked at just about every available pullout. Although I occasionally hunt with archery equipment during gun season, I don't like to do so unless I have a solid plan that involves escape routes, or I am on private property where gun hunting isn't allowed. Neither of those are the case, so I decide to take the remainder of the weekend off, sort of an unplanned vacation in southeastern Ohio. It's time to relax a bit. Though I'm here to hunt, it is also clear to me that bowhunting for whitetails is something that cannot be pursued with a forced hand. In my opinion, a good bowhunter is able to accept changing conditions and deal with them. There are simply times when it is better not to hunt than to hunt. I point my van towards a state park campground about fifteen miles south. The price for a parking spot for two nights is thirty dollars, and the only reason it is worth it is the unlimited access to hot showers. As soon as I check in I pull up to the shower house and dive in. Although I've been regularly dumping cold water over my head at midday and washing outside, nothing beats the real thing. The colder it gets the more uncomfortable those half-gallon wash-downs become. With a whole afternoon to kill I head back to town.

The first stop is, as usual, the laundromat, followed by a visit to the small supermarket to pick up a few things. This takes me about an hour. Now I'm sitting in a town where I really don't need anything, nor do I have any business here. To burn some time I pull into the local sporting goods store. There is nothing that catches my eye, so I'm back out in fifteen minutes. The national forest ranger station is just up the road. Paying a quick visit I check their maps for any new land purchases nearby. There aren't any. This is more difficult than I thought it would be, killing time. On a whim I drive to the old downtown, just looking around. A block past the post office I encounter the city library. Perfect. Certainly it is possible to burn a few hours in a library. On the inside the library is very modern, tidy and larger than I expected. Off to one side is a room full of computers. Following a short sign up procedure I get busy filtering through two and a half months of unchecked email. With this finished I browse the stacks, concentrating on their selection of both deer biology and hunting books, and spending some time with a book about native flora in southeastern Ohio. Finally, I settle into a comfortable armchair with a newspaper. About an hour before nightfall I drive back up to my hunting grounds to count cars. There is only one parked at my favorite spot, but seven more up towards the north end, most of them along the private property.

Yet another hot shower at 3:00 a.m. marks the resumption of my hunting. The short gun season must have made its mark on the deer movement. Despite spending half a day in my sycamore along the creek, and the evening in a deep draw I don't see a single deer. Undaunted, by the lack of deer sightings I park for another night back up along Possum Ridge.

One of the many small bucks I saw while hunting in Ohio.

Tired again from a long day outside, sleep comes quickly. Sometime in the middle of the night I awaken to the glare of headlights. Lying in my sleeping bag I hear the door of a pick-up slam shut. Shortly, the beam of a flashlight bounces around to the back of my van and then to the driver's door. I listen as whomever it is attempts to open the door. This is my cue to jump up and confront the person trying to get into my van. Standing in the window the guy with the flashlight seems startled to see me. Rolling the window open a crack I ask the gentleman if I can help him. In quick, stumbling words he claims to live up the road, and since my van doesn't have front license plates he thought it was stolen. Front license plates are required in Ohio, but not in Michigan. Nothing like a little public service in the middle of the night. "I'm just catching a little shut-eye before getting up and hunting in a couple hours;" the words are barely out my mouth before the guy is back in his Chevy driving away. My clock reads 2:24 a.m. The bars just let out a few minutes ago. After the interrupted rest I can't fall back asleep. In less than an hour I'm up and driving to my hunting spot.

The last gravel road runs steeply down the ridge and curves just a little before it ends at the county highway. The corner is about a half mile from my parking spot. As my van rolls to a stop I have trouble believing my eyes. There, just across the county highway, stands the big ten-pointer. He's only a few yards into the fallow field, angling slightly across the beam of my headlights. With my foot on the brakes I stare at the buck. His rack is unmistakable with its row of three equal length tines. For a full five seconds he stands rock still staring back at me, before turning straight away towards the ridge behind the field. From behind, the curve of his main beams looks a lot wider than his body. Stepping back on the gas pedal I speed to my parking spot. That buck is heading for his bedding area, and perhaps I can cut him off.

As quickly and as calmly as possible I dress and begin my walk into the woods, the whole time mentally working through my options. Twice I've seen this buck at midday along the creek, but now he's heading for the big woods to the south. Perhaps he's entering the bedding area via those woods at the southwest corner. Perhaps he will check the primary scrape area for estrous does. I decide to hunt my hickory in the corner. Covertly as possible but hustling through the long walk along the creek and up the draw, it's well before daylight as I get settled in.

At first light a single doe angles across the draw from southeast to northwest, passing into the bedding area approximately fifty yards from me. For a couple hours nothing else happens, until about 8:30 when movement along the west edge of the draw reveals itself as the red-coated button buck. He passes fifteen yards from my tree before entering the woods to the south and then following the woodline towards the ladder stand in the other corner. To get here he must have walked right by my birch tree, just like he did the last occasion I saw him. About the time I begin to call my hunting spot selection into question, a flash of antler pulls me out of my bout of second-guessing. There he is! The big ten-pointer. Walking like he has a clear destination in mind, he is down the ridge in a matter of minutes. Now in the draw, it looks as though he will come in to scent-check the scrapes. This is the moment I've been waiting for. With my bow in my hand I very cautiously, and painfully slow, get into position for a shot, anticipating the opening he will cross though. Coming ever closer he is now only about seventy yards away. Sixty yards. Fifty yards. My heart begins to race. He doesn't have a clue of my presence. All of a sudden he stops, his nose tight to the ground. He is standing right where the doe walked through early this morning. "No! This can't be happening!" He lifts his head and looks for a split second towards the scrapes. The pause is short, and my fear quickly becomes reality. The next thing I know the buck reminds me of a beagle following a rabbit. Without lifting his head even once he traces the exact steps of the doe right into the thick brush. A halfhearted attempt with a *doe in estrous* call and a grunt tube reaps nothing more than a short glance. After he is gone I look at my watch. It reads 10:30. Hoping for his return I hunker down in the hickory until dark, and spend the entire next day there as well, but he doesn't show.

Thanksgiving morning is my last hunt in Ohio. Up in my birch tree well before daybreak I hope for a little last minute magic. My hopes are dashed when just at daylight another bowhunter walks down the grade carrying a climbing stand on his back. He turns up the draw and passes within twenty yards of me without ever noticing the lurking bowhunter above him. Right in the center of the draw about eighty yards away he stops. Soon the click-click, click-click, click-click of his climber echoes through the forest. I don't mind sharing the woods, and other hunters is just part of the game while hunting public land, but he's a little close and I have an appointment for later today. Before he is even all the way up his tree, I'm down mine. Despite locating a big buck in Ohio, I get to go home empty handed. Not every successful hunt can be measured in inches of antler. However, the journey itself was worth the price. I should be able to make it to my Grandma's house back in Michigan before Thanksgiving dinner.

What To Do

- If your original plan doesn't work out, keep adjusting and looking for new options. The only way you'll be successful is by being adaptive. Remember, this style of hunting demands that you be able to adjust what you planned to do.
- Investigate even the smallest tracts of public ground, there are hidden treasures out there. Tiny five-ten acre jems often lie hidden from most public knowledge.
- Compare public land borders to reliable maps; sometimes bordering landowners shorten things up a bit.

Chapter 9

Michigan: Suburbs and a Refuge in December Snow

Three days after Thanksgiving I'm back at my brother's place. He has three days off work, and we plan to hunt together. It's the end of November and the guns of fall have been blazing for almost two weeks. True to form in central Michigan, the pressure has caused most of the deer to take cover, now moving almost exclusively in the middle of the night. The vast majority of the bucks were killed on opening day of gun season, and the few survivors aren't that inclined to show themselves. Bowhunting now is tough, and the gun hunters, who have lessened the already slim chances of an encounter with a mature buck, slammed most of Jon's hunting spots hard. That is, except for one spot a short drive to the south.

The subdivision was built to give its inhabitants the illusion of seclusion. Its many cul-de-sacs follow the high ground ridges through a remnant of cedar swamp. The swamp is near a river bottom that extends through the surrounding farmland, several parks, an exclusive golf course, and right into town. The patchwork of ownership along the river, with its many protected areas, has led to a very high deer density, probably more than a hundred deer per square mile along its banks. In fact, if you walk through the parks you will find woods that are completely over-browsed with virtually no natural forest regeneration, and a neatly trimmed browse line about six feet high. The few smaller, remaining spruce and cedars remind one of Japanese bonsai, kept miniature by hungry deer. Fortunately, there are abundant crops all around. These deer would suffer badly if we still had occasional long, hard winters. The local hunters haven't missed the fact that there are a lot of deer, and the hunting pressure is extreme where hunting is allowed. On the private property adjacent to the parks the property borders are lined with gunning box-blinds. Nonetheless, due to the protected areas there are always a few nice bucks that survive the onslaught. The houses in the subdivision are of the trophy variety, all very spacious and opulent, and each sits a parcel of five to ten acres. Generally there are two houses at the end of each cul-de-sac. A resident population of deer lives year-round in the subdivision, mostly does and fawns, but also a few bucks. They bed in the yards and in the strips of swamp between the houses during the day and visit the surrounding farmland at night. As soon as the gun hunting begins, the deer population in the subdivision seems to double, if not triple, and usually a mature buck or two arrives just before the lead starts flying. They seem to know very well that gun hunting is prohibited here.

A group of deer bedded in the subdivision. Notice the house in the upper right corner.

Four years ago Jon received experimental permission on ten acres in the subdivision from a landowner whose wife had simply had enough of the deer eating everything she tried to plant. There were only two stipulations. The first was that as many deer as possible must be taken off his property. The second was that he was to keep a very low profile so that the immediate neighbors had no idea hunting was going on, even though bowhunting is perfectly legal in the neighborhood. Apparently the direct neighbors are staunch anti-hunters, and the landowner didn't want any neighborly strife.

Maintaining a low profile means a couple different things. First and foremost it simply means not hanging out the "I'm a bowhunter" banner. The landowner gave him an assigned parking spot, right next to his garage, and asked that no stands or tree-steps be left hanging in the trees. It also means refraining from wearing any camouflage while scouting, and simply not allowing himself to be seen. Hunting is also primarily done on weekdays, when most of the neighbors are at work.

In such a situation short shots at deer are a must for a couple reasons. Ten acres just doesn't allow deer much room to run, and they should fall within sight. Asking the neighbors to pursue a wounded deer across their place could potentially ruin a really good situation. Gut piles must also disappear. The last thing a hunter can afford to do in tight quarters is leave a gut pile in plain sight in the woods. In places like this there is great potential for conflict, and one tiny mistake can cost you your hunting permission. That first fall Jon killed several does, regularly giving a report to the landowner, and offering the family venison from an entire deer. The venison was kindly declined with the explanation that no one in the household would eat venison. The landowner's wife was particularly pleased with Jon's effort, noting that she saw fewer deer out her window since he started hunting. The following year he was rewarded with the permission to hunt five more acres in the subdivision belonging to another neighbor, adjacent to the initial ten. Since then he has sole permission on fifteen acres of prime suburban hunting land. These fifteen acres is our hunting destination.

The outside temperature gauge in Jon's truck reads seventeen degrees as we stop in a convenience store parking lot to change into our hunting clothes about a mile from the subdivision. Normally we dress where we hunt, but in the subdivision our designated parking spot is really close to where the deer are, and close to where the neighbors could see us, so we make an exception. Though we still strive to be as scent free as possible, these suburban deer are somewhat more accustom to human scent than those at most of our other hunting areas. The last mile of our drive ends at the parking spot next to the garage. Stepping outside we silently retrieve our bows and packs from the bed of Jon's Chevy.

My walk is short. At the base of the tree Jon and I wish each other luck. He vanishes into the cedar swamp, and I start with my tree-steps. Shortly, I'm thirty feet up the poplar tree, snug in my saddle. The poplar has grown close to the trunk of a hemlock, whose outstretched branches provide excellent cover. In my tree I'm only about ninety yards from the landowner's back porch, and probably two hundred yards from the neighbor's garage. Looking through the woods I can see four more houses nearby. The way the houses are situated creates a funnel of sorts at this point. The deer skirt the landowner's backyard, on one of four runways that extend between the neighbor's house and another home across the woods, and eventually enter a particularly thick patch of cedars to bed. To the edge of the landowner's backyard is a twenty-yard shot. Actually, if not for a sliding glass door in the way, I could have an open, albeit long, shot all the way into his kitchen and dining room, though I don't imagine many deer sit at the dining room table. The landowner and his family know we are here, and merely have to look out the window to observe me in my tree.

Jon has selected a tree at the opposite end of the property, at the terminus of the cedars. He is hunting the main crossing where the deer return to the bedding in the morning after their night of feeding in the surrounding crops. Here too, it is the position of the houses that dictate the general deer movement patterns. Important for his spot is the row of houses across the road, behind which are large fields. His tree would just be another tree in the swamp if it weren't for the narrow strip of brush and poplars between two houses. It happens to be the only path with cover from the swamp to the fields, and the deer use it, even though it is bordered closely on both sides by houses. His tree is about eighty yards into the swamp from the road. Initially he selected a tree a little closer, but the deer kept running past him as they

My brother, Jon, with one of
his many nice bucks.

dashed into the swamp whenever an automobile approached; rarely do deer just walk across
the road as a car is approaching. As it is now, they stop about thirty yards short of his tree
and resume a more relaxed pace past his tree on their way to bed down. If deer cross the road
they generally do so right before, or just after, daylight. Fortunately, he is also in a position to
intercept lateral movement through the swamp. His tree is at the tip of a narrow opening that
functions as a hub of deer activity at that end of the cedars.

A couple minutes after 6:00 a.m. the lights in the house turn on. One by one the family
members show up in the kitchen. Keeping one eye open for deer I follow the activity in the
house with the other, though I feel a bit awkward and voyeuristic witnessing a family's morning

routine from their backyard. A short while later the garage door opens and the landowner's Jeep pulls out. His daughter in her car follows him. It is just cracking daylight when movement at the other corner of the lawn catches my attention. A doe and fawn are coming my way. It's not even a minute after I spot the deer that the garage door opens again. This time the landowner's son steps out and walks down to the corner. Although he is only forty yards from the deer as he leaves the house, they just stand there and watch him walk away. A few minutes later a school bus rolls up, turns around at the corner, beeping as it backs up, and drives off. The exhaust from the bus has barely dissipated when the neighbor's garage door groans open. Their two cars pull out of the driveway in quick succession. They are out of sight before the door closes. Yellow flashing lights give away the garbage truck before I even see it. It turns into the cul-de-sac, stops, and a garbage man attaches two plastic garbage cans to the hydraulic lift, with a dull thump emptying their contents into the mobile trash bin. As soon as the cans hit the pavement the garbage man slides each in its own direction. It sounds like two base drums rolling across the pavement. The smell of exhaust fills the air as the truck moves on to the next dead end. Through all this raucous the two deer act like nothing at all is happening. As casual as can be, they browse in my direction, and, after crossing by at less than twenty yards, eventually bed down thirty yards from the neighbor's garage, in plain sight between the two houses.

This behavior is a testament to the amazing adaptability of the white-tailed deer. Here, in a severely altered environment, these deer have learned that all of these sounds and actions present little or no danger. Even the stark smell of human scent causes little reaction if it comes from the usual neighborhood sources. They don't even bother to stand up from their beds when a lady walking her golden retriever circles the cul-de-sac mere yards from their selected resting spot. I know, however, that if I make the slightest audible mistake, or if they catch human scent from an unusual spot, they will be on high alert. The deer are able to distinguish between the normal sounds and actions of the neighborhood and any foreign intrusion, regardless of how subtle. About a half-hour later the landowner's garage door opens again, and his wife pulls out in her SUV, passing within thirty yards of the bedded deer. They don't even flinch. Finally, the neighborhood is quiet.

For about an hour the doe and fawn lie there chewing their cuds before standing and meandering off around the corner of the neighbor's house. Those two barely out of sight, five more deer, two does and three fawns, cross the yard, passing within easy shooting distance of the back deck, right into my corner. It appears to be a typical matriarchal group. The lead doe has a big body and a really long nose, giving away her age. She is cautious, stopping every few steps and staring up into the trees. It appears as though she has survived several bow seasons and knows where to look for lurking bowhunters. Sitting perfectly still, and fortunately surrounded by hemlock boughs, I manage to let her pass without getting my cover blown. Accompanying her is a younger doe, and three fawns; two of them are doe fawns and the third a button buck. Following the big doe's lead, the group filters through the corner and proceeds into the cedars out of sight. They aren't gone long before another single deer appears out of the swamp behind me. This time a yearling four-pointer crosses the corner, tracing the steps of the other deer. As the young buck parts I silently wish him luck, hoping that he makes it through the remainder of the season. The muzzleloader season follows on the heals of the gun season in Michigan.

A couple more hours pass vacant of any more deer activity, and my watch informs me that it's time that my brother should be showing up. We agreed to sit until noon. He doesn't show, and another hour passes. With nothing much happening I wax philosophical, thinking about the irony of hunting literally within shot distance of a house. There are most likely more deer in this neighborhood right now than in the more traditional farmland nearby. With sprawl continually creeping out into farmland, more and more bowhunters face the inevitable situation of suburban hunting every year, with its myriad of opportunities and difficulties. The deer are wild and this is hunting, it's just the manmade habitat that makes the situation unusual. The opportunities are obvious. The patchwork nature of development often creates a great deal of protected area, and a lot of edge that deer love. This usually leads

I saw this four-pointer several times on this short hunt.

to an abundance of deer, if not an outright overabundance. This situation can allow some bucks to reach maturity that would be otherwise killed in most other more traditional areas. The houses and other development sometimes create tight funnels that the deer have to use. Finding a spot like this can lead to a wall full of trophy bucks.

The difficulties, however, are just as obvious. Gaining access to good suburban hunting is a challenge, to say the least. It's just not easy, and often requires a stroke of luck to land. Most of the best hunting is in affluent neighborhoods where the lot size is larger and hunters tend not to be the most welcome. The limited size of the properties is also a restriction. You just can't get out after a buck if he happens to be moving through a few hundred yards away. And you have to be able to tolerate typical suburban interruptions, like kids building a fort right in the middle of the bedding area (there happens to be a nice looking fort about a hundred yards behind me) or neighborhood dogs out for a jaunt on their own, or even anti-hunting neighbors. This doesn't even begin to consider the social and political confrontations deer cause in neighborhoods. The rules of engagement change substantially in a suburban setting as opposed to hunting in more traditional settings. Suburban bowhunting will become more and more common in the future, and will also be a source of plenty of local political conflict.

It's now after 1:30 p.m. Jon must have something interesting happening, or he would be here by now. Punctuality is one of his virtues, at least when it comes to hunting. It's an unwritten understanding in our hunting group that being late usually means hot hunting action. Not a second after this thought I catch sight of him clandestinely sneaking through the cedars in my direction. I hurry down my tree and meet him at the truck. His tardiness is quickly explained. After watching several does and fawns all morning, at around 10:00 a.m. a 120-class eight-pointer entered the scene from the south. The buck crossed through the cedars and bedded down just off the other end of the narrow opening, about seventy yards away. A few subtle calling attempts were simply ignored. There was nothing Jon could do but sit and wait, hoping that either a passing doe would bring him in his direction, or just by chance the buck would come closer. Lying in plain sight he watched the deer for almost three hours. Just after 1:00 p.m. the buck stood, but instead of moving closer he walked straight north, crossing a road into another subdivision. Jon is visibly excited as he relates his story. This is the biggest buck he has seen locally in quite some time. In central Michigan a 120-class buck is far more seldom than a 150-class buck in most other areas in the Midwest.

Hunting refuge

We spend the next two mornings hunting in the subdivision. Though each hunt is chock full of deer sightings, including a couple of yearling bucks, neither one of us catches another glimpse of the big eight-point. My season is almost over, but I have five more days planned for a special permit hunt at a place called Shiawassee.

Shiawassee is a wildlife refuge twenty-five miles south of Saginaw Bay. For those unfamiliar with Michigan's geography, Saginaw Bay is the bay in Lake Huron that separates the "Thumb"

Sights like these are quite common in many subdivision all throughout America.

from the rest of the state. The refuge was established in 1953 around the convergence of the Tittabawassee, Flint, Cass, and Shiawassee rivers to protect remaining critical waterfowl habitat along the Great Lakes migration route. The entire area surrounding the refuge is known as the Shiawassee Flats, and is historically one of the largest wetland ecosystems in Michigan. Untouched until the lumber industry showed up in the late 1800's the Flats covered about ten counties. It consisted of flat sandy marshland surrounded by low hills, and was hunting grounds for several early cultures, and later the Odowa, and Ojibwa tribes. Besides the still-present whitetails and waterfowl, they hunted marten, fisher, otter, elk and bear. On the heels of the lumber industry removing the trees came the farmers. Starting in 1903 farmers began draining the marsh and transforming it into farmland. By 1950 a system of pumps, dikes, and drainage created an extensive agricultural area, including the 9,000 plus acres that are now refuge. Nowadays the refuge is not only surrounded by farmland, there are several nearby industrial cities. The Flats is now heavily populated, and the tentacles of a city called Saginaw actually wrap around the refuge directly to the North. It's not a stretch to imagine the refuge surrounded completely by "development" in the not-so-distant future, but for now it offers a decent chance at a mature whitetail buck in December; something that can't be said about too many other places I could hunt in Michigan.

There are a variety of hunts offered in the refuge; there are bow hunts, muzzleloader hunts and shotgun hunts. Each one is by draw-only, based on a point system. Depending on what hunt you choose to apply for, your chances of being drawn range from 10 to 100 percent. With the point system in place, the hunt I applied for is good for a permit about every other year. My five-day bow hunt begins on December 1st. Since I have nothing prepared for my initial morning hunt, I arrive a little after daylight.

The refuge access-point parking lot is full. In fact, it reminds me of a truck dealership. There are fifteen newer, full-sized trucks, all of them four-wheel drive, and most with extended cabs. By the looks of things, you could almost assume a trip to the local Ford or Chevy dealer was a requirement to purchase a refuge permit. My old rusty Astro van is the odd vehicle in the bunch.

It is crisp and cold and my thermometer reads 19 degrees when I jump out of the engine-heated driver's seat into the parking lot. The thin dusting of snow creeks and squeaks under my boots as I step around and slide open the side door. My mountain bike is the first item I pull from my van. The refuge is measured in square miles, so this will be my main mode of transportation to get me back away from the masses. My plan is to ride a couple of miles into the refuge and hopefully hunt undisturbed deer. With the bike leaning on my back bumper I dress lightly, pulling on a single pair of long underwear under my Scent Lok. The remainder of my insulated under layers are first zipped inside plastic bags and then stuffed in my hunting pack. The last addition to my pack is my lunch, the usual mix of granola and chocolate bars, a couple apples, and some water. Finally, with a short length of rope I tie one of its ends to my bow's riser, run it through a loop on my pack, and then knot the other end to the riser. With my bow firmly tied to the back of my pack I can ride without it getting in the way. The rope allows the bow to hang square across my back or, if the trail narrows, it can be spun to my right or left side.

Before jumping on my bike I study my maps and topo-photos one last time; my intended destination is a farm unit surrounded by flood units a couple miles north. The refuge is divided into units: farm units, flood units, and forest units. A system of dikes and pump stations allow controlled flooding of the different units. The flood rotation varies from year to year, and season to season. If the flood units happen not to be flooded, they are great deer bedding areas, usually far away from the woods. This tid-bit of information is from some friends who have hunted Shiawassee previously, and from my single visit to the refuge a few years back during their once a year, weekend in September, open house. My assumption is that most hunters will stick to the woods, as they are accustomed, so I want to attempt to hunt the more open zones from the ground.

Hitting the pedals I roll north, following the lane atop one of the dikes. The dikes are almost all topped with good lanes suitable for large-scale farming equipment, and easy to ride. There are several square miles of agriculture within the refuge. I intentionally take the route out away from the woods. Riding slow, I'm looking for any place with an abundance of tracks in the fresh snow. In the first mile there isn't much sign at all. The second mile proves more of the same. A square flood unit full of cattails, which I pegged on my map as an out of the way bedding area, is unfortunately filled with water. Arriving along the edge of the Tittabawassee River I follow the last dike as it curves back east. Reaching the northern tip of the southern half of the refuge, where a small patch of cattails and trees form a small bedding area about a mile from any woods, my heart sinks. Lying on the edge of the dike are three mountain bikes, exactly where I intended to leave my own. I pause and stare out across the farm unit. After a minute or two my gaze casts upon another hunter who demonstratively stands up from his hiding spot in the cattails. A few seconds later another hunter appears out of the reeds about a hundred yards beyond the first. The two hunters simply stand so I can see them. The message is loud and clear. This corner of the refuge is occupied. Obviously, my hunting plan wasn't nearly as novel as I thought. Okay, time for plan B.

Leaving my intended destination to the other bowhunters I hit the pedals again, riding another mile to the intersection of a forest unit and flood unit. This flood unit is also under water. That was plan B. Plan C? Plan C is to start from scratch, scout, and simply find the deer. Rolling slowly through the woods I glide back south. The forest units consist overwhelmingly of tall, mature maples; most of the trees don't have a branch until about thirty feet. Too many years with too many deer have left the woods wide open, almost absent of undergrowth. There is so little undergrowth in most areas that I'm able to look several hundred yards into the forest. Deer movement through areas like this is just too random for my liking. In a couple areas I discover thin strips of marsh and lowland brush through the forest. Near each of these are mountain bikes lying conspicuously along the two-track. Every decent-looking spot I encounter already has someone hunting there, all the way to the parking lot. My seven-mile bike ride was a real eye-opener. It's going to be more difficult to get away from the masses than I expected.

Frustrated with the fact that mountain bikes have become standard equipment while hunting in this refuge, I attempt to regroup at my van. The good thing about Shiawassee is that it is huge; there are twelve or thirteen square miles open during this particular hunt. There are numerous access points around the perimeter. Preparing to change locations I lift my bike into my van, and quickly stow my Scent Lok, bow, and pack. A little overheated from my long ride, I sit in the sliding doorway of my van and look over my maps and photos, trying to decide where to explore next. Comparing my driving map to my topo photos and to some hand drawn maps from my friends I begin to develop a new plan, or at least compiling a mental list of areas I could scout. My scheming is interrupted as I glance east just as a group of deer burst over a dike that separates a small, cut cornfield from the woods behind it. Tails waving high, seven deer trot to the middle of the field, stop, and stare back towards the woods. Another hunter must have bumped those deer out into the open. Immediately my attention focuses on the big-racked buck in the midst of the group. He is a smoker! His tall, dark antlers are easy to distinguish even at over two hundred yards. The buck is every bit as big as the one I was chasing in Ohio, maybe bigger. For several seconds the deer just stand still, clearly taking appraisal of their situation. Finally, a mature doe resumes the lead and begins to speed-walk straight towards the parking lot. Her pace is just shy of a trot and she clearly wants to get out of that field in a swift manner. Another doe follows. Before long the entire group is strung in a line moving fast in my direction, the buck in fourth position.

Not quite believing my eyes I peer through the tinted windows opposite me to see where they could be heading. Bordering the parking lot on the north side is a fallow field of grass that extends about two hundred yards to an east-west running dike, and half mile west to a small strip of trees along the river. The strip of trees could be their destination. With my attention focused back to the deer I notice they are indeed still coming my way, and if they maintain the same course they will cross within twenty or thirty yards of my van. When opportunity knocks, you'd better answer the door.

A jolt of adrenaline shoots through me. Trying to remain calm I hastily retrieve my bow from its soft case, fish my release and range finder from my pack, and grab my quiver from its resting place atop one of my plastic tubs. Using the red Ford parked two spots over as cover, I slip around the back of my van to the driver's side. Now standing next to the driver's door I'm able to watch the deer through the side, and front windows. Hidden from view I fumble my release onto my wrist and knock an arrow. Right in front of me is a dark brown, wooden fence and a grey boulder half buried in the ground. It isn't exactly a natural ground blind but the van, the fence, and the rock provides awesome cover. Crouching behind the fence I laser, for reference, the distance to a patch of thistle with my range finder. Thirty-three yards. All the time the deer are closing in.

The lead doe drops into the ditch that separates the cornfield from the access road to the refuge. In a second she is across the road into the tall grass. Not erring even a little from her course she is soon standing right in front of me, just short of the thistle patch. Thirty yards. Perfect. Thirty yards from the ground is just about right. Any closer is too close, and any farther is a tough shot. Completely unaware of my presence she is past me in seconds. The second doe is only steps behind and also passes right in front of me without even looking in my direction. Shifting my weight I adjust for the shot by dropping my knees to the ground. From my knees I can shoot over the fence between my van and the boulder. The buck is now standing on the access road and only has come about thirty yards closer. "This can't be happening!" I think. "I'm sitting here in blue and grey, long underwear in a parking lot with a big buck almost within shooting range. Just a little bit closer."

Suddenly, before I even comprehend the change all the deer twist their heads to the south, and the next thing I know white bobbing tails are waving good-bye up over the dike straight north. I was right, it just can't happen like that, perhaps for a first-time hunter, but not for a grizzled, bowhunting veteran like myself.

Wondering what happened I stand and look to the south as well. There, easing up to the last corner is yet another truck. I slip back around to the other side of my van, return my bow to its case, and pull on a pair of jeans. The truck creeps to the end of the road, revs into the parking lot, coming to a stop just a few yards away. The tinted window rolls down revealing a talkative red-faced old farmer. His first question is whether or not I saw all those deer. "Yeah, I saw them alright." Chatting for a few minutes I discover that the farmer lives around the corner a couple of miles and was just out for a drive to see how many hunters were out, and to see if he could spot any deer. After a while, he wishes me good luck and drives off. Perfect timing. Manitou must have been teasing me, and I'll actually have to get out and hunt if I want to kill a nice buck in the Shiawassee Flats.

The next access parking lot proves less popular than the first; there are only three trucks parked there as I pull in. Jumping on my bike I get moving. For two hours I crunch gravel on tractor lanes, getting an overview of the general area, stopping here and there for a couple short jaunts into the bush. Apart from meeting two guys walking down the main access road I don't run into any other hunters. In early afternoon I discover an interesting area that consists of a row of mature maples lining a dike along a branch of one of the rivers. An oval shaped patch of young, thick poplars a couple acres in size near a hundred acres of marshy bedding, all rife with big, shaggy rubs and numerous scrapes, put an exclamation point on the spot. The sheer quantity of buck sign, not to mention the enormous size of both the rubs and scrapes, is more than anyplace I've seen all fall. How incredible it would be to be able to hunt this area in a normal fashion, but the limited access is exactly the ingredient that makes these draw hunts on refuges interesting. Quite optimistic I climb one of the ubiquitous sugar maples and settle in for a cold and uneventful evening. Just before dark, a doe and a fawn amble down the top of the dike, veering off to one side and eventually swim across the river, which surprisingly isn't frozen yet.

After a very cold night parked along a nearby highway I am back up in the same tree well before daylight. Two inches of fresh snow cover the ground and it's still under 20 degrees. Just after daylight movement along the dike catches my attention. A hunter, toting a climbing stand on his back, sneaks in my direction, pausing often. As I watch him I wonder whether he has noticed my footprints, which should be clearly evident in the fresh snow. The closer he gets the slower he walks, stopping occasionally to look into the trees. My hope is that he walks past, and keeps right on walking. However, just twenty-five yards away he stops at the base of a maple and begins to attach his stand. With a short "Hey", I get his attention and let him know that I'm already hunting here. Totally surprised to see me in the tree the guy apologizes and walks farther down the dike. To my dismay he climbs up another tree less than a hundred yards away. In a mild rage I hustle down my tree, and back out to my bike, which I parked conspicuously on top of the dike. The other guy's bike is parked next to my own, and he nearly followed my footsteps into the woods. With a hundred hunters swarming the refuge this week, the rules of hunting etiquette must be different than normal, if there even is such a thing. Bumping into other hunters is just part of the game. The good thing is, mature bucks can appear anywhere at any second, as my parking lot encounter proves.

Nonetheless, to burn off my simmering temper at having my set-up invaded, I jump on the pedals with some gusto and a little cursing under my breath, not sure where I'm heading. As I ride I check for fresh track in the snow. Unfortunately, the majority of tracks are knobby lines left by mountain bikes. Several bike riders covered the mile from the parking lot to the last major intersection, most of them turning north, but some south and two straight ahead. Completely frustrated with the situation I ride towards the parking lot, wondering what I should do next. Perhaps there is an access point with no lanes to ride on. Here and there sets of deer tracks cross the road, but there is no indication of heavy activity until I get close to the parking area. The tracks of about a dozen deer follow a narrow row of thick brush only a hundred yards from the parking lot. It looks as though I have to change my tactics. With all the hunters riding back to the far corners of the refuge, it seems the deer have moved up front. I too, shot right past without giving this area much consideration. The tracks lead into some thicker woods behind an overgrown field bordering the parking spot. It's time to set out on foot.

Heading for the corner of the thicker woods I cross the opening that was once a field. Along the back edge lies an oval of red willow about thirty yards long, and ten yards across. Just as I begin to circle the red brush, a buck bolts out of its center, tail at half-mast. The 100-class eight point flees straight north disappearing within seconds. He was bedded eighty yards from the parking lot, and probably watched half a dozen hunters, including myself, ride right by! Continuing on, I cut through the corner and run into an ancient ditch that creates the only noticeable rise in the ground in this entire section of woods. In areas where there isn't much terrain variation, even the smallest change will attract activity. As I suspected, a well-used runway traces the edge of the ditch. Taking a hint from the deer I follow the ditch straight north. It parallels the edge of thicker brush, and eventually extends into a marsh of tall reed grass near one of the rivers. The ditch is a travel route from this bedding to the crops about a half-mile away. There are a few rubs, but nothing spectacular. This area is, at first glance, not as obvious as the others I've attempted so far, but the best thing is: there aren't any boot tracks in the snow. Perhaps I will encounter some more normal deer movement here. Just shy of the reed grass, I select a tree at an intersection of two runways. The first runway is the one I walked in on, and the second circles the edge of the marsh. My hope is that a buck will either wander out of the reed grass on his way to the crops this evening, or trace the edge of the marsh. Maybe that eight-point from the patch of red brush will circle back, or perhaps another hunter will push a big buck past me. Considering all the hunters working these woods, anything can happen.

The hours pass slowly and I'm unable to relax. The irritation at the collapse of all my hunting plans for the refuge so far plagues me, even though I've already seen two bucks I would shoot in the first two days. At around 2:30 I'm still grumbling to myself when from the south a deer appears in the snow, walking in my direction. The yearling six-point follows almost my exact steps along the old ditch, under my tree at twenty yards, and into the marsh grass. He moves quickly and stops several times to glance behind, as though he was jumped and wants to make the security of the marsh. This young buck is the only deer I see all day. At prime time, a half-hour before dark, yet another bowhunter still-hunts from the northwest along the edge of marsh, past my tree, towards the parking lot.

And so it continues the next three days. Though I try my best to solve the riddle of the refuge I never see another buck, and another hunter interrupts almost every hunt. I wish there were a dramatic ending to my hunt, but it just doesn't happen that way.

With my last hunt over I load my van and begin my drive home. A beckoning highway gas station pulls me into its more-than-daylight fluorescence. Reaching into the glove compartment for my wallet I jump out to buy a bottle of Coke. Halfway to the door I stop abruptly and return to my van. Before driving away I pull a dollar from my wallet and tuck it in the front pocket of my shirt; the first dollar for next year's budget for on-the-road hunting season.

What To Do

- Near cities, whitetail hunting can be some of the best, providing an opportunity at good bucks.
- Low profile hunting is critical for hunting more urban areas.
- Consider a mountain bike a useful tool for some hunting situations where motorized vehicles aren't allowed.
- Consider applying to limited-entry refuge or state park hunts.
- Be considerate when hunting public land.
- Keep in mind that the only way to hunt public land is with an open mind and a lot of patience. Public means that it is open for anyone to hunt there, and you may encounter someone who had the same idea as you.

Hunting Statistics

- States Hunted: North Dakota, Wisconsin, Missouri, Michigan, and Ohio
- Months Hunted: September, October, November, and December
- Number of Hunts: 70
- Number of Different Days on Which I Hunted: 53
- Travel Days: 10 (Scouting days make up most of the difference.)
- Total Deer Sightings While Hunting: 227 (average; 4.28 per day, and 3.24 per hunt)
- Total Buck Sightings: 52 (average 1 [.98] buck per day, and .74 per hunt) (I estimate 20 bucks at 2 years of age or older)
- Total Doe Sightings: 79
- Total Fawn Sightings: 96
- Average Antlered Buck to Mature Doe Ratio of Sightings: 1 to 1.52 (the ratios varied from state to state)
- Hours Spent On Stand: over 350
    - -(I averaged over 5 hours per sit. That is 8.75 standard work weeks spent sitting in the woods.)
    - -(I averaged 1 deer sighting every 1.54 hours of time on stand.)
    - -(I averaged seeing a mature buck (2 years+) every 17.5 hours of stand time.)
- Shots Taken: 4 (87.5 hours of stand time between shots)
- Bucks Killed: 3 (116.7 hours of stand time between shots at bucks)
- Does Killed: 1
- Weight Lost During the Fall: 9 pounds (I dropped from 153 lbs to 144 lbs by the end of my hunt.)
- Miles Driven on Hunting Trip: 7,844

Hunting Expenditures
for Three Months
of Chasing Whitetails

License Fees:	$687.00 (24% of budget)
Gasoline:	$1176.61 (40% of budget)
Food and Drink:	$428.87 (15% of budget)
Hunting Gear (new boots, gloves, etc.)	$316.89 (11% of budget)
Motel & Camping:	$131.00 (4.5 % of budget)
Miscellaneous (film developing, laundry, etc.)	$95.78 (3% of budget)
Deer Processing:	$75.00 (2.5% of budget)
Total:	$2911.15

During my hunting trip I diligently collected all receipts. These are the results. Admittedly, $2900 taken alone is a good sum of money. If, however, you consider that semi-guided whitetail hunts, which usually means simply access to hunting land, go nowadays for as much as $3000 for a mere five days, the price of my three months of hunting was pretty low. Also considering current lease prices of at least $10 an acre, my fall was really quite reasonable. Not included in my budget was my equipment, which I have been collecting for years. Nor are my normal running expenses included, such as vehicle maintenance, rent, electricity, or insurance.

Epilogue

North Dakota Revisited

Jumping ahead two years it's now early October of 2007. After a 2006 hunting season cut very short by the birth, earlier that year, of my daughter Linnea, I'm back on the road bowhunting. This time, though, definitely not for three months straight. It will probably be a while before I get the opportunity to do that again! During the time between my visits to North Dakota, Dan and I have become close friends. He has moved to a slightly larger town in the northwest corner of the state not far from the Montana line. It's here, along the banks of the Missouri and Yellowstone rivers, that I plan to spend ten days of allotted North Dakota hunting time. Dan has done a little listening to locals, and seems to have gotten the skinny on some good, public, river bottom land nearby.

Arriving at Dan's new house early in the afternoon I'm greeted at the door by his brother Joe, who is visiting from New Jersey, taking a well deserved break from his job in Manhattan. Warned that I was on my way into town Joe is prepared, and offers me a cup of coffee. We take a few minutes to chat while sipping hot java from our mugs. Joe is as forthright and friendly as his brother, and seems to be a fine shot with a shotgun. Dan and Joe have been busy combing the prairie for grouse as of late, and have been quite successful, as is proven by the dinner plans of grouse stroganoff. I can't sit long though, because I have a doe that I killed last evening in Wisconsin to skin and quarter.

On my way out west I stopped for a single afternoon hunt at a new piece of property in south-central Wisconsin to attempt to kill a doe, so I will later be able to concentrate on hunting bucks on my way back through. This new Wisconsin hunting property zone is Earn-A-Buck only, as most hunting units in Wisconsin have become. The Wisconsin farm I hunted the previous years was sold, and my permission to hunt was lost. Stalking to my tree I climbed up, and was barely settled before the doe stepped rather incautiously into shooting range. With no personal qualms about shooting does, I shot without a hint of hesitation, and watched the young deer drop thirty yards away. Within an hour of reaching the woods I had the doe loaded into my van, checked, a fresh buck tag in my pocket, and was on my way to North Dakota.

Joe and I hang the doe from the rafters of Dan's garage and I get busy skinning. With the temperature above seventy this deer has to be turned into venison quick, or at least make it into the refrigerator to firm up. It will make some tender and welcome camp meat. With the deer quickly quartered and in the refrigerator, I'm just cleaning off my knives in the kitchen sink when Dan rolls in from work over at the church. The sun is already sinking pretty low in the

The Missouri river forms the border of this public land.

west, so without too many formalities Dan, Joe and I jump in Dan's truck for a ride down to the river. The purpose of our trip is for Dan to clue me in to where the good places are to hunt. Since it's already late he cuts to the chase and we drive straight to the spot he figures would be the best.

Almost an hour from his house we finally drop down from the open prairie into the river bottom. Here the crops change from what appears to be mostly wheat up top, to sugar beats and alfalfa below. The tract of public land is at the north point of a peninsula surrounded by a huge bend in the river. As we drive north it strikes me that all the fields to the south are still in crops, except the ones directly adjacent to the public land. For almost a half-mile from the public ground the fields are bare dirt, already plowed and disked. Thinking this a little unusual for the first week of October, I ask Dan about it. Apparently, this is brand new public land that was purchased by the state of North Dakota just two years ago. According to Dan's sources (and as the local cowboy pastor he often gets the inside scoop — or at least all the best gossip) most of the area belonged to a single family, and was used as a premier whitetail outfitting operation. The owner was an old man, who got fed up over the bickering about who would inherit his place, so he sold it to the state so that everyone would be able to enjoy it. Since the sale, the neighbors plow the fields closest to the public land to bare dirt as early as they can, in an attempt to keep the mature bucks far to the south, on private ground, which is still controlled by outfitters. At least that's how the story goes. It was in those now-barren fields that Dan counted six bucks in August that he claims all would have easily made the pages of that famous Pope & Young book.

Arriving at the parking spot, a glance is all I need to see this is a really nice, public hunting spot. Right in front of us is a hundred acre field planted in wild rye that is taller than I am. Through binoculars from the truck a food plot of sunflowers is visible in a back corner of the field. Tall cottonwoods line the edges. This will work! The sun is really low on the horizon, and Dan wants to show me another spot down the road before it gets dark, so it's back south after only a couple brief minutes of glassing. Crossing the barren ground we come to the first alfalfa field. In the back corner stand at least a dozen deer. We stop and scan with binoculars. Two yearling bucks are among the does, and a nice two year old eight-pointer feeds close to the wood line.

Driving on we cover another quarter mile to the next alfalfa field, a doe and two fawns are standing about fifty yards off the road, and twenty yards behind them is a big buck! The 140 class eight-pointer takes no notice of us parked on the road and simply continues feeding. Something like this would be practically unimaginable back in Michigan. This buck has it all. His rack is wide, tall and heavy. If I was even somewhat skeptical about hunting this area before, my opinion instantly takes a slightly more positive turn. While we're watching the big buck, yet another buck slides out of the woods about forty yards to the north. Wow! This one is not quite as big as the eight-pointer, but close. The ten-pointer with perfectly symmetrical antlers strolls out and begins feeding close to his pal. Dan, Joe and I all guess a score and come to a consensus at around 130 Pope & Young style points. Both of these bucks are big enough to attempt to kill, and that is all that really matters. Now I'm completely convinced that the tract of public ground up the road is worth a little effort. If there are does up there, these bucks will find the way north, eventually.

We drive on. Another three quarters of a mile up the road we roll up to a sugar beat field with a bunch of deer dispersed throughout its back half. Alone, about two hundred yards off the road, up to his belly in beats stands a huge buck. "Whoa! Monster buck!" bursts out of my mouth, and Dan steps on the brakes. Instantly, in a blur of sunset glistening off antler, and tail tucked, the buck dashes for cover. This old fella must have had some previous encounters with road-hunting violators. For a second or two all three of us in the truck lock eyes on this mega-buck before he bounds to safety, seemingly swallowed by the brilliant sunset. We sit in awe for a second before sharing our various impressions of the antlered monarch. Nobody wants to go first with their size estimate, so I cast out a conservative 160. Dan and Joe agree, but also agree that the buck could be a legitimate Booner. At any rate, in the split second glance I got, the deer had to be in the top two or three biggest bucks I have ever seen, anywhere. The only for-certain bigger buck I have ever seen was one I saw while driving around Chicago one evening a few years back in November. Coming from the north just short of O'Hare, in what I think is the last patch of woods before pure city, a world class buck was chasing a doe about fifty yards off the highway. Even at seventy miles an hour there was no mistaking a buck that could easily grace the illustrious pages of *North American Whitetail*. Although we're now more than a mile away from the public ground, this place is looking better all the time. It's not many times that I've seen three big bucks standing out in the open in the evening while hunting season is in progress. A quick stop at another river bottom, public land spot across the river is all that we can muster before dark. This spot, however, has five cars parked at various points. I decide to concentrate my efforts across the river for obvious reasons.

After a long night of good food and many hunting stories I step out of the feathers a little late. Around noon I arrive back at the public land. This is as much plan as it is circumstance. There is no sense busting out through the woods too early in the morning when the deer will most certainly be on their feet. Donning my scouting gear I start out by inspecting the east side of the public tract. Just as I suspected, the woods is very open, with north to south rows of cottonwoods, mixed with a few thicker patches of aspen. Each strip of trees has several runways through it, most of them also heading north to south. From the topo-photos that I pulled off Dan's computer the general deer movement appears to be straightforward and predictable. The northern tip of the peninsula looks like the thickest bedding area within miles and all the crops are to the south, all beyond the plowed fields. The deer should clearly be moving from north to south in the evening and returning from south to north in the morning. The trick is going to be selecting the best funnel. The only way to accomplish that is to get out there on foot. I spend about three hours carefully picking through the cottonwood strips. The striking thing about this area is that one spot seems just as good as the next; nothing really grabs my attention. There is no lack of trees, so merely to have a spot to hunt for this evening I select a large cottonwood with good cover from multiple trunks. It doesn't require any clearing, so after my selection I march straight back to my van for a late lunch.

It's already afternoon, so I eat quickly before sliding into my hunting gear. Because the weather hasn't changed since yesterday at 70 plus degrees and sunny, I wear Scent Lok and not much more. Within a half an hour I'm hanging comfortably in my new tree. And there I hang for the next four hours, as nothing happens. Not a single deer, nor much else — apart from songbirds — makes an appearance. At one point towards dark I think I hear a deer snorting in the distance, but it is so faint I'm not sure if it is just my imagination wishing for a little activity. I have a feeling something isn't right; the runways through these woods are wide and numerous. There is just too much sign and the understory is too open not to see anything. As soon as darkness falls I silently slide to the ground, and sneak towards my van.

Breaking out of the woods to cross the last opening the potential problem becomes obvious. Bouncing along the edge of the rye field are four halogen headlamps, and three handheld flashlights, all of them far brighter than they need to be. By comparison I don't even have my flashlight turned on, so brilliant is the night sky. The sight of the piercing beams bouncing and circling in all directions reminds me of some old horror film. These guys must have been positioned between my spot and the bedding area, effectively cutting me off. The snort I thought I heard was probably a deer spooked by one of these hunters. Oh well, public land is just that, public. Tonight I was cut off.

At the parking spot I stow my gear as the two pairs of fathers and sons do the same. It strikes me just how well geared they are. All four carry this year's bows, and new packs, and are wearing new Scent Lok. They take the time to stow their cloths and packs in plastic tubs, and change into street clothes before stepping into their trucks; competition who knows what they are doing! This might be tougher than I thought.

The following morning is practically a carbon copy of the first evening, except in reverse. The sunrise is great, but the deer are absent. Upon return to the parking lot there are two more sets of fresh tire tracks. Someone was hunting again. It seems the word is out about this new public ground. Not one to give up quickly I set out to explore the west and north portions of the peninsula. Judging from my topo-photos, if there is anyplace in this entire area that is going to be really good, it will be up towards the northwest corner, where the obvious bedding and the open woods intersect. Taking the two-track around the rye field and then to the north I follow it towards the location I picked out on the map. At about the halfway mark I encounter a tiny, five-acre field tucked back in the cottonwoods surrounded by a clearly new and tight, barbed wire fence with no trespassing signs on every single post. The field is just grass with a few tufts of alfalfa strewn here and there. Taking the field for its face value I continue on, thinking it a little strange for there to be a tiny, private parcel amidst a large, public tract. It's a solid mile walk to where I want to go, but upon arrival I'm not disappointed. Practically at the exact spot I selected on my map is indeed a good funnel. At least ten runways emerge out of the bedding, crossing a row of cottonwoods into an open forest that eventually leads to rye, sunflower, and further south to more crops. Right at the intersection sits a cottonwood with good lean and a split trunk about thirty feet up providing excellent cover. Careful not to breach the security of the bedding I inspect the general area, and come to the conclusion that this entire tract of public land, probably around six hundred acres, can be effectively bowhunted from three trees in this corner, all within a hundred yards of each other. One of the three trees already has someone else's stand in it.

The one I prepare for myself has been hunted from before, and the third has a treestand not fifty yards away. Hoping to hunt here this evening I make for my van, following the two-track opposite the direction I came from, but since this is a peninsula, all trails eventually lead back to the parking lot. Along the way I keep an eye open for more promising-looking spots, but nothing catches my eye that even slightly rivals what I just found.

A mile long hike later I'm sitting in my van relaxing, enjoying the pleasant sunshine, while very slowly preparing to return to my new tree. Glancing down the road I notice a truck approaching, pulling a trailer with two quads loaded on top. It rumbles into the parking lot and stops in front of the metal gate. Two young guys jump out, and while one unlocks the gate the other messes around with something in the bed of the truck. Neither one of them seems to take any notice of me. Considering the numerous signs declaring foot traffic only, and the fact that they have a key to the lock, I assume they must be Game and Fish employees. Closing the gate behind them they drive along the rye field in the direction of the small private plot. They aren't out of sight for two minutes before yet another truck pulls up. Two more twenty-something guys jump out, but this time they walk up and give a friendly greeting. We talk for a few minutes. These two are out scouting. I relay the fact that game and fish guys just went off to the west, so they head east to scout where I just hunted for the last two days. As soon as they are out of sight I slip into my hunting gear.

I'm just steps from my van as the howl of racing quads catches my attention. Towards the back of the rye, two blazing machines rip across the two-track and blast off into the woods to the east. One of the quads does a fast circle around a patch of cottonwoods before disappearing. Hmm! This sure doesn't look like typical state employee behavior! The quads grunt and roar in the distance as I start my hike. About a half mile into it the two riders burst out onto the lane about fifty yards in front of me, one of them screams down the two-track along the bedding area, while the other spins a doughnut before speeding along the edge of the woods heading back west. These two "gentlemen" are obviously doing their best to create a disturbance. Putting the numbers together in my head, and adding them to the background that Pastor Dan gave me, I come up with a theory to the riddle of what they are doing. I surmise that somehow in the land deal someone in the old man's family got to hold onto that tiny field, which means they also hold a key to the public land gate. Just like the barren ground fields separating the public land from the private, this type of disturbance is probably another attempt to keep the deer to the south, and reduce the chances of success for hunters on this public tract. Unfortunately, deer hunting doesn't always bring out the best in people. I just shake my head and walk on, wishing that my cell phone had reception here. I'm sure any conservation officer would be interested in the present situation. Why am I always fortunate enough to run into strange situations like this? Perhaps a little of the unexpected is an essential ingredient to any adventure, perhaps to keep one on his toes.

Undaunted, but honestly a little miffed, I continue on and set up in my new tree. My hopes for a good buck have, however, severely diminished; but, I at least want to hunt this funnel before changing to a new location. The hunting pressure, uneventful hunts, and now this has me thinking hard about hitting the road for Ka-Tah-O-Kuty. Shortly after I settle in I hear the quads being loaded back on the trailer and that truck drive off. At least there won't be any ATV's buzzing my stand tonight; things are looking up. Within an hour the weather abruptly changes, clear skies turn matt gray, and the temperature drops a couple degrees. Almost the instant I notice the change, a buck stands up about twenty yards inside the bedding area. At approximately eighty yards from me his rack is easy to see, narrow tall tines, probably a two-year old, eight-pointer. He does a small loop through the brush and vanishes again.

A few minutes later a doe and two fawns tiptoe out of the bedding. Casually, they walk right past me, making their way toward the rye. It isn't ten minutes later that the buck returns. This time he follows the same path as the doe and fawns. Right below me, at fifteen yards, I get a really good look at his antlers. He is indeed an eight-pointer with about a thirteen-inch spread, and main beams that come way around in the front. If he lives through the fall, he will be a very

Despite the signs to the contrary, some irresponsible ATV riders purposely abuse this public land.

nice buck next year. After he passes, it is as though the dam breaks. Twenty-one does and fawns follow, all picking their way south. A half-hour before dark a bachelor group of bucks stroll out of the bedding. The first buck is probably a hundred-inch eight-point, but the next two are both a year older, and definitely shooters. The second is a ten-pointer, and the third another eight-pointer. Although I get a good look at them the closest they come is about seventy yards. A little coaxing with a *doe in estrous* can and *grunt tube* proves futile.

The fun, though, isn't over. Just before dark another single deer slips out of the bedding about a hundred yards away. Immediately, by the size of its neck and chest, I can tell it's a buck. Reaching for my binoculars I get a glimpse of a row of long tines for about a second, before he disappears behind some Russian olive bushes. Exactly how big he is I can't determine, but he is larger than the other two nice bucks that passed earlier. The path he takes would lead him right under the tree stand I found earlier today. What a crowning moment to the evening. After two hunts without a single sighting, twenty-seven deer walk by in a one afternoon, including three good bucks! I wait a half-hour after dark to climb down in order to give that buck some time to put a little distance between the two of us. My biggest concern now is to get out of here without spooking all the deer that passed through this evening. Fortunately, one of the lanes makes a wide circle behind the woods and crops, a perfect exit. Tomorrow morning I will be back.

During the night the weather takes a turn for the worse. The wind picks up and the rain begins. If you've never experienced prairie wind, it is something to behold. When I wake up at

4:00 a.m. and step outside the rain feels like it is coming in horizontally from the west, striking like tiny, ice-cold needles into any bare skin. Instinct tells me to crawl back under my blankets, but visions of those bucks draw me out. Donning my impervious rain gear I sleepily start my march, all the time repeating a mantra about toughness, attempting to convince myself that I'm indeed not crazy. Perseverance is key to regularly scoring on mature bucks, and this weather, as uncomfortable as it is, is a condition in which mature bucks tend to move. Perhaps they don't like sitting still in the ice-cold rain and wind either. You can't kill a mature buck unless you're out hunting. At my tree it's the usual rainy morning routine. Set and ready, I tuck in all the loose ends, fire up a few activated charcoal-body warmers, and hunker down for a long wait. The wind is so strong that I'm forced to hold on to my bow so that it doesn't fall off its hook. For six hours, I tough it out without a single deer sighting. By 11:00 a.m. I've had enough. The wind has worked through the tiny cracks in my armor, and I'm beginning to feel a little chill. "Where are all the deer?" is the burning question.

Twenty-seven deer including three nice bucks walked through this opening during a single afternoon. Notice the thick bedding in the background.

The answer comes in the form of white bobbing tails, about twenty of them in all different directions, when I reach the sunflowers. It looks like I got down a little early today. I should have stuck it out for another hour, at least. With the inclement weather the deer probably just stayed out in the open later than usual. Oops!

Back at my van I stow my gear, placing my wet, outer layer in plastic bags for a trip to a laundromat, if there is one nearby. While I'm doing this two different trucks pull up into the parking spot, stop to look for a minute or two before driving off. There is just too much hunter traffic here compared to the single, really good funnel. The weekend begins tomorrow, which means there will probably be even more hunters cruising through. And who knows if there will be any more neighborly visits. On impulse I decide to break camp. I have a burning feeling that I need to get back out to Dan's cabin, despite the good bucks I saw yesterday. Things are just not right here down along the big Missouri.

Back in town an hour later, Joe and Dan are a little surprised to see me, and immediately and optimistically assume I arrowed a buck. Their assumption is quickly negated as I relate to them the events of the last three days. I happen to arrive at lunch hour just in the nick of time, and am able to join in on some delicious, Wisconsin doe backstrap. Cut into six inch chunks, browned quickly in a hot pan, and then placed in the oven for about ten minutes, crisp on the outside and red in the middle: now this is real food and a big improvement over my on-the-road, cold, canned soup and vitamins. Dan has that whole deer worked into steaks and hamburger already. I'm surprised to catch him not working, but as it turns out, this is the last day of Joe's visit. Joe has to catch a train back east this evening, so Dan took the day off work to spend time with his brother.

After lunch I ride along on a visit to the local archery shop. Joe has had so much fun out on the prairie grouse hunting, and listening to us talk of bowhunting that his interest in the passion is rekindled, to say the least. He had bowhunted previously and even killed a couple of deer in his younger years, but college, a job on the east coast, and some other commitments pulled him away from hunting. The purpose of our visit to the archery shop is so that Joe can buy a new bow, his first since he sold his last bow about a dozen years ago! Welcome back to the fold, my friend.

Leaving the two brothers alone I make for the cabin. It's about an hour and a half drive back to the southeast. Dan will meet me there sometime in the evening. The wind and rain haven't let up a bit from this morning, and the driving is a bit touchy at times, especially since there are mule deer all over the roads. Even though I drive slow and careful, eluding deer collisions requires constant concentration. A couple of times there are only mere yards between my bumper and roadside cervids. Arriving just at dark there isn't much to do except dry my wet rain gear, re-activate my Scent Lok, and make myself comfortable. Dan arrives about two hours later.

With no hunting spots prepared I sleep-in the following morning. Following a breakfast feast of more venison, we jump in Dan's truck and go for a ride to superficially inspect the area. The main purpose of this is to see where the local ranchers, and Game and Fish employees have planted crops this year. Our first stop, though, is Dan's own property. Dan proudly shows me his food plot, ten acres of corn, about four-foot tall. Corn is tricky business out here, with as little annual rainfall as there is, but this year the rain was just enough and came at just the right moments. Checking the perimeter of his field, it is clear that the corn has increased the local deer activity dramatically. Though his property normally has a small resident population of whitetails, it is out at the end of the local deer herd's movement pattern. The corn has changed that. His land now attracts deer from all around. Dan claims to have counted thirty-two deer enter his plot in a single evening. Good to know! Heading up the road we drive to the public land. Numerous trucks are cruising all over the place. It happens to be the pronghorn rifle opener. Fortunately, most of the antelope are farther out on the prairie, away from these brushy draws, so most of the trucks are just passing through. However, there are four trucks parked along the access roads, probably bowhunters. The crops are situated completely different than they were two years ago. Together we make a couple of short walks to gain a better vantage point for some long distance scouting. Before long we are back at the cabin.

Getting my stuff together I wait until most hunters should be out of the woods before returning to the public land. My interest is focused on the corner where I killed that eight-pointer two years ago. The long walk over the bluff is met with disappointment. There is virtually zero deer activity. The wheat stubble out across the prairie seems to have been left fallow, and now there are cattle grazing there. Turning my attention to other areas I take a long hike around the bluff, and come up empty. Though there is some sign, the ultimate spot eludes me. I just don't like to set up on singular sign, and that is really all that I find.

Back at the cabin Dan and I plan for the evening. Dan will be hunting from a tree along a deep, thick draw that is lined with rubs. My less-than-glorious solution for this evening's hunt is to walk out to the edge of Dan's cornfield and hunker down behind a buffalo berry patch. As usual, this hunting trip is a work in progress. Not expecting much I tuck in between two drab patches, about thirty yards away from the edge of the corn. My hiding spot is right at the lip of a subtle draw that is dotted with similar clumps of buffalo berry. From what I can read of the deer situation, deer bed in various places across the prairie and use this draw, along with the cover provided by the patchy brush, to get to the maize in the evenings. The spot is decent in that I can see for a long way in the direction the deer should be coming, which should give me plenty of time to prepare for a shot if they come close. The weather has dried up, so using a jacket as a cushion I lay down right on the ground. In this position I can watch the corn through the bush with nothing more than the top of my hat visible in that direction, and even the outline of that is broken by stems and leaves. This is definitely improvisation!

For about two hours I doze, opening my eyes occasionally for a look around. An unusual rustle in the corn catches my attention. Slowly I lift my head up over the slight ledge. There stands a single doe at the edge of the corn, pulling on an ear of corn. She munches for a few seconds before turning and walking straight towards me. I scarcely allow myself to breath in an attempt to go unnoticed. I can only hope her course veers a few yards to the right or left, otherwise it looks like she will step on me. As she closes in, her course, fortunately, takes her to my left, but not by much. As she crosses into the gap, where I am now wide open, she is a mere five yards away. With nothing between us but air, she instantly halts, sending a burning stare in my direction, at what must look to her like a strange lump on the ground. Perhaps I even resemble a cougar, of which there are plenty around these parts. The doe is crosswind, so she can't smell me, but still she doesn't like the look of things and in a split second bounds down the draw, surprisingly without snorting, or circling directly downwind in an attempt to catch my scent. She is still moving at a solid pace even at the last point I catch a glimpse of her, about a half mile away.

For the next couple of hours deer pop up all across the prairie, twelve total and nothing closer than several hundred yards away. Enjoying the show I curiously watch through my binoculars. A little too busy with my binoc's, I'm almost startled when two deer suddenly appear about forty yards to my right, filing up the edge of the draw. Casting my attention on them I watch as they cross the opening into the corn, coming to within about twenty-five yards. The first is a doe, and the second a yearling spike. Neither of them has any idea of the danger lurking nearby and casually work their way into the corn. Both the doe and the buck would have been an easy shot. It feels good to know that a makeshift, ground ambush can indeed work.

With just a few minutes of shooting light remaining I decide to stand up to glass the great wide open one last time to see if any bucks have appeared. While concentrating on a new group of deer about four hundred yards behind me, movement, again to my right, catches my attention, this time closer than before. There, crossing the opening towards the corn is a shooter eight-pointer probably gross scoring in the mid 120's, moving fast and only twenty yards away. Now I have a problem! Caught flatfooted, my bow is lying on the ground at my feet. The way he is angling, this deer will make the corn in a couple seconds. No time to hesitate. In a single motion I drop to one knee, slip the binoculars to the ground, pick up my bow, draw, and take a single step out from behind the cover. Instantly the buck stops and looks right at me, standing a single step from the corn, exactly thirty yards away. Second pin on the middle of his chest, I am just dropping my release finger as the buck spins and sprints back in the direction from which he came. A couple of short mmmaaa mmmaaa mmmaaas spontaneously burst out of my mouth, but to no avail. This buck certainly isn't going to wait around to get killed. Never have I been so close to releasing an arrow and not gotten the shot off. The time it takes for my finger to move a half an inch, is how far away I was from releasing. Down the gully I can hear the buck snorting, warning every deer within miles of the danger he just encountered. A glance out across the open prairie to the other deer makes it clear they are now all focused on this little draw. Once again, I blew it! It isn't the first time an encounter with a nice buck has gone awry, and it definitely won't be the last time. There is nothing left to do other than pack up and make for the cabin.

A while later Dan joins me. He, too, had an encounter with a buck this evening. The two-year old, eight-pointer was broadside at ten yards, but Dan let him pass. This is big country, and there are other bigger bucks roaming this badland edge. Packing up quickly Dan breaks for home; tomorrow is Sunday morning and he has to prepare his bowhunting-cowboy, prairie-pastor sermon before heading to work bright and early. He promises to return late Sunday to be able to hunt the remaining days of my visit. Left alone and already five days into a ten day hunt I decide that the first half of my Sunday will be dedicated to finding some new places to hunt.

Both Sunday and Monday turn into marathon efforts. In the course of two days I walk many, many miles, and though I hunt in the evenings and morning, the real news is the discovery of three great spots. The first, and best, spot is over a mile and half walk from the nearest road, that consists of a small patch of aspens at the mouth of a deep thick draw. Only a single aspen is big enough to hunt out of, but it sits at the convergence of about ten runways that meander in from across an expanse of open prairie, and lead down into bedding. The deer bed in the draw and make a nighttime jaunt about three quarters of a mile away to a neighboring rancher's fields in the distance. The second is a circle of out-of-place oaks on a saddle that funnels deer across a low sloping mountain (or at least what is called a mountain in North Dakota) five fifty foot tall, white oaks over a mile off the road, with nothing but open grassland and low brush all around. Runways, scrapes and rubs litter the area. The third is a short, bur oak at the end of a row of them, in a draw about a half-mile from Dan's corn plot. As I glassed on Sunday morning three nice bucks, including a really

This rubbed buffalo berry bush was near my hiding spot..

good, tall, narrow ten-pointer passed right by this little oak. Each tree is several miles from the other. The hard work done, my plan is to fill out the remaining days of my hunt with a rotation of these three spots.

On Tuesday morning the alarm clock unpleasantly jolts me awake seemingly in the middle of the night. Half grudgingly and half eager I sit up and mechanically make for the shower. It is the seventh day of my ten-day hunt and, with all the walking and hunting I have been doing, I'm beginning to get run down. When I start to feel fatigued on a hunt I like to jump in the shower before my morning outings, if that is possible. The warm water wakes me up, warms me up, and a pre-hunt, scent eliminating qualities of a shower is always a good idea anyway. Now awake and clean, I quickly pull on my underlayers and grab by pack from its airtight tub. Just as I'm about to walk out the door Dan pops out of his bedroom. Groggily he says, "Hey, I have to tell you something. I just dreamt that you shot a huge buck with all kinds of points, and its body was so big it reminded me of a rhino." My reply is dismissive and something along the lines of, "Okay Dan, that's great, now get up and go hunting."

A step out the door I already forget about Dan's premonition. There is a long walk and potentially a long hunt ahead of me. Arriving at the parking spot I don the last of my scent control armor and begin my hour-long hike to my promising poplar. Normally, I walk to my stands without the aid of a flashlight, and this particular October morning it strikes me that it is extremely dark. There is neither moon nor stars. A thick blanket of cloud cover rolled in during the night. About half way to my tree it suddenly gets even darker when incredibly thick fog suddenly envelops me. Covering the remainder of my walk mostly by feel, I make it to my tree over an hour before first light. Within a few minutes of my arrival I'm sitting comfortably in my saddle.

For an hour I half doze, with an ear open, futilely attempting to audibly detect any approaching deer. As daybreak arrives I can't help but wonder at the fog. The air is so full of moisture the fog is actually more like a mist, and I can only see about forty yards. I am just thinking that I will have to be on high alert, because the deer will be on top of me before I can react, when suddenly, standing in my shooting lane a mere twenty yards away, is a huge buck. One split second glance is all it takes to decide, "Big enough."

The buck is ghosting steadily by, so hurriedly I pull my bow from its hanger, attach my release, and draw. The few seconds it takes to complete this is too long, and by the time I draw, the buck crosses just out of my shooting lane. I let back up. But, I must have made a tiny bit of noise, because just past my lane, the buck freezes. Now he's standing a mere ten yards away, completely blocked by understory. He stands rock solid motionless for what seems like an eternity. Once, I even look away and then back to reassure myself that he is still there. The buck has two choices, either he can continue on his chosen path, which would give me a nine yard shot in two more steps, or he can turn and walk straight away into the draw, and disappear unscathed. With a quick flip of his tail the buck steps forward. Immediately I maneuver around the tree, draw, anchor and select a hole to shoot through. The buck takes that second step, and though my only open shot would put my arrow a touch high on his chest, I decide that it is now or never, and let fly.

Crack!!! The buck folds to the ground, falling straight away from me, but in a rolling flash is back up. He scrambles straight towards me, under my tree, and within two seconds collapses in a branch-snapping heap only twenty-five yards behind me. He doesn't make another move, not even a single kick. Silence. I have never seen a deer die so fast in my entire life! Slumping back in my saddle I'm in a mild state of disbelief. Did that just happen? The way the buck is laying, right in the middle of the aspen patch, I'm unable to see his antlers from my tree. After that initial glance at his rack I was so concentrated on making the shot that I hadn't even peeked again. My thoughts are simply, " I sure hope he is as big as I think he is."

After gathering my gear together, along with my composure, I scale down my tree and walk over to the buck. His antlers are no disappointment; they are actually bigger than I expect, fourteen-points, long tines, and good mass. This is the biggest buck I've ever killed.

A couple days of heavy scouting reveal three great spots. The first a patch of aspens on the edge of a deep, brushy draw, the second a circle of oaks on a good saddle, and the third a heavily traveled point of short bur oaks.

It seems luck was on my side this morning. Reaching into my pack I pull out my camera and snap a few quick shots, and then get busy gutting my deer. I working automatically, not thinking about anything, still in a mild state of shock. Wondering at the deer's sudden collapse I inspect its lungs. The arrow cut through the entry side lung right at the top, down over the heart and through the middle-front of the exit side lung. A definite double lunger, but even so, a buck this big shouldn't have collapsed that fast. Looking a little closer, and sticking my fingers through the holes to get a better idea of the arrow's path I notice that the main artery coming up from the heart is sliced with a nice X; cut off the oxygen to the brain and the lights go out, fast. There is still another question that has to be answered. Why did the buck run back under my tree and what was the loud crack on impact? This is a little more straightforward. My arrow hit the opposite lower leg bone, and shattered it. The broadhead stopped just under the skin in the opposite shoulder.

As soon as I am finished I grab my gear and hike back to my van. With such a long drag ahead of me I decide to get Dan to come and help. I drive to the spot where he is supposed to be hunting, but his truck isn't there, so I continue on to the cabin. There I find Dan still in bed.

"Dan, get up!"

This was my first close-up view of the big prairie buck.

"Did you get one?"

"Yeah!"

"How big is he?"

"He's alright. Take a look." I hand him my camera.

"That's the buck out of my dream, you got the Rhino buck!"

It's only then that I remember Pastor Dan's dream. I guess when your hunting partner has other worldly connections you should listen to his premonitions.

Two days later my van is loaded up, venison frozen

This big 14 pointer made for a great culmination to another cross country hunt.

solid in a cooler, and I'm on my way back east. There is twenty acres along the eastern edge of Minnesota where I received permission to hunt, that new spot in Wisconsin, a couple old trees in Michigan beckoning to be hunted, and some public land in Indiana I want to check out. When you see a rusty old Chevy van parked along the edge of some hunting ground somewhere, you just might know whom it belongs to. If you've made it all the way to this page, you'll have noticed that there is no secret to bowhunting big bucks on a small budget. It is something anyone willing to put in a little effort, time, and creativity can do, including you. So get out there, answer the call that has been burning at you for so long, and go on a whitetail adventure.

› ⇉⇉ › · ⇇⇇ ‹

About the Author

Chris Eberhart was born and raised in whitetail rich Michigan where he hunted exclusively his first fifteen seasons. Although he is a whitetail bowhunting fanatic, his job commitments and family keep him away from whitetail country a great deal of the time. With limited time and money Chris has developed a system to maximize his success on mature whitetails all across the United States. His techniques will work in any location. He is the author of two whitetail hunting books; *Bowhunting Pressured Whitetails* and *Precision Bowhunting*. His writing has appeared in numerous hunting magazines including *Deer & Deer Hunting, Bow & Arrow Hunting, Petersen's Bowhunting,* and *Michigan Out-of-Doors*. Chris has also appeared in episodes of *American Archer Television*.

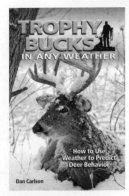

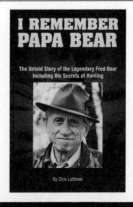